Pop \

Pop Warner

A Life on the Gridiron

JEFFREY J. MILLER

McFarland & Company, Inc., Publishers

Jefferson, North Carolina

ISBN 978-0-7864-6497-5 (softcover : acid free paper) ∞
ISBN 978-1-4766-2274-3 (ebook)

LIBRARY OF CONGRESS CATALOGUING DATA ARE AVAILABLE

BRITISH LIBRARY CATALOGUING DATA ARE AVAILABLE

Front cover; Stanford football coach Glenn Scobey
"Pop" Warner (Stanford University Libraries)

Printed in the United States of America

*McFarland & Company, Inc., Publishers
Box 611, Jefferson, North Carolina 28640
www.mcfarlandpub.com*

To Cathaline and Benjamin,
my home team

Table of Contents

Acknowledgments

This book would not have been possible without the support, assistance and encouragement I received from so many friends and colleagues along the way. As I write this, I can only hope that I have not neglected to thank anyone who helped—and if I did, I am both sorry and embarrassed!

First and foremost I wish to thank John Maxymuk and Jeff Mason, who diligently proofread my manuscript and offered advice. The book you are holding is the result of five and a half years of work, and these two wise gentlemen were there all the way, indulging my countless emails and phone calls. I should also point out, however, that any errors are my own.

Thanks also to Tom Benjey, the world's preeminent authority on the Carlisle Indians football team. Tom was always available with information and to answer questions, no matter how inane they might have seemed. Renowned football historian and author Terence Jon Troup provided invaluable insight into Pop Warner's single- and double-wing offenses, as well as other essential elements of the leather helmet days of football. Chris Willis, head research librarian at NFL Films and author of many books, offered much needed encouragement along with access to NFLF's vast film collection at their facility in Mount Laurel, New Jersey. Alan V. Manchester is a retired educator, historian, author and proud grad of Cornell University. He is also Springville, New York's foremost authority on all things related to Warner, and gave me access to his vast collection of Pop-related items. John Richards is a talented artist who doubled as my point man in Palo Alto, California. He was helpful in obtaining information and items at Stanford University. Dan DiLandro and Peggy Hatfield, my friends at the E.H. Butler Library at Buffalo State College, were helpful in securing hard-to-find articles and information. Richard Tritt, photo curator at the Cumberland County Historical Society, was helpful in my search for images from Pop's days at the Carlisle Indian School. Don Orton, curator of the Pop Warner Museum in Springville, went above and beyond in helping me in my pursuit of images and information on the Warners. Jolene Hawkins at the Lucy Bensley Genealogical Research Center in Springville was helpful in locating information on Pop's family, and in providing access to Springville's old newspapers and historical archives. Thanks also to Lois Batt Lane, great-niece of Tibb Warner, for providing insight into Tibb's childhood and family. Thanks to Pete Dygert, owner of the Springville property on which Jim Thorpe trained for the 1912 Olympics, for sharing information about his family. Thanks to E.J. Borghetti and Celeste Welsh at the University of Pittsburgh's Media Relations office for their assistance. Thanks to Michelle Futornick, Stanford Library News Service, and Jenny Johnson, Stanford Special Collections, for their assistance with photos.

I also wish to express my gratitude to Ken Crippen of the Professional Football Researchers Association; Tex Noel of the Intercollegiate Football Researchers Association; Bob Wheeler, noted historian and author of *Jim Thorpe: World's Greatest Athlete*; Lars Anderson, staff writer at *Sports Illustrated* and author of *Carlisle vs. Army: Jim Thorpe, Dwight Eisenhower, Pop Warner, and the Forgotten Story of Football's Greatest Battle*; Joel Maul; Lud and Judy Sternad; and my wife, Cathaline, and our son, Benjamin. Yes, it's finally finished!

Last but not least, a special "thank you" goes out to my third grade teacher, Jane (Little) Neureuther, for encouraging me to take on the task of writing a biography of Springville's most famous citizen. I hope I have made you proud!

Preface

In the spring of 2009, I had just completed work on a book I had co-written with Buffalo Bills Hall of Fame coach Marv Levy called *Game Changers: The Greatest Plays in Buffalo Bills Football History*. It wasn't long before I began considering ideas for my next project. One subject that kept coming to mind was unquestionably the most famous person from my hometown of Springville, New York, and is buried in a cemetery about five or six football fields from my house.

As a football historian and writer, I was familiar with Glenn "Pop" Warner's name, but I had never really delved deeply into his life or even the many contributions he had made to the sport. He was always there, on the periphery, but since my focus had always been on the professional variety of the sport, he rarely came up in my research. Yet the more I started to think about him, the more intrigued I became. My preliminary research only scratched the surface of the Warner mythology, which included misleading information and out-and-out inaccuracies.

This unsatisfactory appetizer, as most researchers will tell you, resulted in both increased frustration and curiosity. Warner was given credit for many of the same football-related inventions and innovations that were credited to contemporaries such as Knute Rockne, Amos Alonzo Stagg and John Heisman. It was impossible for the casual fan to find out which of these legendary figures actually invented the hidden-ball trick or was first to use the three-point stance.

I wanted to know more and believed there were others who felt the same way. I hoped to fill some of these holes in Warner's biography and give a fair and balanced account of the events that shaped his life and legend. Recent biographies of Rockne and Heisman reinforced my belief that there was still very strong interest in the early history of the game and its pioneering figures.

When I finally committed to writing this book, I purchased a copy

1

of the 1993 book *Pop Warner: Football's Greatest Teacher* by Mike Bynum. I could not believe that this was the only book ever written about Warner, who was the winningest coach in college football history when he retired and is credited with providing the blueprints for the game as we know it today. Furthermore, Bynum's terrific book, essentially a ghost-written autobiography, was told strictly from Pop's perspective. It gave plenty of insight into the man's motivations and feelings about certain games or issues but skipped many aspects and events in his life. This, I found, was a frustrating tendency of Warner's. For example, in all of his writings (books, magazine articles, newspaper series), the coach rarely, if ever, spoke about his childhood or his family. He almost never wrote about his wife, Tibb. His writings related to the Jim Thorpe Olympics scandal were, regrettably, disingenuous at best. Nor did he ever adequately cover the congressional investigations into conditions during his time at the Carlisle Indian School.

I found plenty of reference material as I navigated Pop's history. He had written a couple of books on coaching, a 60-part series of articles in late 1928 and early 1929 focusing on his career in football, and a six-piece series for *Collier's* magazine in 1931, as well as several columns and articles that appeared in various ephemera during his lifetime. But these writings, while informative and providing a foundation for a larger biographical work, provided little that revealed the man or told me much about his personal life away from the football field. Since Pop and Tibb had no children, insight into their personalities and private lives is sketchy at best.

Following every lead, no matter how tenuous, I was able to piece together what is, in my opinion, a fuller picture of Pop's personality and private life than was previously available. I found answers to most of the questions I had when I began peering into this coaching giant's life more than five years ago. Some questions remain, along with some skepticism as to why he did some of the things he did, but I feel this book presents a more complete and accurate depiction of the legendary Pop Warner than has been offered before.

ONE

Childhood

It might be a bit of a stretch to proclaim the Western New York town of Concord as the birthplace of modern football. Yet if one were to bear in mind the fact that the man some historians consider to be the father of today's game was born and raised in the small farming community nestled inconspicuously in the southern-most part of what is now Erie County, then perhaps it's not such a far-fetched notion. While Concord might not resonate with the same timbre as, say, Canton or even Cooperstown, it is in that very community that Glenn "Pop" Warner, who at one time was recognized as the winningest coach in college football history and is credited with many of the innovations that transformed the game into the one we recognize today, was born to a Civil War cavalryman and his school teacher wife.

Glenn Warner's story actually begins in the nearby town of Ashford, where his maternal grandfather, Alexander Scobey, settled his family in the 1830s. The Scobeys, like so many of the region's pioneers, migrated from New England, lured to the Genesee country after reading pamphlets circulated by agents of the Holland Land Company. The area's first inhabitants arrived about 1807, and by 1815 the population was a robust 85. Undaunted by cruel winters, unforgiving terrain and the occasional wildlife encounter, these pioneers took little time in clearing the land and erecting log houses at every turn. Though the soil on which the settlement was made was considered ideal for the cultivation of grains and vegetables, the principal industry in Concord's formative years was dairying.

Not so, however, for Alexander Scobey. Figuring that cows needed barns for shelter and feed for sustenance, Alexander established one of the area's first saw and grist mills on Cattaraugus Creek—which marks the boundary between Ashford and Concord—and operated the business successfully for the next 40 years.[1] He built the family home nearby and fathered nine children with wife Sarepta. The seventh of these children was daughter Adaline, born November 8, 1840. When Adaline came of age, she was enrolled in the nearby one-room school, and later attended high school at Springville Academy. After graduating, she became a teacher in the town's southside district, where she remained for the next sixteen years. It was said she was an extremely intelligent woman with an infectious sense of humor. She was also a talented writer, and several of her poems were published in local newspapers.

William Henry Warner was born in the nearby town of Collins in 1840, the son of Samuel and Mary (Sanders) Warner, and spent his childhood on the family farm. He contracted martial fever when the War Between the States erupted, enlisting in the 4th Arkansas Cavalry in June of 1861. He spent his entire military career in the Western theater, and by the time he mustered out four years later, William had risen to the rank of captain. He returned to Western New York after the war and took Adaline Scobey as his bride. They settled on a farm atop Nunweiler Hill near what is now the intersection of Boston and Genesee roads in the town of Concord in 1867. Five children were born to them: Alice, Nettie, Glenn, Fred, and William. Only the boys lived into adulthood, as Nettie died in infancy, and Alice at age 18 in 1886.[2]

Glenn Scobey Warner was born in the family farmhouse on April 5, 1871. Being reared on a farm and the oldest male sibling meant that Glenn learned early on the responsibility of rising before the sun to stoke the fire, tend the animals, and perform whatever other tasks were required to help his father prepare the household for the day ahead. After school, there was homework and more chores, but Glenn always managed to find time to enjoy boyhood activities with his brothers and friends living nearby. In 1878, at

Adaline (Scobey) Warner, Glenn's mother. Date not known. (Concord Historical Society, Concord, New York.)

age seven, Glenn witnessed the arrival of the Springville & Sardinia Railroad, the first trains linking the sleepy little town with the outside world. Until the age of ten, he walked to a one-room school located on Genesee Road about a mile due east of his home.[3] In 1882, Captain Warner moved the family into a house he himself had built on East Main Street within the village of Springville, the commercial hub of the town of Concord. At the time, Springville was home to slightly over 1,200 souls, and for a boy accustomed to the open spaces of Concord's outskirts, Glenn recalled, the bustling village "seemed like New York City."[4] He was enrolled at Griffith Institute, located on what is now Academy Street in the heart of Springville's burgeoning business district, about a half-mile walk from his family's new home.

Glenn was rather plump for his age, and it wasn't long before some of the boys in town saddled him with the unflattering nickname of "Butter." His somewhat oversized posterior became the inevitable target for hooligans bearing summertime slingshots and wintertime snowballs. There came a day, though, when Glenn decided he had taken enough abuse and mustered the "spunk to retaliate upon my tormentors." The reckoning occurred one wintry afternoon as he was making his way home after school. As usual, he was accosted by one of the village bullies, who grabbed the hat from Glenn's head, threw it into a puddle of mud and stamped on it.

"Right there ended my passive submission," Warner remembered. "I gave him a good licking with the other kids looking on in open mouthed astonishment at my sudden change of front." It was a cathartic moment for the youth, who discovered that a

William Warner, Glenn's father. Date not known. (Concord Historical Society, Concord, New York.)

show of strength and fearlessness sent a message to other would-be bullies: Glenn Warner was no one's patsy. "That battle showed me the way," he said, "and after a few more youthful scraps I was held in the respect befitting my size and strength by the grade and high school combined."[5]

The Warners' Main Street home became a popular gathering spot for Glenn and his growing circle of friends. The story is told of the time when a neighbor commented to Glenn's mother that the boys were damaging her front lawn with their roughhousing. Mrs. Warner responded blithely, "I'm raising boys, not grass."[6]

Somewhere along the way, Glenn developed a talent for artistry, watercolors in particular. There were no athletic teams when he arrived at Griffith Institute, nor was physical education even part of the school's program. "Throughout my boyhood," he recalled, "athletics of all kinds were regarded as an extracurricular activity, and schools and colleges did nothing to promote them."[7] All of the physical exertion enjoyed by the students took place during recess when they gathered to partake in horseplay, or perhaps attempt to get in a bit of an actual sport such as baseball or football on the school's front lawn. The lawn measured the approximate length of a standard football field, with cross streets at each end acting as goal lines and a walkway leading to the building's main door designated as the kickoff line. No one in town owned an actual football, so the boys fashioned one by inflating a cow's bladder. And since no one really knew the rules of this relatively new sport, noted Warner, what they were playing more closely resembled soccer than football. "That was all the football I could play until I went to Cornell."[8]

It's not surprising, then, that Warner never considered the gridiron sport to be his favorite. Rather, it was the game of baseball that captured his fancy as a teenager. He played for the local team, wearing pants crafted by his mother from an old pair of work overalls. Glenn was a good catcher, but his best position by far was pitcher. He combined a good fastball with an aggressive spirit, making him much sought-after by other area teams. Childhood friend Ralph Waite recalled that Glenn was a fiercely competitive young man. "He was a hard loser," said Waite, who later in life gained fame of his own as the developer of the first dental anesthetic. "But to me, this is a symbol of a great man and a great athlete."[9]

Glenn was still undecided about his future when he graduated from Griffith Institute in 1889. He had no intention of going to college, at least not until one of his former teachers suggested he take the entrance exam for the United States Military Academy at West Point. As a boy, Glenn had fantasized about following in the footsteps of his father, who had been a cavalry officer during the Civil War. But as a young adult, the idea of a career in the military no longer appealed to him. However, with no prospects on the horizon—and after a bit of coaxing from his teacher—Glenn decided to give the exam a go. He made the 55-mile trek to Niagara Falls, where the exam was being held, and gave it his best shot.

"I took the physical part of the examination and passed," he remembered. "Then the other parts of the exam were started." He recalled that a group of 40 young men were present for the test, but only four made the final cut. "I did my arithmetic problems all right, but I was too slow. I did not hustle to put them on the examination papers after working them on the scratch paper. Before I could get started I heard, 'Hand in your papers, examination over.'"[10] So much for the Army.

The following autumn, Glenn's father purchased a cattle and wheat ranch in the Wichita County, Texas, town of Iowa Park, near the Texas-Oklahoma border. The entire family was heading west and the eldest son, still unemployed, was going with them. The next three years proved one of the most contented periods in Glenn's life, as he reveled in the rough and rugged existence of a Texas cattle rancher and found an outlet for his artistic pursuits. He spent his first full day on the ranch riding horseback alongside his father and brother Bill from one end of their spread to the other. The painter within him was inspired. "The sights I saw that day were both intensely wild and beautiful."[11]

As with any farm, the work required was hard and demanding. Glenn, his brothers Fred and Bill and their father performed all of the labor that first season, clearing the land, herding stock and planting the crop. That rugged, non-stop work transformed the fat that once drew boyhood taunts into solid muscle. During his second summer in Texas, a local tin-

Glenn Scobey Warner as a teenager. Date not known. (Concord Historical Society, Concord, New York.)

smith, aware of Glenn's interest in art, invited the young ranch hand to come to work for him as an apprentice. Glenn had been a frequent visitor to the tin shop and marveled at the many designs and implements there. Once he discovered how much he could earn in this line of work, Glenn eagerly accepted the offer. He worked hard, and this, coupled with his natural artistic ability, quickly earned him a promotion from his apprenticeship to actually managing the shop at $15 per week.[12]

Glenn's passion for baseball also followed him out West, and he was soon playing for a local team. In his first season, he led his team to the state amateur championship game—which they ultimately lost to a squad from Waxahachie. It was during his time in Texas that Warner developed a fervor for another sport of sorts—gambling. He would later recall his first foray into the world of wagering, in which he bet that a cow pony he owned could beat a friend's mustang in a sprint, and was so certain of it that he staked his first week's earnings on the outcome. Glenn had failed, however, to take into consideration the weight of the jockeys. He himself, at nearly 200 pounds, would be riding the pony, while the mustang would be ridden by a man weighing in at a mere 140. The race was over almost from the moment it began. The mustang tore out from the starting line, leaving Warner and his pony struggling simply to gain full speed. He had lost the race, as well as his week's wages, but gained a new passion that stayed with him for the rest of his life.[13]

The young man had assimilated easily into life in northern Texas, calling his time there "about the happiest of my life," yet he never lost his love for his home town back in Western New York.[14] In the summer of 1892, Warner returned to Springville for what was supposed to be a vacation, but things didn't play out as he had planned. He hadn't been back long when he was invited to pitch for the Springville town team in a five-game series against a rival team from the neighboring burg of Gowanda. The towns enjoyed a mutual civic hatred, and the series promised to be spirited. The event began with both teams fielding only local players, but the will to win overcame whatever sense of honor either team possessed, and by the second game both had a couple of paid ringers on their rosters. By the fifth game, both rosters were almost completely composed of imported talent. One of the players recruited for the Gowanda nine was a young shortstop from a western Pennsylvania minor league team. That shortstop, John McGraw, went on to an illustrious career as a player and manager in the major leagues, but for now was little more than a hireling brought in to tip the scales in the favor of the Gowandans. Warner managed to remain as one of the few local boys not displaced by paid talent, and though his team was able to force the series to go the full slate of games, McGraw and his crew won the fifth and final outing and claimed bragging rights. This chance meeting between the two future legends proved valuable to both men in years to come.

Rather than return to Texas as originally planned, Glenn decided to extend his stay and visit Buffalo—some 30 miles north of Springville—to see what the booming city had to offer. It just so happened that the Grand Circuit—a touring harness racing series—was in town at the same time. His wallet still bulging from money earned as a tinsmith, Glenn decided to try his luck. He believed he had a foolproof system in wagering small sums on each race and allowing the cash to accumulate slowly, instead of attempting to strike it rich quickly with large bets. "I won fifty dollars," Warner recalled, "and straightaway jumped to the conclusion that I knew everything there was to know about horses."[15]

Emboldened by the ease with which he had been able to make a quick fifty bucks, and with no immediate plans to return west, Glenn opted to follow the Grand Circuit for the rest of the racing season. Employing his foolproof system, Warner projected that he could rake in profits of $50 to $100 per week. But cold reality set in after he lost not only his recent winnings but also most of his tinsmithing earnings the following week in Rochester. All he had managed to salvage was enough money to cover the cost of return fare to Springville.

Glenn had plenty of time to reflect on his options while the train made its way back to Erie County. "I dared not write to my father and tell him I was broke," he reasoned. "I would have to explain what had become of the money he knew I had when I left home."[16] He also saw no reason he could give to justify remaining in New York. After some serious internal debate, Warner's fertile mind hatched an idea that incorporated the kind of skullduggery for which he would later become famous.

William Warner had always hoped his eldest son would take up law, so Glenn devised a plan that both satisfied his father's dream and actually prompted him to send the secretly struggling son some much needed money. Glenn found a catalogue for Cornell University Law School and enclosed it in an envelope along with a letter declaring his intention of pursuing a law degree. His letter pointed out that he needed funds to defray some of the expenses, such as tuition and textbooks. A few weeks later, Glenn received a response from his father in which William expressed his happiness with Glenn's decision. Even better—the letter contained a check for $100! The ruse had worked. Glenn had been spared the humiliation of having to explain how he had lost all his money.

Figuring he had better not push his luck any further, Glenn decided to enroll at Cornell while he still had the funds to do so. "My sudden decision to enter Cornell was caused by the result of a horse race which shows again what seemingly trivial things may change a person's whole life," he observed. "I had no thought of going to college when I finished high school. But what I considered at the time a great misfortune turned out to be about the luckiest thing that ever happened to me. I would probably never have gone to college but not for that turn of the wheel of fortune."[17]

Two

Pop Warner, Football Player

On September 27, 1892, 21-year-old Glenn Warner departed Springville headed eastward by train toward the central New York town of Ithaca, home to Cornell University. Somewhere along the 150 miles separating the two communities, Warner became acquainted with a fellow traveler named Carl Johanson, who was also studying law at Cornell and just happened to be captain of the varsity football team.[1] Johanson was entering his second year with the Cornell eleven, after spending the previous four starring at Williams College.[2] Quickly sizing Warner up as one bearing the physical attributes of a solid football lineman (six feet, 215 pounds), Johanson inquired as to whether the Springvillian had ever played the game. Warner confessed to having never played football on a formal level, and also that the only actual ball he had ever seen was the one he and his schoolmates had fashioned from a cow's bladder.

Johanson then asked Warner if he had experience in any other athletic pursuits. "I explained that I played quite a bit of baseball," Warner recalled. "He told me to report at the [football] field that afternoon and he would see that I was outfitted."[3]

Later that day, Warner made his way to football practice as instructed. The Cornell football team, established in 1887, held its practices and games at Percy Field, a Spartan facility located on a seven-acre piece of land that served as the primary site for all of the school's athletics. "The football field was little more than a corner lot," Warner remembered. "The bleachers along the field would hardly accommodate 2,000 people. We dressed and undressed under the battered old wooden grandstand, a few cleated boards our only privacy."[4]

After being outfitted with the requisite gear, Warner hustled onto the field and found Johanson putting the team through its paces. Johanson welcomed his new player and immediately assigned him to the left guard position. The team had already been practicing for two weeks prior to Warner's arrival, and was brimming with confidence after having defeated the Syracuse Athletic Club in a warm-up game three days earlier. Warner would have a great deal of catching up to do, so Johanson kept his first lesson straightforward: "All you've got to do," he instructed, "is to keep 'em from going through you and spoiling the play when we've got the ball, and when they've got the ball, knock the tar out of your man and tackle the runner. Perfectly simple."[5]

Warner later recalled struggling through that first practice, as might be expected for someone with no formal experience. But even though he made a few errors, captain Johanson was impressed with Warner's determination and hustle. At the end of the workout, Johanson instructed the squad to take a final jog around the playing field before retiring to the dressing room. As he was about to join his teammates, Warner was called back by Johanson, who told him that he was not expected to run with the rest of the men, since it was his first day. But Warner demurred. "I thought it would make a hit with [Johanson] if I took all the work, so I followed the bunch thinking it would only be once around and I could stand that." He soon regretted his decision, for the team was not running one lap, but one *mile*—four laps![6]

Unfortunately for Warner, there wasn't much time to recover from that brutal first practice, as Cornell was scheduled to host Syracuse University the very next day—a Wednesday. On a warm, early-autumn midweek afternoon at Percy Field in Ithaca, Glenn Scobey Warner received his gridiron baptism, playing the entire game and helping his Cornell University team defeat Syracuse, 58–0. "I can't remember that the game was marked by any large amount of science," said Warner. "Both teams used only straight bucks and slants off tackle, but lack of trick plays was more than made up for by vigor." Warner recalled a feeling of satisfaction when the official blew the whistle to end the contest, believing that he had acquitted himself as well as could be expected against men he presumed to be grizzled veterans.

"This is my first game," Warner said as he shook hands with a Syracuse lineman. He was surprised by the reply.

"You've got nothing on me. It's my first, too!"[7]

First game or not, Warner was hooked. It had taken just two days of organized football for baseball to be supplanted as his favorite sport.

And he wouldn't have to wait long for his second game, as Cornell hosted Bucknell just three days later—Saturday, October 1—and registered another whitewash, winning 54–0. Three more huge wins over Dickinson (58–0), Lehigh (76–0) and Williams College (24–12) brought Cornell to 6–0 before traveling to Springfield, Massachusetts, to face Harvard (which, along with Princeton and Yale, made up college football's "Big Three") on November 23. Despite outscoring their previous opponents by a combined 286–12 (an average of better than 47 points per game), Cornell could manage only 14 points against Harvard's tough defense, and went down to defeat for the first time that year, 20–14. But Johanson had the Red Men back on the beam three days later when the University of Michigan visited Percy Field, walking away with a convincing 44–0 win. This was followed by victories over MIT (44–12), the Manhattan Athletic Club (16–0), and Michigan (30–12, this time at Michigan).[8]

In Warner's debut season, Cornell posted a sparkling 10–1 record, and outscored its opponents 434–54. He later wrote that much of the credit for the team's success belonged to Charles Courtney, the school's rowing coach, who doubled as the football team's athletic trainer. Warner learned a great deal about conditioning from observing how Courtney trained his athletes. Courtney prescribed vigorous exercise and strict diets, which forbade desserts such as pies and ice cream sodas. He even banned apples on the Sunday hikes he had made compulsory. Transgressors were dealt with harshly, as his rowing team found out when it came to Courtney's attention that they had partaken of some strawberry shortcake prior to one particular race.

Glenn Warner became "Pop" after joining the Cornell football team in 1892, when he was given the nickname for being the oldest player on a squad at the age of 21. (Concord Historical Society, Concord, New York.)

Proving that he wasn't kidding or playing favorites, Courtney suspended
the whole team and replaced them with a backup crew, which ultimately
won the intercollegiate title and went down in school lore as the "Shortcake Crew."[9]

Warner's first autumn at Cornell was significant for at least one other
event. Having taken three years off between graduating from Springville's
Griffith Institute and enrolling at Cornell, Warner was now a full-grown
adult of 21 years. "In the old days," he recalled, "the boys didn't get to college as early in life as they do in the present day. Therefore, most of the
college teams of those days were composed of more mature players."[10]
Still, at 21, Warner was older than the other freshmen on the squad, and
his advanced age soon made him the subject of some good-natured rib-
bing. It wasn't long before a teammate, whose identity is lost to history,
referred to Warner as "Pop" during a practice. The other players shared a
hearty laugh at the offhand remark, but the appellation stuck, and became
the name by which Warner was best-known for the rest of his life.[11]

As the year 1893 dawned, Warner's eye was caught by a posting on a
campus bulletin board announcing tryouts for the upcoming baseball season. The diamond sport had been Warner's first love, and with dreams of
a major league career spurring him, the young man now known to everyone at Cornell as Pop reported for the first day of practice. The captain
of the Cornell team was Harry L. Taylor, a lanky infielder who, despite having played the past three seasons for the big-league Louisville Colonels,
was returning to his alma mater to resume his amateur career. That first
day, Taylor caught while Warner took the mound. Taylor cautioned Warner
not to throw too hard, since this was the first workout and he would not
want to overdo it and cause injury to his pitching arm. Arrogantly disre-
garding his captain's admonitions, Warner decided to give it his all. "I'll
show this bird Taylor something," he thought to himself before unleashing
a roundhouse curve. He proceeded to mix curveballs with fastballs, putting his all into every pitch while paying no heed to the damage he was
doing to his arm in the process. The next day, Glenn's arm was so sore he
could barely throw. Rather than easing up as advised, however, he tried
to throw even harder, worsening the injury and any chance he had of making the team.[12]

With his hopes of becoming the next Cap Anson or Willie Keeler
dashed, Warner determined to try his hand as a pugilist. Despite an admitted lack of formal training in boxing, Warner enjoyed more success in the

ring than he did on the diamond. Using his size advantage and self-taught "rushing" tactics, Warner managed to win Cornell's heavyweight title, defeating the man who had held the crown for the previous two years. In the spring, Warner tried out for and made the Cornell track team. He competed in several events, including the mile walk and the two-mile bicycle race, but Pop's best events were the shot put and the hammer throw. His best effort in the shot measured 35 feet even, just three inches shy of the Cornell record. He managed to hurl the hammer 84 feet, a little more than a foot short of the school best.

During the offseason prior to the 1893 football campaign, the Cornell players elected a new captain—halfback George P. Witherbee, a very popular classmate as well as a member of the Cornell rowing team. But that summer, Witherbee's teammates were jolted with the news that their captain had drowned in Lake Champlain when the sailboat he and several others were in was overturned by a strong wind. It was reported that Witherbee lost his life while attempting to save one of his mates.[13] Elected to fill the captaincy was tackle Charles J. Barr, whose reign proved one of the lowest points in the history of the team, as the Cornellians struggled to replace not only Witherbee, but also Winchester Osgood, the team's top halfback, who had left Cornell to play at the University of Pennsylvania. Barr was not up to the task, and compounded the issue by pushing the players to the point of exhaustion with daily scrimmages. "We scrimmaged almost every day," recalled Warner, "until we were bruised and crippled, and all the life and ambition and spirit we had was pounded out of us." The team limped to a dismal 2–5–1 record, its first losing season since the inaugural campaign in 1887. The fact that both of Cornell's victories came in the year's first two games lends credence to Warner's assertion that the team was in better shape at the season's start than it was at the end, with the campaign ending in an embarrassing 50–0 loss against Osgood and the University of Pennsylvania.

Following the 1893 season, halfback George P. Dyer was elected team captain for 1894. Of course, it mattered little to Warner who the captain was going to be, since he was graduating prior to the start of football season and hoped to be practicing law by that time. By the summer, however, no prospects for gainful employment had developed. During the previous summer break, Glenn's father had helped subsidize his son's room and board, but this year was different. His two-year curriculum complete, Glenn was now on his own. Making matters worse was the sharp economic downturn brought on by the Panic of 1893, the worst depression in U.S. history to that point. He returned to Springville and lived hand-to-mouth, performing odd jobs to earn food money. It was during this time that Warner began to find an audience for his artwork and was able to raise a little cash from the sale of his street scenes and landscapes.

Meanwhile, Cornell's football team had been decimated by the large number of players graduating that spring. Team manager William F. Atkinson visited Glenn in Springville and suggested that he return to Cornell for another year. All he would have to do is take a few graduate courses and he'd be eligible to play football. Glenn was intrigued, but didn't have the $200 he estimated was needed to cover the costs of school, plus room and board. No problem. Atkinson offered to purchase some of Warner's artwork for exactly that amount.[14]

Eighteen-ninety-four was the first season in which Cornell had a formal head coach, relieving the captain of the responsibility of running the team. Marshall Newell, a four-time All-America tackle at Harvard—whom legendary coach John Heisman considered the greatest football player he ever saw—was hired.[15] Newell was a staunch proponent of the teaching of fundamentals and drilled his players constantly in the proper techniques of blocking and tackling. Warner, ever the student, soaked up Newell's teachings like a dry sponge. The results were immediate, as the Cornellians defeated Syracuse (39–0), Union (37–0) and Lafayette (24–0) to start the season at 3–0.

During the week following the Lafayette tilt, the Cornell players assembled at Percy Field for the purpose of electing a permanent captain for the '94 campaign. George Dyer had been given the position on an interim basis until it was clear which players were returning for the season. With the roster solidified, Newell now felt it was time for the players to choose the man who was to lead them on the field for the balance of the schedule. On the afternoon of Wednesday, October 17, Warner's teammates paid him the ultimate tribute by electing him to the post.[16] It was Pop's first real position of leadership, and he came to relish the role.

Warner's captaincy began on a sour note, however, as Cornell lost its next game, a 12–4 thriller at Princeton that saw the new skipper score his first touchdown as a collegian on a three-yard line buck.[17] Cornell then traveled to Cambridge to play Harvard and, despite Warner's second touchdown in as many weeks (this time after recovering a blocked punt in the end zone), the Red Men came out on the short end of a 22–12 decision. Yet Warner was anything but disheartened by the defeats—in fact, quite the contrary. He viewed his team's ability to score upon two of college football's so-called Big Three to be a "great feat" for Cornell, which was still considered a relatively small school at the time.

Newell and Warner had the team back on track the following week with a 22–0 victory over visiting Michigan, but this was to be Newell's last game with Cornell for several weeks. He had been asked to return to Harvard to help prepare his alma mater for its upcoming game against archrival Yale. As captain, Warner was placed in charge of the team for the duration of Newell's absence, the timing of which could not have been worse. Pop had just two days to prepare the squad for its next game, a Wednesday afternoon contest with the Crescent Athletic Club in Brooklyn, which was to be followed three days later with a game in Albany against Williams College.

The Cornellians made light work of the Crescents, however, walking away with an easy 22–0 win, and that initial taste of success inspired Warner's daring side. Football in the early 1890s was a straight-on affair in which players used brute force to advance the ball toward their opponent's goal line. Instead of running the ball where the other team is waiting for you, he thought, why not run it where they won't be expecting you to? Warner's pencil worked feverishly as he sketched out a play he believed could fool the Williams defense and possibly result in a long gain, or even a touchdown. The next practice found Warner providing a crash course in the running of his new play, the first of literally thousands he would unleash on gridirons over the next forty-plus years. The play had three of the backs feigning an end run to the left side of the line while the quarterback turned and handed off to the left guard, who in this case just happened to be the team's interim coach. The left guard would then run to the right with no interference and, hopefully, no defenders in his path. Scoring that touchdown against Princeton after spending two-and-a-half years toiling in the trenches of the forward line had made Warner thirsty for another opportunity to lug the leather, a privilege not normally entrusted to guards and tackles.

Warner had his team practice the play, dubbed "Number 39," over and over until he was satisfied it could be executed without error. As the game was winding down to its final minutes, the score was deadlocked at 0–0. With Cornell in possession of the ball at midfield, Pop turned to quarterback Clinton Wyckoff and whispered that it was time to run the special play. The players then took their positions at the line of scrimmage, and Wyckoff barked out the signals and received the snap from center. Everyone on the Cornell side of the ball surged left—everyone, that is, except Warner, who took a step back and turned to his right. The quarterback drew in the defense by faking a pitch to the halfback before handing off to his left guard, heading in the opposite direction. After sprinting around the right side of the line, Warner looked upfield to see no one between himself and the opponent's goal line. The deception, just like the one he had used to convince his father to send him money for college, had worked beautifully. With all of the speed his 215-pound frame could muster, Warner made for the Williams end zone. But it was late in the game and, being a lineman, he was unaccustomed to sprinting long distances. After about 20 yards, he was already slowing down. He clutched the ball tightly to his chest using both hands, wanting to make sure he didn't fumble. A moment later, Warner was grabbed from behind by a Williams defender, making a valiant tackle to save the game. Warner held the ball in front of his torso in an effort to soften his landing, but as soon as he hit the ground, the pigskin popped free and was recovered by the defense. Williams held on until the final whistle, preserving the scoreless tie. Cornell hadn't won, but Warner didn't have time to be upset about it. His first trick play was a success, and his head now stormed with ideas—ideas that would eventually revolutionize the game of football.[18]

Cornell then suffered a heartbreaking road loss at Penn, losing 6–0 after holding the favored Quakers to a scoreless tie at halftime. Then it was on to Buffalo, where Michigan avenged the earlier season loss at Ithaca by vanquishing Cornell, 12–4.

Warner's swan song as a collegiate gridder was played November 29, Thanksgiving Day, against the visiting Lehigh eleven. Cornell prevailed in a contest cut short when Lehigh walked off the field early in the second half. The dispute erupted after Cornell halfback Frank Starbuck returned a Lehigh fumble for a touchdown, giving the Red Men the lead in the game. The Lehigh boys argued that the whistle had blown, but the referee refused to waver—the touchdown stood. The visitors, incensed, stormed off the field. But that wasn't the end of it. The referee then ordered Cornell to attempt the conversion, which they did successfully, giving them a 10–6 win. Despite the ignominious ending to Warner's final outing, it was his block and subsequent recovery of a first-half Lehigh field goal attempt that was ultimately the difference in the game.[19]

Pop Warner's playing career was now over, and it was time to buckle down and start earning a living. Armed with a prestigious Bachelor of Laws degree from Cornell University, Warner prepared to begin life anew as an attorney. But for someone who had spent his first 23 years going from one vigorous pursuit to the next (family farm, town-team baseball, cattle ranching, tinsmithing, university football), the prospect of spending the rest of his life in the day-to-day drudgery of legal work was more than he could bear. Fortunately for Warner, he wouldn't have to for very long.

THREE

Pop Warner, Coach

During the 1894 football season, while still engaged as the starting left guard and captain of the Cornell University football team, Warner managed to find time to study for and take the New York State bar exam. Unlike his attempt at the West Point exam three years earlier, Warner passed and was duly licensed to practice law. After playing his final game, he accepted an offer from the law firm of Scott & Scott in Buffalo, and the following January began what proved to be a very brief legal career.[1]

But as Pop struggled to settle into what was supposed to be his life's work, his thoughts kept returning to his true love—football. How unfair it seemed that it had taken nearly three years for him to fully grasp the game, and just as he was playing the best football of his life, his career was over. "It wasn't until I was almost finished playing that I learned the game's primary fundamentals such as blocking and kicking," he said. "Sometimes I wonder if I could have been selected to Walter Camp's All-America team had I gotten more football experience while in high school."[2]

His yearning was short-lived, however, for that spring Warner was contacted by the business manager of the Cornell football team, who was relaying an offer from Iowa State College of Agriculture & Mechanic Arts (now Iowa State University) to coach that school's football team the following fall. Warner hadn't been practicing law long enough to make a respectable living, and figured that he could augment his regular salary by coaching football on autumn weekends. Iowa was offering $25 per week, plus expenses, with the condition that he be present to start practices in mid–August. Warner was thrilled: "Twenty-five dollars a week sounded like big money to me." But Iowa was a long way from Buffalo, and since he had a little time before having to respond, he decided to do a little research to see if there were any other schools out there looking for a football coach. Employing the *World Almanac* as his guide, Warner compiled a list of nearly 100 schools and sent letters of inquiry to a select few.[3] He was pleasantly surprised when he received a reply from the University of Georgia, with an offer to begin at $35 per week starting in mid–September. Suddenly, a light bulb went on in his head. Why accept one job and collect one salary when he could accept both and pocket all the money being offered? He sat down and composed a letter explaining to Iowa State officials that he had already accepted a position at the University of Georgia, but added that he was more than willing to come up to Ames in August and spend a month preparing the squad and coaches for the upcoming football season. To his delight, the proposal was accepted, with a counteroffer of $150 plus expenses for his four-and-a-half weeks of service. The school would arrange to have former team captain Bert German work closely with Warner to learn his system and take over after his departure. In the meantime, Warner notified the University of Georgia that he was accepting their offer, and would be present and ready to begin practices on September 15.

In early August, Warner arrived at Ames to begin his first head-coaching job. He had no prior knowledge of the talent he had to work with when he blew his whistle to signal the first practice on August 15. The team had never had a proper head coach, and it was clear upon first inspection that they had much to learn. It didn't help, as Warner later confessed, that the coach was also learning on the go. He had full grasp of the guard position, of course, but the other positions were a different matter. As a result, Warner was forced to learn more about the game of football in the next month than he had in his entire three seasons at Cornell. But he was equal to the challenge. "What little football knowledge I did possess, I imparted fairly well to the players," he recalled. "The players were mostly farm boys who had never played football before entering college, but they were all good pupils." Warner drove his players hard in the very warm late-summer heat, and by the time the Iowans were scheduled to play an exhibition game against the Butte (Montana) Athletic Club in mid–September, he felt they were in top physical condition.[4]

Iowa State had received an invitation to come out to Butte shortly after Warner's arrival, with a financial guarantee "sufficient to cover the team's expenses." Because the Butte mines ran three shifts six days per week, the game was scheduled for a Sunday so the miners could attend. But even with the financial incentive, playing on the Sabbath was not going to sit well with the powers-that-be at Iowa State, so Warner "informed" school officials that the game was being played on Saturday. The trip was approved.

"At that time," Warner recalled, "Butte was the toughest and sportiest town in the United States, everything wide open both night and day. We found the good people of Butte full of confidence in their team and, figuring it a safe bet, I put up all the money I was to receive for my season's coaching." But once again, Warner's powers of prognostication proved lacking. While he was correct in believing his team better conditioned and disciplined, he failed to take other variables into account. The field was hard and devoid of grass—the result of toxic fumes emanating from the nearby ore smelting plants—and this made the passing of the ball between the center and the quarterback a tricky proposition. The referee was handpicked by the home team, and his bias was evident from the opening whistle. Whenever the Iowans neared the enemy's goal, the referee would invariably make a call to blunt the drive. "We soon discovered that the referee didn't mean to let us win," Warner observed. "When we finally threatened to leave after a series of unfair decisions, he calmly told us we could whistle for our expense money if we did." But perhaps the most disconcerting distraction was the crowd gathered to watch the fiasco. "The Butte cheerleaders were whiskered gentlemen who kept up a continuous fusillade with six shooters. Almost every man in the crowd had a large gun on his belt, and anytime Butte pulled off a ground-gaining play, out came those guns and harked their applause."[5]

Trailing by ten at halftime, and with his players exhausted and hurting from the overly aggressive play of the Montanans—and no doubt anxious to save his bet—Warner decided to suit up and insert himself into the game. It didn't help much. When the game was mercifully called after the third quarter, nearly every Iowa State player's uniform, Warner's included, was torn and tattered. Not only had they lost the game by a 13–10 score, Warner also found himself $150 dollars lighter in the pocket. But the rookie coach waxed philosophical about the experience. "We went back to Iowa a sadder but wiser bunch of boys," he recalled. "But that wager was a good investment, for it taught me a lesson. I have never been overly optimistic over the outcome of any game since that unexpected setback. That feeling has been strengthened since then by the fact that some of the defeats my teams have suffered came at the time when I was most confident of winning."[6]

Shortly after returning to Ames from the disastrous road trip, it was time for Warner to depart for Athens, Georgia, where he was scheduled to take over as coach at the University of Georgia. Before leaving, Warner instructed assistant coach German to give the players a week off to recover from the Butte trip before preparing them to face a very good Northwestern team at Evanston, Illinois, on September 28. The advice was sound, as the Iowans responded by trouncing Northwestern 36–0.

When Warner's train arrived in Athens, he was met by the graduate manager of the football team, who helped the coach load his belongings onto a horse-drawn wagon that was to serve as the transportation from the depot to the school. As the humidity soared and temperatures hovered around 90 degrees, he was taken to the athletic facilities, and immediately felt a sense of regret. He surveyed the parched football field and caught sight of the rickety bleachers, which he guessed held 150 spectators at best, and momentarily considered turning tail and heading back to Iowa. But the team manager convinced him not to be discouraged by the school's less-than-stellar facilities. The team, he boasted, possessed enough talent to surmount any shortcomings one might notice in a cursory tour. His concerns somewhat allayed, Warner opted to stick it out.

But Warner's list of concerns grew as he called his players in for the first practice of his tenure at Georgia. When Warner counted no more than a dozen bodies populating the practice field, he thought, "Up against a pretty tough proposition out there."[7] But the first-year coach soon discovered that his men, though short in number, were long in pluck. He came to the conclusion that players from southern regions tended to be both leaner and meaner than their northern counterparts. The two best players on the squad were junior halfback Rufus "Cow" Nalley and senior fullback Herbert Stubbs, the team's captain.

Warner drilled his players incessantly, applying the same attention to the fundamentals of blocking, tackling and discipline that he learned from Marshall Newell at Cornell. He rousted the players from their beds at six o'clock in the morning and forced them to run five miles before breakfast. Afternoon practices could last as long as three hours. He was demanding and not above belittling a slacker with insults and profanity.[8] But by the time of the season-opening game against Wofford College on October 19, the team had been whipped into shape and won easily, 34–0.

An act of historic proportions brought Georgia (which would not officially adopt the nickname of Bulldogs for another 23 years) its first loss of the year when it faced the University of North Carolina in Atlanta on October 26. With the score deadlocked at 0–0, a North Carolina drive stalled on its own 13-yard line. Warner watched from the sidelines as the opposition went into punt formation. The ball was snapped to the punter who, seeing his forward line breached by a horde of on rushing Georgians, scrambled to his right. In an act of desperation, the punter heaved the ball in the direction of left halfback George Stephens, who was making his way downfield to cover the return. Stephens caught the ball at his own 20 and raced the remaining 80 yards for a touchdown. The only problem was that the forward pass had not yet been legalized. As the North Carolina side of the field erupted with cheers, the Georgia faithful were apoplectic. Warner was beside himself and argued vehemently with the officials that the play should not be allowed. But the referee inexplicably claimed he had not seen the throw and refused to call the play back. The touchdown stood as the margin of victory, and Georgia fell to 1–1. Despite Warner's protests over the game-winning forward pass, he would eventually soften his stance and become one of the tactic's most frequent users in the early days after its legalization.[9]

Two days after a second North Carolina loss (this time a 10–6 final), the Georgians crushed Alabama 30–6 to bring their record to 2–2. Warner had more than two weeks to rest his men before traveling to Atlanta to face Sewanee on Monday, November 18, and won 22–0. It was then on to Nashville to play Vanderbilt the following Saturday, losing 6–0.

The season was scheduled to end with a contest against a hated rival, the Agricultural & Mechanical College of Alabama (generally then, and now officially, known as Auburn for its home city), on Thursday, November 28—Thanksgiving Day. Warner had been told by seemingly everyone on campus that the annual Auburn game, which has since become recognized as the Deep South's oldest football rivalry, was the most important of the season. The teams had met only twice before, but it was now tradition that they end their seasons against each other. Since Warner had never seen Auburn play, he had little knowledge of the team's personnel or playing style. He asked the team manager and alumni members whether it might be wise to send someone to scout them and bring back a report. The reply was always the same: "Georgia defeated Auburn last year and as Georgia has a much stronger team this year there is no need except as to how big we will make the score."[10]

Auburn was coached by 26-year-old John Heisman, who was in his first year at the school after spending the previous three seasons at Oberlin and Buchtel (now Akron). Heisman was destined to become one of the most successful coaches in college football history, but for now was guiding his team through a rather mediocre 1–1 season. The Georgia team was also at .500 with a record of 3–3, but all of their victories had been lopsided, and all of their losses had been by six points or less. Warner recalled that his team arrived in Atlanta "a very confident and somewhat cocky outfit." Georgia rooters spent much of the time leading up to the game visiting every saloon and hotel in the city, trying to place bets with their Auburn counterparts. Despite being offered two- and even three-to-one odds, few Auburn fans were biting.

Too bad, for Heisman had his men well-prepared for this grudge match. Unbeknownst to Warner, Heisman had been in the stands to witness the October 26 contest between Georgia and North Carolina, and had come away with some insights that proved useful in helping Auburn grind out a 16–6 triumph.[11] And just as he had in previous instances when his teams came out on the short end of the score, Warner was able to find a lesson and learn from it. "In my desire to turn out a winning team," he observed, "I had brought the boys up to their final game in an overtrained condition and this, together with their over-confident and self-satisfied feeling, not to mention the unexpected strength of our opponents, brought us to Waterloo."[12]

To his surprise, he was reassured by alumni that it was they, and not Warner, who were to blame for the loss, since he was advised that scouting Auburn was simply unnecessary. Georgia's final record of 3–4 was a comedown from the previous year's mark of 5–1, but school officials were happy nevertheless with the team's performance and offered Warner a contract— with a five-dollar-per-week raise—for the 1896 season. Meanwhile, Iowa State, implementing Warner's system and weekly advice, finished with a mark of 3–3. They too expressed their desire to have Warner return the following season.

Despite an aggregate record of six wins and seven losses, Pop Warner entered the 1896 season with votes of confidence from both of the schools he coached in 1895. With Iowa State starting its practices and season much earlier than the University of Georgia, he was able to repeat the arrangements of the previous season. He was another year wiser, and would utilize the lessons he had learned in his first year to bring unprecedented success to both schools in his second.

Iowa State opened its season with a 46–0 destruction of Iowa Falls and a 50–0 laugher over Cornell (Iowa) College. But just as he had in 1895, Warner was expected to be in Athens by mid–September to begin whipping that school's squad into shape. Before departing, Warner left assistant coach Bert German specific instructions on how to run every aspect of the team during his absence.

Georgia had a short schedule in 1896—just four games, in fact—and didn't play its first until October 24 against Wofford, winning 26–0. Victories over North Carolina (24–16) and Sewanee (26–0) brought the Georgians to 3–0 and, with just one game remaining, a legitimate chance at an undefeated season.

The traditional season finale pitted Georgia against archrival Auburn. Determined not to make the same mistake that had befallen his team when Georgia lost to Auburn the previous year, Warner sent scouts to several Auburn games, and the reports they brought back revealed some tendencies he felt could be exploited.

Warner noted one particular tendency of Auburn's was to position a single man in a forward position about ten yards from the ball when they were receiving kickoffs. The remaining ten players were spread out much farther behind him. Warner devised a scheme that had the kicker punch a short kick to the left. He then stationed two of his fastest players to that side of the field and instructed them to sprint and try to beat the opponent to the ball.

Warner called for the on-side kick to be used as the beginning of a chain of interlocking plays that were intended bamboozle the opposition. If the on-side kick proved successful, the first play of the series called for all of the players to line up on the right side of the ball on first down. The center would then hike the ball sideways to one of the backs, who would then follow his blockers. This runner then, in turn, would lateral to a trailing back, who would carry the ball until tackled. The next play repeated the steps of the first, only running everything in the opposite direction.

There was no chance to use the plays in the fiercely contested first half, but his team was able to stake out a slim lead heading into the locker room. Warner instructed fullback Hatton Lovejoy to initiate the sequence on the opening kickoff of the second half. It could not have played out more perfectly. Lovejoy's kick was recovered by Rufus Nalley, and the Georgia offense moved into position on the right side of the ball. Just as Warner had planned, the Auburn defense was totally confused. The ball was snapped, and Georgia gained considerable yardage on the first play. The second, begun with all the Georgia players now on the left side of the ball, was good for another long gain. Two plays later, halfback Walter Cothran crashed into the end zone, giving Georgia a 12–0 lead. Heisman's boys never knew what had hit them. Auburn managed to score late in the game, but the successful employment of Warner's plan had provided the margin of victory.[13]

"That trick kickoff and the two trick plays following it won the game for us," he reasoned, "but it is only about once in a lifetime that such a series of three plays can be worked without something going wrong. As everything turned out perfectly we were called a very smart team. Had luck been against us the coach would have been hailed as a very dumb person. Such is football!"[14]

The win brought Georgia its first undefeated season and Warner's name to the attention of every school looking to hire a creative, proven coach for their football team. But any school that was thinking they had a chance at signing the up-and-coming Warner was going to be disappointed. If he was going to leave the University of Georgia, there was only one school that could hope to sign him—the same place where he was introduced to the game as a 21-year-old college freshman—Cornell University.

Four

Back to Cornell

The successes enjoyed by Warner during his two seasons coaching simultaneously at Iowa State and the University of Georgia brought his name into national prominence. It was inevitable that other schools, looking to advance their programs, would come to Athens armed with attractive offers. One such school was Warner's alma mater, Cornell University, which hadn't replaced former coach Marshall Newell after he left more than a year earlier. A three-man committee—consisting of team Captain William McKeever, Team Manager Daniel M. McLaughlin and university professor L. M. Dennis—was charged with the responsibility of luring one of its most famous alumni back to Ithaca for the 1897 season. Induced by the offer of $600 per season—double what he had been earning at Georgia—Warner signed his contract on January 30, making him the first Cornell grad ever to return to coach the team.[1] And, since the Cornell season didn't start until September 25, Warner was able to return to Iowa State for a third year.

Warner was pleased to learn that Joe Beacham—a teammate of his at Cornell and captain of the team in 1896—had already been hired to be his assistant coach, but it wasn't long before the good will and harmony that were present upon Pop's arrival began to erode. At the time, the duties of the college head football coach were still in the early stages of development. He hadn't realized that school officials, alumni, or anyone else with an opinion felt comfortable offering the coach advice, anytime or anywhere, on how the team should be run. A particularly bothersome incident involved a freshman guard named Mark Faville, who had been assessed by some observers as being too cowardly to play football at the university level. According to reports, Faville had played on a local high school team and had "shown a yellow streak and was not to be depended upon." Warner patiently thanked the meddlers for their advice, but let it be known that he intended to be the judge of who was and who was not going to suit up for the Cornell football team. The coach, demonstrating his firm grasp of the use of psychology to motivate his players, pulled Faville aside one day and told him the things he had been hearing, believing it would goad the youngster into working hard to disprove his detractors. It worked.

"He thanked me and explained that he had been crippled the entire season the year previous and had been unfit to play," Warner recalled. "No head guards with ear protectors were worn then, and Faville developed a pair of very sore cauliflower ears. Yet with those painfully sore ears Faville continued to dive under the mass offensive players and played a great game all season."[2]

Despite the distractions, Warner found ways to develop a strong and successful team. He didn't have the material that the big schools such as Harvard, Princeton and Pennsylvania had, but he believed hard work and exacting execution would give his team a chance to win, no matter the opponent. Applying his customary focus on fundamentals and discipline, Warner had his team ready by the time the season opened on September 25 against Colgate, winning 6–0. The Red Men then defeated Syracuse (15–0) and Tufts (15–0) before tying Lafayette (4–4) to bring the season record to 3–0–1 as they prepared to face the powerful Princeton Tigers on October 23.

Princeton arrived in Ithaca at 6–0, having won their previous contests by an average score of 38–0. They had been enjoying this success while employing a close offensive formation called the "turtleback." There were no rules at the time regarding just how a team had to line up for an offensive play, so Tigers captain Garrett Cochran devised a tight configuration that had each player slightly overlapping the man next to him and the ends slightly behind the line. The quarterback, standing directly behind the center, was backed up by the remaining backs, who stood about three yards from the scrimmage line. From this formation, one of the backs would receive the ball from the quarterback and attempt to smash through the line while the other backs pushed him from behind. No one seemed able to find a way to stop it.

Including Pop Warner. His game plan was uncharacteristically conservative: keep it close and hope to pull it out with a fourth-quarter flourish. The plan was working until late in the first half, as Cornell found itself down by a narrow 4–0 score. With two minutes remaining, Cornell faced a third-and-two at Princeton's 30-yard line. At the time, a team had only three downs in which to make a first down, so Warner instructed his quarterback to punt, believing his team had little chance of scoring. A punt would pin the Tigers deep in their own territory and allow Cornell to hold out for the remainder of the half. But when the Cornell offense lined up for the ensuing play, Warner could only watch in disbelief as his team instead ran a play in an effort to pick up the first-down yardage. The play, as Warner could have predicted, was unsuccessful, and Princeton assumed possession. The Tigers had just enough time to march down the field and score, extending the lead to 10–0 as the teams retired for halftime. Cornell fought valiantly in the second half, but the score at the end of the second half was the same as at the end of the first.

Warner was indignant. "Our squad had foolishly given away the other six points to Princeton," he remembered. After the game, he locked himself in a small room and sobbed. It was the low point of the young coach's career. "My tears were based on youthful ambition [on the player's part] and my own desire to win." But many years later, as a more mature and wiser man, Warner moderated his opinion, realizing that his quarterback's actions were exactly the same as the ones the coach himself would have taken in the same situation. "He was playing to win, which is the only way I would have wanted him to have played."[3]

Cornell lost by an even bigger margin the following week, falling 24–5 to Harvard. After going undefeated while at the University of Georgia the previous year, back-to-back losses were too much for the highly competitive Warner to bear. He determined to pull out all of the stops to ensure a victory in the upcoming matchup with Penn State.

While putting together the game plan to be used against State, Warner decided to activate a play the team had been tinkering with at practice throughout the season. The play, later dubbed the "hunchback" or "hidden ball trick," had been used successfully by the Cornell scrub team in scrimmages against the varsity, and the coach believed it could work in an actual game. The play was not new. In fact, it had first been employed by John Heisman's Auburn team in a game against Vanderbilt two years earlier, but no documentation exists that can verify whether Warner was aware of Heisman's prior usage. And though Heisman had indeed used it first, the play became associated with Warner for his successful employment of it on at least two occasions—the first time in this game against Penn State, and later, more famously, while he was coaching at Carlisle.[4]

As Cornell halfback Allen Whiting recalled years later, Warner had the team practice the play throughout the week leading up to the contest. "Pop arranged to have a strong elastic placed in the bottom of my jersey," said Whiting. "He then got us out on the field to coach us in the new play. It could only be used on kickoffs. As soon as I realized it was well placed [under the jersey], I would yell and the whole team would yell and start, fan-shape in all directions. I would go straight down the field."[5]

As it turned out, the trick play wasn't even needed, for Cornell dominated from the opening kick and held a 40–0 lead late in the game. But with 30 seconds remaining and Penn State preparing to kick the ball to Cornell, Warner decided to run it anyway. He sent a substitute player onto the field with instructions to run the play.

Whiting positioned himself to receive the kick. "When Mechesney kicked off," reported *The Free Lance*, Penn State's student newspaper, "the Cornellians at once bunched together, and while State was vainly searching for the ball, Whiting, with the pigskin neatly tucked beneath his sweater, was making tracks for our goal line, which he reached in safety, to the intense amusement of the cold, shivering spectators."[6]

Cornell laid waste to Williams College the following week, winning 42–0 to improve to 5–2–1 with only the traditional season finale against the University of Pennsylvania left on the schedule. The Quakers had destroyed Cornell 32–10 in the final game of the 1896 campaign, leaving the Red Men with a final record of 5–3–1. Warner would have liked nothing better than to defeat Penn and finish the year a game better at 6–2–1. The Cornellians gave it their best shot, and nearly pulled off a major upset, but lost by a narrow 4–0 score, leaving the team with the same record it compiled the year before.

Warner's first year at Cornell had been a moderate success, and he was asked to return for the 1898 season. To his delight, the offer came with a $200-a-year raise, bringing his annual salary at Cornell to $800 (about $23,600 in today's dollars). In addition, Warner would continue to coach the Iowa State football team for four weeks each summer to supplement his income. But even with the raise and the stipend coming from Iowa State, he was making barely enough from coaching football to support himself for the whole year. During the break between seasons, Warner returned to Buffalo to resume his law practice. His thoughts, however, never strayed far from the gridiron. His mind was a torrent of X's and O's as he daydreamed about the upcoming campaign. It couldn't arrive soon enough.

When Warner returned to Cornell on September 16 after his customary four-week stint at Iowa State, he was greeted by his new assistant coach, Tommy Fennell, a Cornell alum and teammate of Warner's on the 1894 team. Fennell had been selected to fill the post left vacant by Joe Beacham, Pop's trusted aide from the previous year, who had enlisted in the U.S. Army and would be stationed overseas. Fennell, too, had just arrived at campus, having spent the last two weeks conducting a training camp in Richfield Springs, some 100 miles to the east of Ithaca.

Despite the loss of such key players as end Lyndon Tracy, guard Mark Faville, and team captain William McKeever, Warner had eleven boys returning from the previous year and was confident that a successful season was in the offing. "I do not know anything about our [new] material at present," said Warner, "but according to all reports it seems to me that we will find a fair number of desirable candidates among the entering class. We will go in to turn out the strongest team old Cornell has ever had, nevertheless."[7]

Warner's powers of prediction were improving, as the Red Men stormed out of the gate with blowout wins over Syracuse (28–0), Colgate (29–5), Hamilton (41–0), Trinity (47–0), and Syracuse again (30–0) to start the season at 5–0. The team was flying high, but all the while, unbeknownst to Warner, his assistant coach had been scheming to supplant him as head coach at the end of the current season.

When the Carlisle Indians came to town on October 6, it was truly an event. It was Carlisle's first visit to Ithaca, and the crowd overflowed, as football fan and curiosity seeker alike turned out to witness the battle between the unbeaten Cornell eleven and the exotic Indian team they had been reading so much about.

As he stalked the sidelines prior to kickoff, nervously dragging at his ubiquitous Turkish Trophy cigarette, Warner was more interested in watching his opponent warm up than his own players. He had had the opportunity to scout the Indians earlier in the season and came away with a sense of foreboding. They were outweighed by every college team in the nation, but it mattered little because their style wasn't like any other's. Carlisle was a team that relied on quickness and agility rather than size and strength. They weren't going to try to beat their opponents standing toe-to-toe, the way the game had been played since its invention. The Indians represented the game's future, where speed and deception would overcome brawn. Simply put, the Indians' style was very much in line with Warner's way of thinking.

And it was "Warner's way of thinking" that the Carlisle eleven lacked at this point, as the Indians—in just their sixth season of organized football—were consistently fooled by Cornell's use of the "double pass," which was, in essence, an early version of the reverse.[8] One of these plays resulted in a 55-yard touchdown scamper by Allen Whiting.

It was a ferocious contest, as both teams indulged in extra-curricular activity from the outset. "Throughout the entire game," reported the

Philadelphia Record, "there were disputes and the playing was very rough." Depending on which side of the field one sat, it was the players on the opposite bench who were responsible for the brutality. The *Record* pointed its finger at the Indians: "In the second half there was more or less foul playing, and the linemen of the Carlisle team lost no opportunity to participate in this."[9] But the *Carlisle Daily Herald* pointed right back: "Slugging was indulged in openly by the Ithacans."[10]

Cornell prevailed 23–6, but Warner had seen enough of the Indians to know that a team like this could ultimately change the way the game was played. They were the perfect team to run the types of plays Warner had been formulating since filling in as interim coach of the Cornell eleven back in 1894. For the remainder of the season, visions of the Carlisle Indians—their speed, their agility, their athleticism—lingered in his subconscious.

The Cornellians had no problem with the University of Buffalo team the following Saturday, walking way with a 27–0 win to improve to 7–0 before having to face Princeton, a team they had not beaten in six previous tries. And this year was to be no different, as the Tigers wrecked Cornell's perfect season with a closely fought 6–0 triumph. But the Red Men then reeled off three straight victories over Oberlin (6–0), Williams (12–0) and Lafayette (47–0) to improve to 10–1 heading into the last week of the season.

As it had the previous three years, Cornell University was scheduled to play the University of Pennsylvania to close out the campaign. The teams were evenly matched, with Cornell standing at 10–1 and Penn at 11–1. Despite the fact that the game was being played in Penn's home city of Philadelphia, Warner believed his team had the upper hand. What he hadn't taken into account, however, was the weather, which he later cited as the difference-maker in this game.

When the Cornell squad boarded the train for the trip to Philly, the weather in Ithaca was very mild for late November. But when the train arrived at its destination, Warner's boys were greeted by a freezing rain storm that kept up for two days. The field was reduced to a quagmire as the precipitation continued, driven by strong winds that the coach likened to a hurricane, resulting in what he considered perhaps the worst field conditions he'd ever seen.[11] Still somewhat inexperienced as a coach, and considering the moderate temperatures when his team embarked at Ithaca, Warner had not thought to bring spare uniforms for his players to change into in the event of inclement weather. The oversight proved costly.

Cornell played strong in the first half, and actually led 6–0 as the teams went to their locker rooms at halftime. But it was in those very locker rooms that the game was ultimately decided. Cornell retired to a rickety, unheated barn whose slats allowed the whipping winds to pass through, making it impossible for the boys to find warmth or comfort as they rested on bales of hay or the bare dirt floor. "I looked around to notice my players, still wearing their water soaked uniforms, shivering or their teeth chattering." In stark contrast was the heated Penn dressing room, which welcomed its players with a change of dry uniforms and trainers providing alcohol rubdowns. "This additional treatment was a benefit to Penn," Warner observed, "but it was a severe handicap to Cornell. We would have been much better off by not having an intermission at all."

Fully refreshed, the Penn boys came storming out for the second half. Using the "delayed pass" (in essence a fake sweep to one side that draws the defense over before the ball is given to a lingering back who scampers around the opposite end), Penn was able to ring up 12 unanswered points. Warner had prepped his team to be watchful for this play but, cold and tired, his ends simply couldn't defend it. Nor were they able to mount a comeback under the conditions, and the Quakers held on for a 12–6 victory.

Once again, as if taking continuous notes that might one day be used as the basis for a book on the fundamentals of football, Warner found a moral in the loss. "The Penn game taught me a valuable lesson," he said. "Afterwards, I made a rule for myself and my equipment manager that we would never go on an out-of-town trip without an extra set of uniforms so that we could be prepared for bad weather."[12]

Upon returning to Ithaca, Warner was made aware that Fennell had been lobbying behind the scenes to take over as head coach at the conclusion of the season. He must have had his suspicions, since Fennell seemed to be going out of his way throughout the year to assure Warner that he had no aspirations of coaching beyond the current campaign. Still, Pop felt that his overall record of 15–5–1 was good enough to provide some degree of security. But there was a division among the players, some of whom wished to retain the current coach, and some who preferred a change. In those days, the team captain held great influence over the choice of coach, and with current captain Allen Whiting graduating in the spring, a vote was set to elect a new skipper for the 1899 season. Two candidates emerged: Edward Sweetland representing the pro–Warner camp, and Daniel Reed representing the Fennell faction.[13] Warner did his best to stay out of the fray, but he realized that the controversy itself reflected poorly on his stewardship of the team. "Cooler heads were sure to select a coach who was not mixed up in the scrap in any way," he thought. It was at this juncture that Warner began looking for a new team to coach.[14]

One of the first schools he thought of was the Carlisle Indian Industrial School. Despite the fact that Cornell had defeated Carlisle 23–6 that year, Warner had come away intrigued. "The Indian boys," he confessed, "appealed to my football imagination."[15] Warner wrote to Captain Richard H. Pratt, superintendent of the school, and expressed his interest in coming to Carlisle to coach the football team. He asked Walter Camp, the Yale coach considered to be the ultimate authority of the sport at the time, to send a letter of recommendation on his behalf to Pratt. Pratt was interested, and within a few weeks responded to Warner with an invitation to come to Carlisle to discuss the matter. Just a few days later, Pop was on a train bound for the famed Indian school located in the heart of the Cumberland Valley in south-central Pennsylvania.

When Warner first met the 59-year-old Pratt, resplendently attired in his Army officer's uniform, he sensed an immediate connection. Captain Pratt, like Warner's father, had been a cavalry officer during the Civil War, and as the two made small talk inside Pratt's office, they likely discovered that they had even more in common. Both hailed from small western New York towns (Warner from Springville and Pratt from Rushford, about 30 miles east), and had spent time as apprentices to tinsmiths prior to finding their lifelong career paths.[16] But this was a business meeting, and Pratt eventually got to the point. When he asked Warner what he expected as a salary, the self-assured coach set his price at $1,200, plus expenses. Despite the school's tight budget, Pratt didn't flinch. He knew Warner was the man for this job. After hammering out some minor details, the two shook hands and the deal was done.

Warner's resignation from Cornell came as a surprise to most of the team's followers, who were unaware of the machinations transpiring behind the scenes. He did not want to leave, but felt he had no choice. "It was with great regret that I left Cornell," he recalled. "I had visions of becoming to football what the great [Charles] Courtney was to the Cornell crews."[17] But it wasn't to be. Warner's departure left the head-coaching position open for his rival, but school officials decided exactly as he predicted they would. The school opted to go with an outsider—Percy Haughton, former Harvard great—who had no involvement in the events that ultimately led to Warner's resignation.

Cornell University, however, had not heard the last of Pop Warner.

FIVE

Carlisle

The Carlisle Indian Industrial School was the brainchild of Lieutenant Richard Henry Pratt, a Union cavalry officer who spent the years following Lee's surrender overseeing Indian prisoners at Fort Sill in the Oklahoma Territory. In 1875, Pratt was given the task of transporting 72 of these prisoners from Fort Sill to St. Augustine, Florida, for incarceration at Fort Marion. Pratt, the son of a Christian missionary, believed the Indian's only hope for survival in the "civilized" world was for him to assimilate as well as he could into the white culture, or, as he put it, "kill the Indian, save the man." This was a very progressive, and controversial, notion, for there were many at that time who believed in the outright extermination of America's native population. Over the next three years, the inmates at Fort Marion were given instruction in the English language, introduced to Christianity, and provided training in various trades. In 1879, their sentences now complete, 17 of Pratt's charges were convinced to pursue further education at Hampton Institute in Hampton, Virginia, a boarding school founded a decade earlier by General Samuel C. Armstrong for the purpose of educating recently freed slaves. Pratt envisioned a model similar to the one used at Hampton and lobbied the United States government to set up a school exclusively for children of Native American descent.

Pratt's bold concept was initially met with resistance, but he continued to lobby federal officials and eventually won the support from Carl Schurz—secretary of the interior under President Rutherford B. Hayes—and was granted use of the decommissioned Army barracks at Carlisle, Pennsylvania. The base was the country's second-oldest military facility, having at one time housed Hessian troops captured by General George Washington's army during the Battle of Trenton in 1776. By the 1870s, the facility was no longer in use, and was available for Pratt's purposes. On October 6, 1879, Pratt and the first group of 147 students arrived. Many of Carlisle's original students were children of tribal leaders, sent by their

famous fathers to learn the ways of the white man. Oglala Sioux Chief
American Horse entrusted several of his children to Pratt's care, as did
Brule Sioux Chief Spotted Tail and Kiowa Chief Lone Wolf II.

At Carlisle, students divided their days between academic studies and
vocational training, while also receiving a healthy dose of religious instruction. They wore military uniforms and lived regimented lives, and were
forbidden to speak their native tongues. Extra-curricular activities included
music, debate clubs, and athletics. During summer breaks, students received
practical experience through the school's "outing" system, in which the children were assigned to white families to perform various types of menial
labor, such as housekeeping and farming. The students had the opportunity to earn money, but did not have access to it until they either graduated
or left the school. In addition to the acquisition of vocational skills, the
outing system served other important purposes. First and foremost, by
keeping the children from returning to their homes during the summer, it
ensured that they would not backslide into their tribal cultures. Additionally, the government saved money by not having to house and feed the
students while they were living with their host families.[1]

When football fever began to spread across college campuses in the
1870s and '80s, the Carlisle students were quick to contract the bug. They
took it upon themselves to grade the playing field and raise money to pur-
chase a real football. By the late 1880s, the students had organized into
intramural teams that played games against one another, but soon became
bored playing amongst themselves. In 1890, the Carlisle boys played their
first game against an outside team from nearby Dickinson College. But
when Pratt—from whom the players had kept the game a secret—learned
of a serious injury suffered by Carlisle student Stacy Matlock, he was hor-
rified. "This produced such a revulsion against the game that I said, 'This
ends outside football for us.'"[2]

It would be another three years before Captain Pratt finally relented
and lifted the football edict. Sometime in 1893, 40 boys filed into the superintendent's office and pleaded with him to allow them to play. Their
spokesman gave a long, well-thought-out oration on the benefits of the
game. "The genius of his argument almost compelled me to relax my judi-
cial mien and release my pent-up laughter," Pratt recalled. He was won over
even before the speech concluded. "When he had finished, I waited a little
and then said: 'Boys, I begin to realize that I must surrender and give you
the opportunity you so earnestly desire. I will let you take up outside football again, under two conditions: First, that you will never, under any circumstances, slug. That you will play fair straight through, and if the other

fellows slug you will in no case return it. Can't you see that if you slug, people who are looking on will say, "There, that's the Indian of it. Just see them. They are savages and you can't get it out of them." Our white fellows may do a lot of slugging and it causes little or no remark, but you have to make a record for your race. If the other fellows slug and you do not return it, very soon you will be the most famous football team in the country. If you can set an example of that kind for the white race, you will do a work in the highest interests of your people.'"

The boys voiced their agreement. Then Pratt gave his second condition: "In the course of two, three or four years you will develop your strength and ability to such a degree that you will whip the biggest football team in the country."

When the team spokesman stated that they would try, Pratt exclaimed, "I don't want you to promise to try. I want you to say that you will do it. The man who only thinks of trying to do a thing admits to himself that he may fail, while the sure winner is the man who will not admit failure. You must get your determination up to that point."[3]

The boys again agreed. Football was back at Carlisle.

The following fall, the Carlisle Indians, under the tutelage of school disciplinarian William G. Thompson, played their first season of intercollegiate football. The team played just three games, all against minor schools, winning two and losing one.

It was clear to Pratt that if the Carlisle football program were to advance, he would need to bring in someone with credibility and knowledge to coach the team, or, in the modern parlance, a "football man." He found just the man for the job in Vance McCormick, a former All-America quarterback at Yale who was living in nearby Harrisburg. It just so happened that a member of the Carlisle faculty, Miss Anna Luckenbaugh, was a former teacher of McCormick's. She sent a letter to the Yalie asking him to come to Carlisle to instruct the boys in the finer points of the game. McCormick accepted, offering his services as a volunteer. He arrived in September of 1894, and the results were immediate. McCormick spent several weeks drilling the players in the proper techniques of blocking, kicking, tackling, recovering fumbles, receiving kickoffs and punts—basic concepts in which none of the boys had had any formal training. He led by example, often ending up in the middle of the action or the bottom of the pile—sometimes still in the suit and tie he was wearing upon arrival— as the team ran through its plays. The Carlisle boys were quick studies, and soon were performing as if they had been doing these things all their lives.

The added benefit of McCormick's involvement at Carlisle was the

instant respectability it brought the school's football program. The team
was able to arrange a greatly expanded schedule in 1894, playing nine
games against the likes of Lehigh, Navy, Bucknell and Franklin & Marshall.
Despite the fact that the Indians' only victory came against a high school
team from Harrisburg, they played well enough throughout the season to
attract the attention of some of the biggest schools in the nation, including
Yale and the University of Pennsylvania, both of which added Carlisle to
their schedules in 1895.

When the Indians faced off against Pennsylvania on October 16 of
that year, it was a watershed moment, a sign that the team was on its way
toward fulfilling the promise made to Pratt two years earlier. And though
they were crushed 36–0, it was no mean feat being on the same field as the
powerful Quakers. Three weeks later, the Indians fell to Yale, 18–0. Despite
these losses, Carlisle posted an impressive 4–4 record on the season.

Unfortunately, McCormick was unable to commit to a third season.
He recommended former Yale teammate William Hickok to take his place.
The two-time All-America delivered another .500 season (5–5), but
proved unpopular with both Major Pratt and the players and was not asked
to return for a second term.[4] Taking over for Hickok was a third Yale man,
William T. Bull. Under Bull, the team enjoyed its first winning campaign,
finishing with a 6–4 record that included an 82–0 triumph over Gettysburg. Yet another Yale alum, John Hall, followed in 1898, resulting in a
rather disappointing 5–4 record.

After five years under the Eli influence, the football program seemed
suddenly to be going backward. The time had come, Pratt believed, to take
the team in a new direction. He wished to bring in a coach who not only
possessed fresh ideas, but someone who was dedicated to the mission of
making the Carlisle Indians one of the top teams in the game. Based upon
Walter Camp's recommendation, 27-year-old Glenn S. "Pop" Warner, formerly coach at Cornell University, was offered the position.[5]

The school's entire enrollment at the time of Warner's arrival was
approximately 1,000 boys and girls ranging in age from 12 to 21 (and sometimes older), about one quarter of whom were boys of football age.[6] From
that number were culled the 15 to 20 players that made up the Carlisle
football team. Warner was fortunate to have several veterans returning
for the 1899 season, a few of whom he later considered to be among the
best he ever coached at the school. The team's captain was tackle Martin
Wheelock, a 25-year-old Oneida Indian hailing from Wisconsin. He had
been playing varsity football at Carlisle since 1894 (and would continue
until 1902, a total of nine seasons). Isaac Seneca, a member of the Seneca

Nation from the Cattaraugus Indian Reservation in Western New York, was the team's star halfback and, later, its first-ever All-America selection. Quarterback Frank Hudson, a 133-pound Laguna-Pueblo from New Mexico, was considered one of the greatest dropkickers of the pre-forward pass era.

But in early September, when Warner called the players in for his first practice, he was not encouraged by what he saw. "My first view of Carlisle's football material was anything but favorable," he remembered. "The boys who reported for practice were listless and scrawny, many looking as though they had been drawn through a knothole. My heart went down into my shoes, for I was getting twelve-hundred dollars a year and felt that only an ever-victorious team could possibly justify such an enormous salary." He vented his worries to Major Pratt. "I protested that the squad ought to be trying for beds in a hospital rather than places on a football team."

Pratt, to Warner's surprise, seemed unconcerned, reassuring the coach that there was no cause for alarm. "They have been on farms all summer," he explained. "These Pennsylvania farmers insist on getting their money's worth. The youngsters will soon begin to pick up weight, so don't worry."[7] As predicted, the players eventually put on some bulk, but not much. In fact, Warner's teams at Carlisle were fated to be at a disadvantage in size every year he coached at the school, and only once would he have a team averaging in excess of 175 pounds.

Warner approached this job a bit differently from his previous stints. There was still emphasis on the teaching of fundamentals, but unlike his time at Georgia, where he was remembered for driving his players from their beds for five-mile, pre-dawn runs, Pop had come to learn that such grueling work could result in more harm than good. "It is a mistake to start the training season with hard, rough work before the players have gradually worked up to such work," he now believed. "It is generally in the first two weeks of practice, when the players are full of ambition and determination, that they are most likely to overdo or get laid up with an injury. The game and the practice require such hard work that it is a waste of energy which might better be applied to learning the game to engage in such exercise as running around the track or the gridiron, calisthenics or setting up exercises. A player can get all the exercise he needs in practicing the rudiments of the game and engaging in daily practice."[8]

His initial workouts with the Indians proved problematic, for several had limited understanding of English, while others could barely speak the language at all. The one thing most did understand, however, was profanity. Centuries of all types of bigotry and abuse had taught Native Americans to recognize what a white man meant when he was swearing at them. Their new coach, having been raised with "all the prejudices of the average white man" and trained by "some rather hard-boiled gents," believed that the most expedient way to communicate with his players was through gesticulation and profanity, the latter of which Warner was well-versed.[9] But as Warner soon learned, the tactics he found to be effective at other schools were not only ineffective with the Indian boys, they soon resulted in a minor revolt. "I took a fairly extensive vocabulary with me to Carlisle," he recalled, "and made full use of it."[10] After the first week of practices, he began to notice his squad's numbers diminishing on a daily basis. He questioned the remaining players of the whereabouts of their missing teammates, and learned that they were offended by the coach's gruff language and had decided to quit. The Carlisle school, after all, had been teaching the boys to be Christian gentlemen. This revelation gave Warner pause. He called a mandatory meeting for all of the players and explained to them that his use of foul language was not meant to offend them, but rather to "impress certain things more forcibly upon them." The coach apologized "profoundly and sincerely," feeling he had been taught a valuable lesson by "those so-called savages." After being assured by Warner that he would make every effort to tone down his language, the players agreed to return to practice.[11]

It took some time, but the players eventually came to trust their new coach, and Warner's outlook improved as the boys began to show their many talents on the field. Not only were they gifted athletically, but they were fast and eager learners. "In addition to speed and skill in the use of feet and hands," he observed, "they also had highly developed powers of observation handed down through many generations."[12] And unlike many of the players he had coached at other schools, the Indians did not second-guess or seem preoccupied with doing things the way they had always been done. Their willingness to try new things allowed Warner to fully express his creative side, for just as quickly as he could draw something up on the chalk board, they were able to bring it to life on the gridiron. One such innovation was the "body block." "Up to that time," he noted, "all blocking was done with the shoulder, a method that had a good many drawbacks. In the 'Indian block,' as it came to be called, a man left the ground entirely, half turning as he leaped so as to hit an opponent just above the knees with his hip, and following through with a roll, thus using his entire length. The Indians took to it like ducks to water, and when they blocked a man, he *stayed* blocked."[13]

hen there was the use of deception, a stratagem he had experimented with at his previous coaching stints and would employ with even greater success with the Indians. Warner saw the potential in this group of players when his Cornell team faced them the year before, and now he was marveling at it on a daily basis. One particular afternoon, he called the players in and explained his concepts to them.

"When you're on the defense," he began, "and the other team starts a play in which they all move to your right, what do you do?"

Team captain Martin Wheelock provided the answer: "Slide along to the right with them, find the ballcarrier and drive in."

"Right," Warner replied. "It's only natural."

The coach then had his second-stringers—referred to on campus as "the Hot-Shots"—line up on offense. He instructed them to move to the right at the snap of the ball. He then whispered to the halfback to feint toward the right and then hightail it around the left end. The ball was snapped and the scrub linemen moved to the right. The defensive players followed and a pileup ensued. But the ball wasn't there—it was nestled in the bosom of the Hot-Shots' halfback, who was skirting the opposite flank en route to an easy touchdown.

"Here's what I want you to remember on this play," said Warner. "Get the other team moving in one direction, so your ballcarrier can go the other. And the best way to do it is for all of you to move that way. All except the guy with the ball."[14]

Warner's tenure with Carlisle began auspiciously, with victories over Gettysburg (21–0) and Susquehanna (56–0). But these games were merely warm-ups, the modern-day equivalent of exhibition games used to prepare the team when it entered the heart of its schedule, which for Carlisle arrived in Week 3, when they were slated to face the University of Pennsylvania, a team they had not beaten in four previous meetings.

Pennsylvania, of course, was a nationally recognized power, by now elevated to the pantheon of football's elite teams that included Harvard, Princeton and Yale. They had lost only twice since 1893, and were a lock to once again vanquish the upstart Indians from nearby Carlisle. But Warner's boys were well prepared, playing a flawless game to upset the slower, heavier Quakers by a 16–5 score. "There was no fluke or chance about it," wrote the *New York Times*. "It was a clear-cut victory. The Indians won because they played the better football." It was, without a doubt, the biggest win in the history of the school, and if any follower of the game had not noticed them by now, this surprise defeat of one of college football's Big Four brought the Carlisle Indians into the consciousness of even the most casual of observers.

The Indians had a minor letdown the following Saturday when they defeated Dickinson by a rather modest score of 16–5. Their lackluster performance could well have been a lingering aftereffect of the Penn upset, but it was more likely that the team was looking past Dickinson in anticipation of their October 28 matchup with hated Harvard.

Harvard was heavily favored, of course, riding a winning streak that by this time had reached 18 games. But they came out flat, perhaps themselves a bit guilty of looking past the Indians in anticipation of their own contest with Penn, scheduled for the following week. When the Indians jumped out to a 10–0 first-half lead on a successful 35-yard dropkick by Hudson and a 50-yard fumble return by guard Thaddeus Redwater, Warner observed, "the Crimson players quit looking bored."[15] Somewhat embarrassed, the Harvard boys emerged for the second half with a renewed sense of purpose, which included some rough play. At one point, Carlisle fullback Jonas Metoxin was carried from the field and taken to the hospital after suffering a blow to the head. The Indians were simply overpowered, surrendering 22 second-half points en route to their first loss of the season.[16]

Warner had his team back on track two weeks later with a 32–0 drubbing of Hamilton College before traveling to New York to take on Princeton in their third tilt with a Big Four team in less than a month. The Indians again found themselves in the position of underdog, as bettors were offering ten-to-eight odds in favor of a Tiger victory.[17] Despite suffering their first shutout loss (12–0) in two years, the Indians' play continued to garner notice from Eastern newspapers. "The result was a crusher for the red men," observed the *Philadelphia Record*. "Their victory over Pennsylvania and their double score against Harvard warranted a better showing from the Indians, although they put up such a formidable game that they proved themselves worthy of the respect which is paid them in the football world."

An 81–0 skunking of Oberlin, in which Carlisle led 52–0 at the half, brought the Indians to 6–2 on the season. Their only losses had come against the two best teams in the nation, and they had played well in both of those games. The Indians were making headlines everywhere they played, but the tinsmith-turned-coach continued to tinker, looking for anything that could give his undersized team an edge when it faced bigger squads. Warner wondered if there was some way that his backs could get off the snap of the ball more quickly, thus giving them the advantage of being a step ahead of their opponent as a play was unfolding. At the time, backfield men normally started from an upright stance, with feet apart and hands resting on their knees. It occurred to him that sprinters started from a crouched position, with one or both hands on the ground, allowing them to bolt from the starting blocks with an immediate burst. "I figured that if sprinters could get away faster by partly supporting the weight of the body on one or both hands, it was logical that backfield players could obtain the same results."[18]

Pop had some of the players try it during practice and liked what he saw. Backs starting from a three-point stance hit the line much quicker than those standing upright. He had them work on all of their plays using the new stance throughout the week. They would use it on Thanksgiving Day when they faced Columbia University at Manhattan Field (aka The Polo Grounds) in New York City.

The Lions came into the weekend sporting a 9–2 record, which included a stunning victory over Yale. It didn't matter. Right from the Indians' first possession, the Columbia defenders were caught off guard by the crouching start. The smaller Carlisle backs exploded into the line, pushing the heavier Columbia lineman all over the field. Huge holes opened in the Columbia forward wall, allowing halfback Isaac Seneca to run wild, ripping off gains of 30, 30, 40 and 55 yards and scoring two touchdowns.[19] It wasn't even close: Carlisle 45, Columbia 0. Warner's latest innovation proved so effective that it was soon adopted by every team in the nation. There was no doubting that the Carlisle Indians had come of age and were indeed living up to their promise to Superintendent Pratt.

With the defeat of Columbia, Carlisle's season was presumed to be over. However, the Indians received an invitation to come out to the West Coast to play the University of California on Christmas Day for a nominal East-West championship. Warner, never one to shy away from a challenge, was eager to accept. But there was concern that his players, who had just completed a long and rough season, would be plumb worn out. There was, of course, no need to worry. Warner convened a meeting with the players and put the proposition to a vote. Not surprisingly, he received a unanimous affirmative response.

Major Pratt, however, was reluctant to give his blessing, but soon realized that the educational value of the trip outweighed the rather significant amount of classroom time the players stood to lose while they were away. According to Warner, Pratt consented to this—and, ultimately, future trips—because he believed " ... the education they received from traveling and their contact with other college men more than offset the time they lost from their regular school work."[20]

While the Indians' train wound its way toward the California coast, Warner took necessary steps to keep his boys in shape. He had them jog alongside the train as it climbed and descended steep Rocky Mountain passes.[21] At every stop he had the players disembark to stretch and exercise. The sight of a dozen and a half Indians tossing a pigskin around on the lawn of a railroad depot was sure to attract the attention of locals. "In one Western town," Warner recalled, "an old gentleman asked me who they were and where they were going. When I told him it was the Carlisle Indian football team going out to San Francisco to play California, he stroked his whiskers and remarked, 'Well, they are going a darned long ways to get the hell kicked out of them.'"[22]

Of course, the old man couldn't be faulted for his temerity, since the Californians had brought home an impressive 7–0–1 record on the year, including a 30–0 pasting of Stanford. But the Carlisle Indians were no pushovers either and, since they hadn't played a game in nearly a month, were sure to be eager and well rested.

When he walked out onto the field for the pre-game warmups, Warner's mind undoubtedly flashed back to his first game as a head coach when his Iowa State squad traveled to Montana to face a team of roughnecks intent on playing by their own rules. It began with the selection of the game ball. Chosen by the home team, the proposed ball was much larger and heavier than the regulation-sized ball to which the Indians were accustomed. Then there was the playing field which, much like the one in Butte, was devoid of grass. It had been covered with a heavy layer of sand, making dropkicking difficult and footing tenuous, neutralizing the speed and athleticism of the Indians. It was clear that Gerry Cochran and Ted Kelly, California's coaches, were intent on keeping Carlisle's explosive offense from igniting.[23]

It is not surprising that the game was completely devoid of offensive fireworks. Even the normally sure-footed Hudson missed several dropkick attempts. The afternoon eventually devolved into a punting exhibition as the teams sought alternative ways to improve their field position. But when Cal's punter fumbled a snap in his own end zone, the opportunistic Indians swarmed in to force a two-point safety. It was all the offense they needed, as the points stuck as the margin of victory.[24] When the final whistle blew, Pop Warner and the Carlisle Indians had settled the question of Eastern football supremacy, at least for the time being.

As the train carrying the Carlisle football team snaked its way through the American Southwest on its path back to Pennsylvania, the coach—mindful of the educational and diplomatic importance of the trip—made it a point to visit several Indian schools en route. One of the first stops was in Arizona for a visit to the Phoenix Indian School, an institution based on the Carlisle model. While there, the superintendent of the school asked

Warner if his boys might be up for a game. Pop initially declined, again citing player fatigue, but eventually agreed—after all, there might be some undiscovered talent lingering out in the Arizona desert. On New Year's Day, with temperatures hovering around 90 degrees and the Phoenix boys clad in ridiculous all-leather uniforms, Carlisle rolled to an easy 83–6 win.[25]

Twelve days later, the Carlisle train pulled into Lawrence, Kansas, home to the Haskell Indian School. The Haskell students gave the Carlisle boys a royal welcome, feting them with a lavish breakfast, dress parade and inspection. Many of the Haskell students were awestruck just to be breathing the same air as the famous Carlisle football team, many of whom, like Isaac Seneca and Martin Wheelock, were held in higher esteem than the president of the United States. One student particularly awed by the visiting titans was a ten-year-old Sac and Fox boy named Jim Thorpe.

The long 1899 football season was finally over and had been, by all accounts, hugely successful. Carlisle won eight of its regular-season contests while losing just two, those coming against traditional heavyweights Princeton and Harvard. Casper Whitney, editor of *Outing* magazine, ranked them as the fifth-best team in the nation. Halfback Isaac Seneca became the first Carlisle player to be chosen a Walter Camp First-Team All-American, the highest honor that could be bestowed on an individual player. The trip to California was the farthest any college team had traveled for a football game. In addition to the accolades, the achievements of the Carlisle football team shed a very positive light on the Indian school system. Not only were they successful on the field, but they were courtly and well-mannered when they were on the road. As far as Major Pratt was concerned, the Carlisle football team had come to symbolize his idea that the Indian could be "saved" by exposure to the white man's educational system and culture. Dr. Carlos Montezuma, the school's medical director who had accompanied the team out West—and himself a Yavapai Apache—noted in an article written for the *San Francisco Examiner* that the purpose of the trip was more than the game itself. Rather, it was an opportunity "to demonstrate what education means to the Indians when given under the same conditions and with the same environment enjoyed by the white boy."[26]

On their long road trips, Warner noted, "The team always traveled first class and stopped at the best hotels. They were always welcome because the were a gentlemanly and very quiet bunch of boys who were always complimented for their appearance and conduct wherever they went."[27]

For his role in the success of the Carlisle football program, the team's head coach was rewarded with a promotion to the post of athletic director, a year-round position that put him in charge of all athletics at the school.

Up to that point, Warner had considered himself a lawyer first and foremost, still maintaining an office back in Buffalo when not overseeing football programs each fall. He later claimed to have actually been considering giving up coaching in favor of his legal career, but the thrill of athletic competition—the strategy, the execution, the pageantry, the winning—had made the law profession "seem pretty tame" by comparison. Of course, the raise in salary to $2,500 (roughly equivalent to $74,000 in today's dollars) didn't hurt.[28]

Warner's new role as Carlisle's athletic director required him to coach the baseball and track teams in addition to football. Carlisle had never participated in track competitions against other schools and, despite having been a member of the track squad during his undergraduate days at Cornell, Warner knew very little about coaching and training for the numerous events. He immediately began research, purchasing all the latest texts on the sport, and in the spring of 1900 oversaw the school's first actual track team. The squad found little to distinguish itself in its debut season, but over time the program would foster several athletes who brought the school to the international stage.

Baseball, on the other hand, was right up Warner's alley. It had always been his favorite sport. The school team had enjoyed some success prior to Warner's arrival, but never quite received the same level of emphasis from Major Pratt as the football program. After the first few practices, Warner observed that the players were skilled in the basic fundamentals of the game, such as hitting and throwing, but "did not use good judgment nor put as much into their baseball as did the college boys." This, he concluded, was because the boys "were not as far advanced educationally."[29]

One of the top players was Louis Leroy, a full-blooded Stockbridge who hailed from Omro, Wisconsin. Leroy was a fun-loving kid who, like Warner in his youth, aspired to a career in the majors. He was known to rub his right arm and tell his teammates, only half-jokingly, "This is a ten-thousand dollar arm." And while he may have possessed at least one valuable appendage, Leroy was afflicted with a condition that repeatedly tried Warner's patience—wanderlust. Leroy was a chronic runaway, and on several occasions—usually after spring baseball season—Warner was forced to light out in search of his star pitcher, who was usually found hurling for some far-flung Pennsylvania semi-pro team.[30]

But Warner's most outstanding prospect was an Ojibwa Indian named Charles Albert Bender. As a young teen, Bender often pitched to the older boys during winter practices held in the school's gymnasium, and developed into a bit of a prodigy by the time Warner took over as coach. Warner immediately recognized Bender's ability and assigned him to the varsity team. He was initially placed in center field, but was also used as a relief pitcher. The following year, Bender was elevated to the team's starting pitching rotation and became the ace of the stable. Given his humble beginnings, there was no way anyone could have predicted at the time this was just the beginning of a career that would eventually land Bender in the Baseball Hall of Fame.

As the 1900 season neared, Pop Warner's stature in the world of college football was on the rise. Successes at Georgia, Cornell and, more recently Carlisle, had placed his name at or near the top of his profession. Major Pratt rewarded Warner with the promotion to the post of athletic director, which brought with it a substantial raise in pay. His authority at the school was second only to the superintendent's, and at times seemed to supercede it. Since Warner was now a year-round employee of the school, accommodations were made for him and his wife, the former Tibb Loraine Smith, to whom he was wed in Springville on June 1, 1899.

What is known about Tibb Warner is sketchy since Pop, in all of his writings, rarely mentions her. She was born and raised in the nearby village of Franklinville. She attended school there until her family relocated to Springville when her father, Heathcoate D. Smith, opened a dry goods store on Main Street in the village.[31]

Local tradition has it that she and Pop were high school sweethearts, and their romance somehow continued after the Warner family relocated to Texas in the early 1890s. One can only conclude that he, or perhaps they, made a conscious decision to keep their private life just that. Whatever the reasons, Tibb Warner's apparent willingness to remain in her husband's shadow is consistent with the few first-hand observations available. She was described by one acquaintance as "a standoffish sort" and "very reserved." Tibb was also described as seeming uncomfortable around children, an observation that seems relevant in light of the fact that she and her husband would have none of their own.[32]

When Warner perused the list of players expected to come out for the upcoming football season, he couldn't help but notice how thin—both figuratively and literally—the roster appeared. He would be lucky to snag a player weighing close to 200 pounds very few times during his years at Carlisle, but this season's team came up short not only in weight, but also in number. Gone from the 1899 squad were several of his top performers, including All-America halfback Isaac Seneca, fullback Jonas Metoxin, end Joseph Shoulder, and quarterback Frank Hudson. With his ranks so depleted, Warner was forced to do something to which he was fairly unaccustomed—go on a recruiting trip. At Cornell, the recruitment of players was as simple as spotting large, athletic-looking boys around campus and talking them into trying out for the team. "I used to hang around the registrar's office when the freshmen came to college," remembered Warner, "to look over the material and try to persuade the bigger boys to come out for football."[33] But the team's recent trip through America's heartland had inspired him, and in early August Warner set off for Oklahoma to scout western reservations for potential material for the Carlisle football team.

Major Pratt got in on the act also, sending letters of inquiry to Indian agents across the country in hopes of weeding out a player or two who could bolster the team. "Have you not a small number of exceptionally good boys and girls to send to Carlisle? If you should by chance have a sturdy young man anxious for an education who is especially swift of foot or qualified for athletics, send him and help Carlisle compete with the great universities on those lines and to now then overcome the best."[34] But their combined efforts produced very little, for only one player—a marginal talent named John Walletsic—found his way into a Carlisle uniform as a result.[35]

The 1900 campaign opened at home against Lebanon Valley. Behind the brilliant running of backup halfback Manuel Ruiz, the Indians prevailed 34–0. Yet despite the lopsided score, it was clear that Carlisle was not quite the team it had been in 1899. "The Indians," observed the *Philadelphia Record*, "have lost a number of last year's stars and it looks as though Coach Warner has an uphill task." Still, five more wins over second-tier teams (Dickinson 21–0, Susquehanna 46–0, Gettysburg 45–0, the University of Virginia 16–2, and the University of Maryland 27–0) created the illusion that the Indians were a formidable team. That was all about to change.

Harvard was up next. The Indians had not beaten the Crimson in three previous tries, but in the process had come to think of the boys from Cambridge as the essence of perfection both on and off the field. Any feat of excellence, whether athletic or otherwise, was said to have been done "Harvard style." At the same time, the Indians had developed an extreme distaste for the elitist Harvard players. The week leading up to a Harvard game was sure to be filled with the Carlisle boys, even those with limited mastery of English, derisively mimicking the distinctive New England accent, with special emphasis on the broad *a* (HAH-vahd).

Coach Warner had installed some new tricks during the week that "completely befuddled" the Crimson, who were "used to the orthodox style of the game." The Carlisle offense lined up with everyone to one side of the field, then swept around to the opposite side as the ball was being snapped, creating a devastating charge that combined Warner's characteristic deception with old-school momentum. Throughout the first half, the underdog Indians dominated play, taking the game's first lead on a touchdown by fullback Jesse Palmer. The domination continued until late into the contest, at which time the Crimson finally deciphered the Carlisle attack and managed to evade a major upset, coming from behind to win 17–5.[36]

Warner took the team to Pine Grove, an eastern Pennsylvania mountain resort about 55 miles northeast of Carlisle, to recover after the tough loss and prepare for the upcoming game against Yale.[37] But the change of scenery was no help, as the listless Indians fell to the Eli 35–0, Carlisle's worst defeat since a 36–0 loss to Penn five years earlier. Things continued to go badly a week later, as the Indians lost their third straight to a Big Four team when Pennsylvania laid a 16–6 drubbing on them. They experienced a slight rebound with 5–5 tie against with Washington & Jefferson before heading to New York to face Columbia and close what had turned into a very disappointing season. After beginning the campaign at 6–0, Carlisle had since posted a terrible 0–3–1 record. Still Warner, at least to the press, remained optimistic that his team could salvage the season with a victory over the Lions, whom the Indians defeated the previous year using the new three-point stance. "I think it is going to be a hard and close game," he told the *New York Times*. "The team is going to play to win, and I feel sure that we will win." But there were no novelties to rely on this year, and with the uninspired Indians eager just to have the season over, the Columbians cruised to an easy 17–6 Thanksgiving Day win.

The Indians had compiled a respectable final record of six wins, four losses and one tie, but this was a big comedown from the 8–2 mark of the previous year, which also saw defeats of Penn, Columbia and California. They were never quite able to overcome the departures of Hudson, Seneca and Metoxin (three-fourths of the starting backfield), and seemed to lose interest after devastating back-to-back mid-season losses to Harvard and Yale. Unfortunately for Warner and the Carlisle faithful, things were not going to get any better in the upcoming campaign.

For the second straight year, Coach Warner found his roster seriously wanting as training camp loomed. Not only was the team small in size and number, they were also short in experience. Only four starters from the previous season were returning in 1901, forcing Warner to carry more scrubs than he normally would have.

One such player was newcomer Nikifer Shouchuk. A 160-pound candidate for center, Shouchuk was a native of the Aleutian Islands, an archipelago extending some 1,200 miles westward from the Alaskan Peninsula below the Arctic Circle. Shouchuk had never ventured away from the Aleutians before coming to Carlisle, and Pennsylvania's late-summer warmth made for a difficult adjustment. He also spoke virtually no English when he arrived, making instruction problematical. "Nikifer was a bright lad and learned English very quickly," Warner recalled. "But I sometimes doubted if he understood the signals. So one day I called him over and asked, 'Nik, what do you do on 15–25–36?'"

"Me run," Shouchuk replied happily. "Yes sirree, Mister Pop. Me run most fast."[38]

The coach appreciated his pluck, but Shouchuk was a work in progress. His turn as a regular was still a year away. For now, Pop had Antonio Lubo, a full-blooded Mission from California who had spent the better part of the past four seasons with the Hot-Shots, penciled in at center. The four regulars returning this year were linemen Martin Wheelock and Charles Dillon, end Nelson Hare, and quarterback James Johnson, the team's star player. At least four positions were being held down by men in their first year with the team. Indeed, 1901 promised to be the most challenging season Warner had faced as a helmsman since his rookie year coaching simultaneously at Iowa State and the University of Georgia.

The season opened against Lebanon Valley on September 21. Lebanon Valley was a traditionally weak team, and Carlisle's annual meetings with them were looked upon as mere warmups. As such, Warner saw this game as an opportunity to closely examine the material with which he had to work, and started his second-stringers against Lebanon's first team. Carlisle still managed to win comfortably 28–0. A week later, the Indians played host to a team from the Gallaudet School, a university for deaf and hearing impaired students. The Gallaudet players used hand signals to communicate and call their plays, leaving the Carlisle players frequently scratching their heads.[39] What was expected to be a rout was turning into an upset by halftime, as Gallaudet held a 6–5 lead heading into the locker room. However, the Indians managed to pull themselves together in the second half and escape with a 19–6 win.

The lackluster showing against Gallaudet carried over into the Indians' next game against Gettysburg, a team which had never even scored a point in four previous meetings with Carlisle. But when the final score read Gettysburg 6, Carlisle 5, there was serious concern regarding the condition of Pop Warner's team. Yet another close game followed when Carlisle barely squeaked by Bucknell, 6–5. The Indians then pummeled Haverford College 29–0 in their final home game before embarking on a road trip that was to last the remainder of the season, which included seven games over the next five weeks.

Warner had the October 19 meeting with Cornell at the Pan-American Exposition circled on his calendar since the beginning of the season. The Exposition was a world's fair set in the city of Buffalo, at that time the eighth-largest metropolitan area in the United States. It was intended as a celebration of nascent American influence in the Western Hemisphere and overseas. At every turn one could witness evidence of recent technological and scientific advances. Perhaps the most impressive sight came each night when every building on the grounds was illuminated through the use of power generated by hydroelectric turbines located at nearby Niagara Falls. It was an awesome display of American ingenuity and cast the Queen City in a very positive light, both figuratively and literally. Coach Warner, who until recently maintained a law office just four miles from the fairgrounds, was sure to be delighted.

But the buoyant mood of the fair came to an abrupt end on September 6 when President William McKinley, attending a reception at the Exposition's Temple of Music, was mortally wounded by an anarchist named Leon Czolgosz, who stepped out of a crowd and fired two shots from a concealed revolver into the president's belly. McKinley's death on September 14 cast a pall over the fair that was still evident five weeks later when the elevens from Carlisle and Cornell were slated to meet in the Exposition's stadium.

There was another compelling side story to this game, too, for not only was Warner facing his alma mater for the first time, it also marked the first instance in which he'd be going up against his brother Bill on the gridiron. While Pop had been busy the past several years making a name for himself as one of the top young coaches in football, Bill Warner—ten years his junior—had graduated high school back in Springville and earned himself a spot on the Cornell football team. After his sophomore season with the Red Men, Bill was elected captain and was considered by many to be the equal—and by some to be the better—of his older, more famous sibling. As far as Pop was concerned, this game meant as much if not more than any other he had ever participated in. Not only were family bragging rights at stake, he was also intent on proving to Cornell officials that they had erred grievously when they let him leave Ithaca without so much as a cursory plea. But this was not the game in which Pop should have been planning his redemption, since Cornell was considered one of the top teams in the nation, having gone undefeated in its five previous outings while outscoring opponents by a combined 136–0. Pop knew his small and inexperienced team was no match for the Cornell machine, and remarked to reporters prior to departing for Buffalo that he wasn't optimistic about his team's chances. "Don't expect too much of us," he said, "as you know how lack of weight and experience count."[40]

A crowd estimated between 16,000 and 18,000 was squeezed into a stadium built for only 12,000. The overflow forced their way through locked barriers and past helpless ticket takers. A few poor souls were stopped by security guards, and some even pummeled with nightsticks, but several thousand still managed to gain entry without paying a dime. The game itself seemed anticlimactic by comparison. As expected, the heavier and more experienced Cornellians controlled the line of scrimmage and the flow of the game from the opening kickoff. After losing captain Wheelock to injury midway through the contest, Carlisle's line averaged less than 160 pounds per man. The game was never in doubt as Cornell emerged on the upside of a 17–0 decision.

Pop gave grudging credit to his brother's team after the loss. "There was an element of luck in Cornell's playing," he sniffed. "One touchdown was made on a fluke and her second, while entirely creditable, was a long run. Despite this, her team won on its merits and I have little fault to find. I wish our men could have been in better shape, but it's all over now and I don't intend to offer excuses."[41]

Things got worse the following week when the Indians traveled to Cambridge to play Harvard and were crushed 29–0. Warner's demoralized troops then headed westward to take on the University of Michigan. Already shorthanded as a result of injuries, the Indians found themselves down two more men when Louis Leroy (the baseball star and unremitting runaway) and Edward DeMarr, filling in at the halfback positions, were reported absent from the team's hotel the morning of the game. "I at once realized that they figured Detroit was pretty far west and thought it a good opportunity to beat it back to their reservation," said Warner. "This left us in a pretty tough hole."[42]

With barely enough bodies to put a full team on the field, Warner pleaded with Fielding Yost, the Michigan coach, to shorten the length of the game. Yost wouldn't hear of it. To make matters worse, Carlisle lost another man early in the game when one of its ends was helped off the field after dislocating a shoulder. Michigan won in a rout, 22–0. Among the 8,000 in attendance were Wu Tingfang, Chinese minister to the United States, and Russell A. Alger, the former U.S. secretary of war.[43]

It was then on to Annapolis to face Navy for the first time since 1895. The banged up Indians managed to outplay their opponent for much of the first half, taking an early 5–0 lead on a 40-yard double pass play by Johnson. That score held up until the second half, when Navy regrouped to score 16 unanswered points and claim victory. It was a fierce battle that saw several Carlisle players carted from the field. Warner complained to the press that the Navy boys were "the dirtiest aggregation of players his men had run up against this season." He accused the cadets of twisting legs and trying to "intentionally maim and injure his men" and using language that was "profane, offensive and ungentlemanly."[44]

Carlisle was now 5–5 on the season, the first time they had not been above the .500 mark this late in a season during Warner's tenure.

The Indians pulled themselves together and very nearly pulled off what should have been the biggest upset of the entire season when they faced Pennsylvania on November 16. Carlisle, according to the *Philadelphia Record*, "outplayed and outgeneraled" the Quakers, taking a 12–5 lead into the locker room at the half. But Penn, capitalizing on a couple of horrendous calls by the officials, managed to battle back and snatch victory from the jaws of defeat.

Another strong effort against Washington & Jefferson resulted in 0–0 tie, bringing the Indians to 5–6–1, with the final game of the season coming up against Columbia. A victory would leave Carlisle at .500 and provide some measure of redemption in what was now officially the team's worst season since 1895. The Columbians, however, were not in a charitable mood, and clobbered the Indians 40–12. It was the most points ever given up by a Carlisle team.

It was clear that the Indians were not the team they had been just two years earlier. Much of the decline could be attributed to the lack of size and experience, but outside observers, including Walter Camp, felt there was more to it. The Carlisle boys had become, in Camp's opinion, too refined. "[The Indians] have nearly reached a state of equilibrium," he observed in a post-season article for *Outing* magazine. "The time was when the Indian team went blindly and fiercely into the arena, and were ready to go up against anything that the pale faces could devise. Now the Indians have settled down into a more civilized frame of mind where they are looking for an occasional match and reputation rather than the old untrammeled method, which lent them a unique reputation." And though

Camp didn't reproach Warner directly, it was obvious he felt the coach should bear some of the blame for the team's collapse. "In spite of the ability of Warner," Camp continued, "the Indians did not make much advance last season, and in order to improve further this year they must have some new plays, and discarding those that are well known, take the initiative with some good, strong, close formations."[45]

The dearth of new plays might well have been an indication that Warner was preoccupied, for it was unlike him to stand pat and not be constantly crafting new ways to beat the opposition. In spare moments, which, for Warner, were few and far between, he liked nothing better than to retreat to the campus workshop. There he might be found crafting some new piece of equipment or taking apart an automobile engine, just to turn around and put it back together again. He combined his artistic skills with those he learned as a tinsmith to create golf clubs and fancy walking canes, which he gave to friends as gifts.

The football equipment at the time of Warner's first tenure at Carlisle was still fairly primitive, offering little in the way of protection against hard, direct contact with other players. Padding was soft and became heavy when soaked with perspiration or nature's elements. "I figured that protectors which would fit closely to the parts to be shielded and distribute the impact at hard knocks over a large surface would afford much better protection and be less clumsy and not act as sponges," said Warner. He had been looking for a material that could potentially improve the protective value of the paddings currently in use. Sheet metal was against the rules, and plastic was not yet in common usage. Then one day while visiting a local haberdashery, Pop found it. "I bought a pair of shoes and was given a shoe horn," he remembered. "This shoe horn was made of light fiber about one-sixteenth of an inch think and I at once figured that was the material I had been looking for." Warner learned where the material was manufactured and that it was available in various shapes and thicknesses. He sent patterns for shoulder and thigh pads to the company, and when the pieces arrived, soaked them in hot water and molded them into the proper shape. Once dry, Warner waterproofed the pieces by applying a coat of varnish. He then lined the pads with felt.[46]

As with many of Warner's other innovations, his improvements to protective gear were soon adopted by coaches at every college in the country. In the summer of 1903, he sold some of his inventions to the A.G. Spalding & Brothers sporting goods company.[47] Other inventions followed, including the first blocking sled, which Warner created to improve a lineman's speed and build leg and back muscles. Improvements to the tackling dummy, which Amos Alonzo Stagg was credited with using first in 1889, are also attributed to Warner. His inventions brought another source of income to Warner, and he would continue to benefit from them for years to come.

Warner was also a composer of some merit, and somewhere along the line found time to write a hymn to honor the school, which the student body would sing at assemblies.

School Song

(Sung to the tune of "O Tannenbaum")

Nestling 'neath the mountains blue,
Old Carlisle, our fair Carlisle.
We n'er can pay our debt to you,
Old Carlisle, our fair Carlisle.

While the years roll swiftly by,
In our hearts thou 'rt always nigh,
To honor thee we'll ever try,
Old Carlisle, our fair Carlisle.

All your precepts we hold dear,
Old Carlisle, our fair Carlisle.
The world we'll face without a fear,
Old Carlisle, our fair Carlisle.

Rememb'ring thee, we'll never fail,
We'll weather every storm and gale,
While o'er life's troubled sea we sail,
Old Carlisle, our fair Carlisle.[48]

While at home in Western New York for his customary summer vacation, Warner learned that Louis Leroy, the half-hearted halfback/pitching prospect who bolted from the football team on the morning of the previous season's Michigan game, was in town playing for the minor-league Buffalo Bisons. Warner decided to surprise Leroy by visiting him at the ball park one afternoon. Unbeknownst to Leroy, Warner was friends with George Stallings, the Bisons' manager, and was able to slip into the team's dugout without Leroy noticing. As Leroy sat alone at one end of the players' bench, Warner sneaked up, slapped him on the back and exclaimed, "Come over here a minute!"

"The boy turned as white as red skin possibly could," Warner recalled.

"Where to?" Leroy stammered.

"Back to Carlisle!" Warner replied.

Leroy was crestfallen, and who could have blamed him? The last time Pop came looking for him, he found Leroy pitching for a semi-pro team in Lancaster, Pennsylvania. Warner brought him back to Carlisle, where he was placed in the guardhouse for the remainder of the summer. But Leroy was now a young man of 23 years, and the coach had no intention of forcing him to return to the school. Warner paused for a moment before letting out a chuckle and informing Leroy that he was just kidding with him.[49]

Stallings gave Leroy the starting assignment against visiting Providence that day, and Louis pitched spectacularly in guiding the Bisons to victory. But it was a bittersweet moment, for it was the last time Warner ever laid eyes on the pitcher with the ten-thousand-dollar arm. Leroy's dream of a career in the majors was finally realized three years later, when he signed to play with the New York Highlanders (forerunners to the New York Yankees).[50]

The light at the end of the tunnel in which the Carlisle Indians had been lost for the past two seasons was finally starting to brighten. Several of the scrubs and younger players from previous years were maturing and expected to play significant roles on the team in 1902. Nikifer Shouchuk was ready to take over at center, allowing Antonio Lubo to move over to guard. Arthur Sheldon and Charles Williams were now starters in the backfield. But without a doubt, the most important development of the season was the arrival of Albert Exendine.

Exendine, part Cherokee and part Delaware, came to Carlisle in December of 1899. He had never ventured outside the Indian territory of western Oklahoma before, but longed to travel east ever since seeing a recruitment poster for Carlisle on the wall in his school at Anadarko. He was somewhat shy when he arrived, intent simply on learning a trade and getting an education. Exendine had no experience with organized athletics before coming to Carlisle, but the naturally athletic 16-year-old was convinced to join the bakers' intramural team the following fall. In 1901, Exendine, or "Ex" as he was known to his friends, joined the blacksmiths. A year later, after returning from a grueling summer outing experience on a potato farm at a strapping 165 pounds of solid muscle, Ex felt confident he could hold his own against the varsity boys. When Exendine strode onto the field for his first practice, Coach Warner looked him up and down before asking, "How much do you weigh?"

"One-hundred and sixty-five pounds," Exendine replied.

Impressed, Warner replied, "You should have come out last year."

Warner assigned Exendine to his brother Bill, the Cornell captain who was helping Pop out as a volunteer coach. Bill, at six-feet, four inches and more than 210 pounds, dwarfed his trainee. He instructed Exendine to get into position and try to block him. "The first time I tried to block him, he threw me back," Exendine recalled. "I went at it again and again in that hot sun and got thrown back. Slowly I learned to turn my shoulder, use it and take him that way. When we finished we were both wringing wet. Bill walked over to Pop and said something. I was in uniform the next day."[51]

Carlisle opened the season with its now-traditional matchup against Lebanon Valley, winning 48–0. Gettysburg, which had stunned Carlisle with a 6–5 upset a year earlier, was no match this time around, and was crushed 25–0. The Indians were then upset 16–0 the following week by a surprisingly strong Bucknell team.

They rebounded with a 50–0 annihilation of Bloomsburg Normal, but injuries were once again becoming a concern as the Indians prepared to travel to Warner's alma mater for a rematch with the coach's brother and Cornell University. During the week, guard Martin Wheelock was diagnosed with pleurisy and was ordered to the infirmary by Warner.

"No, no!" Wheelock pleaded. "It's nothing at all. Please don't keep me out of the game."

"But you can't run, Martin," Warner replied.

"Change me to center," Wheelock reasoned. "Then I won't have to run." Given the shortage of manpower at his disposal, Warner had little choice but to do as Wheelock suggested.

Antonio Lubo was also ailing, still convalescing after having a significant portion of diseased bone surgically removed from his arm. Refusing to be sidelined, Lubo fashioned a leather splint that covered the arm from elbow to fingertip.

Prior to kickoff, Pop met up with his younger brother. After an exchange of pleasantries, Bill asked Pop for a status report of his team.

"So-so," said Pop. "I've got a sick chap at center and a one-armed chap at guard."

"Say," Bill exclaimed, "we don't want to play a bunch of cripples!"

"Don't worry, old boy," Pop replied. "You'll find them lively enough."

Indeed he would. There was to be no repeat of the loss suffered against Cornell at the Pan-American Exposition in Buffalo the year before. This time around, it was the Carlislians who controlled the line of scrimmage. "The play of the two cripples was the outstanding feature of the game,"

Pop observed. "Lubo gave him all he could handle, and as for Wheelock, he kept the opposing center on his back all afternoon." When it was all over, the final score read Carlisle 10, Cornell 6, and the score between the Warner brothers was even at one apiece.[52]

A week later, the Indians crushed Philadelphia-based Medico-Chirurgical College, 63–0, to improve to 5–1. But the momentum was lost by the time they arrived at Cambridge for their traditional contest with Harvard. The Crimson boys forced several fumbles, two of which were turned into touchdowns, in handing Carlisle a humiliating 23–0 loss.

The Indians returned to Carlisle for their final home game of the season against Susquehanna. Coach Warner, however, was not going to be at the game. At that time, it was not uncommon for head coaches to skip games against minor teams and travel to rival universities to scout upcoming opponents, leaving the game-day command of the team to the assistants or captains. Never a fan of second-hand scouting reports, Warner opted to take advantage of the weak competition expected from the visitors from Selinsgrove, Pennsylvania, and return to Cambridge to attend that Saturday's Harvard-Penn game—the latter representing Carlisle's next opponent. The Indians didn't miss a beat, winning 24–0.

Warner's scouting trip proved justified when the Indians soundly defeated Penn, 5–0. But the Indians failed to carry the momentum over to the following Saturday's contest against a weak Virginia team. "The betting was 5-to-1 that Virginia would be defeated," wrote the *Richmond Dispatch*, "and even money that she would not score." The 10,000 spectators present were indeed shocked to see the Virginians race to a 6–0 halftime lead and hold off a second-half rally to score an impressive 6–5 victory over the favored visitors from Pennsylvania.

The Indians were able to close the season on a positive note, however, knocking off Georgetown, 21–0, before 3,500 fans on the Georgetown campus on Thanksgiving Day. The next day, they were invited to visit President Theodore Roosevelt at the Executive Mansion. Roosevelt was a well-known follower of the grid game, and spent a lively 45 minutes discussing its finer points with his awestruck visitors. He showed keen interest in each player's background, asking questions about their tribes and great leaders. The president seemed most interested in talking to Nikifer Shouchuk, for whom it was reported he had several questions. Roosevelt, a Harvard man, asked one of the players about the Carlisle-Harvard game, to which the boy had to admit losing 23–0. The president smiled and replied, "That was better than Harvard did with Yale."[53]

Carlisle's final record for 1902 was a fine 8–3, their best in three campaigns. Walter Camp ranked them as the ninth-best team in the nation, while Caspar Whitney had them rated eleventh. Despite the outstanding play of quarterback Jimmy Johnson, however, there were no All-America selections for the Indians.

Pop Warner is remembered as one of the most vocal opponents of the professionalization of football. It wasn't that he didn't like the idea of a man making a buck, for there were few who enjoyed making one as thoroughly as he did. Heck, he didn't even mind cashing in on the outcome of a game with a friendly wager every now and then. But for Warner, playing the game for money was objectionable "simply because there's no future in it."[54] However, if the money was good enough, he could be coaxed into setting aside a principle or two. Such a moment came during the winter break following Carlisle's outstanding 1902 season, when he and his brother Bill were invited to take part in a football tournament scheduled at Madison Square Garden the week after Christmas and culminating on New Year's Day. The tournament, dubbed the "World Series of Football," was conceived by Tom O'Rourke, a prominent boxing promoter and manager of the Garden. O'Rourke managed to sign up five teams for the series, including one representing the Orange, New Jersey, Athletic Club, the Warlow (Long Island) Athletic Club, a nominal New York City team (in reality a collection of "all stars" from Pittsburgh and Philadelphia), another team from New York called the Knickerbockers, and Pop's team, ostensibly representing the city of Syracuse's athletic club.[55]

The Syracuse aggregation was being captained by Frank "Buck" O'Neill, the star end from Williams College. In addition to O'Neill and the brothers Warner, the team featured two of Pop's former Carlisle players in Hawley and Bemus Pierce. Unlike Bill, who was fresh off an All-America year at Cornell, Pop had not played an actual game since donning the togs against Butte seven years earlier. But the chance to line up next to his brother and, better still, the inducement of a $300 guarantee was enough incentive to for him to ignore any misgivings he might have had. "Three-hundred dollars looked mighty good to a man on a small salary," Warner reasoned. "Besides, I wanted a vacation."[56] Some vacation.

Shortly after Christmas, Warner left the comfort of Springville to join his teammates in Syracuse for some workouts preparatory to the heralded event. The team then traveled to New York for the tournament. On Monday, December 29, 1902, the Syracuse Athletic Club locked horns with the New York/Penn amalgam in what can rightly be called the first indoor professional football game. With a crowd of 3,500 watching, the all-stars from Syracuse defeated the "New Yorkers" by a score of 5–0. The score could have been greater, had Pop not failed on the conversion try following the game's only touchdown, and at least three field goal attempts.[57] Although he managed to play every down, this was the only game Pop appeared in, having received such a pounding—including a deep gash on the side of his head—that he opted to sit out the remainder of the tournament. Bill Warner saw it through to the end, helping the S.A.C. claim the first World Series of professional football by defeating the Orange A.C. 36–0 in the final game. Despite the $300 O'Rourke guaranteed each player, Bill was the only man to walk away with the full amount. Pop, having appeared in just the one game, was not so fortunate. To go along with his injured scalp, he received the grand sum of $23 cash. "The tournament proved to be a financial flop," Warner later wrote. "The next morning when I tried to arise I found I was so lame and stiff that I could move only with great difficulty and I had to send for my brother to help me dress. That ended my professional football career."[58]

The squad turning out for the summer's first practice was predictably small and inexperienced, and would test the limits of Warner's abilities as a coach. Pop was happy to have the assistance of his brother Bill, who for the second straight season was on hand for the first week of practices as a guest coach. Bill's purpose was greater this year, however, as he was now officially head coach of the Cornell eleven and eager to learn as much as he could from his famous kin.[59]

On the field, the team was to be led by quarterback James Johnson, now entering his sixth year with the squad. The five-foot, seven-inch, 140-pound Stockbridge Indian was an immensely talented but frustratingly moody player who brought Warner some of his most memorable victories while at the same time giving the coach some of his most severe headaches.[60] By the end of the season, the two could no longer stand to be in the same room.

As usual, Carlisle breezed through the early part of its schedule, laying waste to Lebanon Valley (28–0), Gettysburg (46–0), Bucknell (12–0) and Franklin & Marshall (30–0) before the season's first important game against undefeated Princeton on October 17. Despite fumbling the ball 12 times, the Tigers proved too strong for Carlisle and scored an 11–0 victory. Warner's boys bounced back in the final home game of the season to defeat a weak Swarthmore team 12–5 and improve to 5–1, with the annual trip to Harvard up next.

Ever mindful that his players had a tendency to become bored with the monotony of practice, and perhaps fearful that the boys might fall victim to a collapse similar to the one that befell them in 1901, Warner reached back into his bag of tricks and pulled out an old chestnut sure to capture their attention—the hidden ball play he first used at Cornell six years earlier. "We often practiced this and other trick plays to liven up the daily grind of scrimmaging," Warner remembered. "Sometimes these plays worked successfully, and sometimes not."[61] Either way, the Carlisle boys loved the play, and they pestered their coach to let them use it in a game. After much deliberation, it was decided the play would be used, but it was to be saved for the Harvard game. "Trick plays were what the redskins loved best," Warner observed. "Nothing delighted them more than to outsmart the palefaces." Especially those from Cambridge. "Neither the boys nor myself considered the play to be strictly legitimate. We did, however, know that the play would work against Harvard and, at least, prove to be a good joke on the arrogant Crimson players."[62]

In order for the play to succeed, the ball had to be stuffed underneath a player's jersey and remain secure while the player made his way upfield. Warner had Carlisle's resident tailor, Mose Blumenthal, sew elastic bands into a few of the players' jerseys, but 184-pound guard Charles Dillon was ultimately selected to be the one to carry the hidden pigskin. It was an inspired choice, for if the play was to work as it was supposed to, the confused defenders were most likely to go after someone who normally carried the ball—a back such as Johnson or maybe Arthur Sheldon—not an interior lineman. More importantly, Dillon was extremely fast, and the man carrying the ball was going to have to get away as quickly as possible.

The day before the game, the Indians took the train from Philadelphia to Boston and checked into the Copley Square Hotel. Later that evening, Warner took the team for a walk through the city's darkened streets, where they discussed the upcoming contest and the trick play they couldn't wait to spring on unsuspecting Harvard.[63]

A capacity crowd of 12,000, nearly all of them devotees of Harvard, turned out to witness what was to be the final game ever played at Soldier Field. And while many came hoping to see some of the trick plays for which the Indians had become known, none were prepared for the surprise the visitors had in store for them.

And neither were the Crimson prepared for the onslaught that overrode them in the first half. Harvard, as expected, was taking the Indians lightly, and this attitude almost proved fatal as they were repeatedly fooled by Carlisle's strange formations and Johnson's play-calling, which included a healthy dose of Warner's trademark misdirection. Before the half concluded, the Carlisle quarterback had guided his team to within twelve yards of the enemy's goal line. Harvard held fast, but Johnson managed to boot an 18-yard field goal to give his team a 5–0 lead that stood as the teams retired to their respective dressing rooms.

With Harvard set to kick off at the start of the second half, Warner figured the time was right and instructed his players to give the play a try. Prior to the kick, Warner pulled referee Mike Thompson aside and advised him that the Indians were going to be attempting a trick play, and provided a brief description of what to expect.

The Indians were champing at the bit, but the first kick went out of bounds and had to be repeated. The second effort was right down the middle of the field—perfect. Johnson caught the ball at his own five-yard line. His teammates massed together as if preparing for a V rush. Concealed within the assemblage was Johnson stuffing the ball under the back of Dillon's jersey. Once secured, Johnson shouted, "Go!" The Carlisle players scattered in eleven different directions, those outfitted with a leather helmet clutching it to his bosom to give the impression that he was the one lugging the pigskin. The dumbfounded Harvard boys, clueless as to which Carlisle player had the ball, began tackling every man in an opposing jersey in a vain effort to stop the play—every man, that is, except the one who actually had it. While players scrambled and bodies lay strewn about the field, a small roar could be heard as Dillon made a beeline for the Harvard end zone. The hump in Dillon's jersey, still unnoticed by the Crimson defenders, had been detected by many in the crowd, and the cheering grew louder as more and more caught on. When Carl Marshall—Harvard's last man—met up with Dillon at mid-field, the Crimson captain actually stepped aside, thinking Dillon was attempting to block him. Dillon sprinted into the Harvard end zone, the ball still forming an unnatural bubble in the back of his uniform. Johnson came up behind him, removed the ball and touched it to the ground. Harvard coach John Cranston protested vehemently, but referee Thompson, having been tipped off by Warner prior to the play, declared it within the rules. Touchdown![64]

Carlisle now held a commanding 11–0 lead, but their audacity had awakened a sleeping lion. The Crimson fought back to take a 12–11 lead with only minutes remaining. The Indians were not about to give up either, and mounted one last valiant drive deep into Crimson territory, but Johnson fumbled at the 15, sealing Carlisle's fate.

The hidden ball play was covered widely, the *New York Times* describing it as "one of the most spectacular, unforeseen, and unique expedients

ever used against a member of the Big Four." But the play, though successful, had not resulted in a Carlisle victory. And that was fine with Warner,
who had to confess that he preferred to win by what he considered to be
"legitimate" football tactics, rather than a play he later dismissed as no
more than a fluke.[65]

Carlisle rebounded the following week, destroying Georgetown, 28–
6, and improving to 6–2 on the season. They then traveled to Philadelphia
to meet arch-rival Penn. Games between the two elevens were traditionally
fierce, but the Quakers, who entered this contest at 8–2, were totally outclassed in losing 16–6. "The 'redmen' outwitted and, excepting in a few
instances, outclassed the 'pale faces' representing Pennsylvania," wrote the
New York Times. "The victory is a highly creditable one to coach Warner
and his sturdy team. Had it not been for several fumbles, the Indians' score
would have been doubled in the first thirty-five minutes of play."

Warner conceded that his team was "perhaps a bit cocky following
our win over the Quakers," and "didn't take our next game against Virginia
seriously," despite Virginia's 7–1 record. Quarterback Johnson seemed
more interested in "daring, crowd-pleasing plays" than actually winning the
game. "But in the end result, this exhibition of showmanship didn't help
us win."[66] All the Indians could muster was six points, just enough not to
lose. Final score: Carlisle 6, Virginia 6.

The incensed coach wasn't taking any chances with unbeaten Northwestern coming up. He ordered his quarterback to return to basic football, and the result was a convincing 28–0 triumph in a blinding snow
storm.

Carlisle's record of 8–2–1 was a half-game better than the previous
year's, and the best since the 9–2 mark recorded in 1899, Warner's first
year at the school. But just as he had in that debut season, Warner extended
the campaign by accepting invitations for post-season games from a handful of Western schools. A three-game tour was scheduled, including contests with the University of Utah, an all-star aggregation called the Reliance
Athletic Association on Christmas Day, and finally the Sherman Institute,
another Indian boarding school located at Riverside, California.

On December 14, the Carlisle Indians boarded a train that carried
them on the first leg of their journey out West. It had already been a long
season, and despite the three-week layoff prior to embarking, this may
have been the cause of some irritability on the part of quarterback Johnson, who clashed openly with his head coach. Things came to a head on
the morning of the Utah game, when Warner felt compelled to bench his
star player over an undisclosed rule infraction, most likely insubordina-

tion. Joe Baker, Johnson's understudy, played well in his place, guiding Carlisle to a 22–0 win.

The train carrying the victorious Indians to California was a hotbed of tension, as Johnson stewed over his demotion and Warner struggled to maintain harmony within the ranks. When the team disembarked at San Francisco, they were greeted by a mass of newspapermen eager to get a scoop on the famous Carlisle football team and its two most prominent figures, head coach Pop Warner and star quarterback Jimmy Johnson, who had recently been honored with selection to Walter Camp's All-America team. Unknown to the members of the Fourth Estate, however, was the fact that the two were no longer speaking to one another.

As the Carlisle players milled about in the locker room prior to the game, Warner pulled Johnson and Baker aside and informed them that Johnson was starting. "When I spoke to Johnson individually regarding some matter of generalship," Warner recalled, "he flared up and shouted, 'Listen, I don't care if I never see your ball game!'" Warner was not about to let one of his players get the upper hand on him, and at once turned to Baker and gave him the nod instead. "But the players pleaded with me to let Johnson play," said Warner.

He reminded the team that Baker had done a fine job filling in for Johnson against Utah and, besides, he wasn't comfortable playing a man whose heart wasn't going to be in it. Just then, Johnson stepped forward and said, "I want to play if the boys want me."

It wasn't exactly the apology Warner was seeking, but it was good enough for now. He gave Johnson the start, and was rewarded with what the coach thought was the best game the All-American ever played. "He was in every play," Warner remembered. "[Johnson] caught and ran back punts as few men have ever done before or since, and handled his team in such an inspiring and capable manner that the critics agreed that Camp had made no mistake." The result was a spectacular 23–0 victory for Carlisle.[67]

A week later, the Carlisle eleven met their counterparts from the Sherman Institute. With Johnson calling signals on the field, the Indians relied predominantly on trick plays instead of straight football. To Warner, the team seemed more intent on "trying to see if they could succeed in pulling off more gadget or hocus-pocus plays than their opponent." Carlisle came away with a modest 12–6 win in a game that should not have been close.

Upon returning to the school, Warner and Johnson met separately with Major Pratt and aired their respective grievances. Warner demanded that Johnson be punished for his transgressions, but Pratt was not inclined to agree. After all, Pratt pointed out, Johnson was now 25 years of age and had already begun studying at nearby Dickinson College, and therefore it seemed inappropriate to administer any type of punishment on him. In addition, there had never before been complaints against Johnson that would substantiate the behavior of which Warner was now accusing him.

What now? If Pratt was not going to back Warner up, the coach would lose credibility with his players. He could not go back now and maintain absolute authority, knowing the players would feel they could circumvent any of his unpopular policies or decisions by going directly to the superintendent with their complaints.

Fortunately for Warner, Cornell University, just as it had twice before, stepped in at just the right moment to provide the solution to the coach's conundrum. Representatives from the school paid Warner a visit and asked him to return to Ithaca to coach both the football and baseball teams. He was intrigued, but there were several glitches, not the least of which was the fact that his brother, Bill, was still under contract as the school's football coach. "When the Cornell representatives initially approached me about returning to the Ithaca campus, it was not a flattering salary offer which turned my head. Instead, it was the fact that I sincerely didn't want to see my brother get caught up in the middle of any kind of tug-of-war match with the Cornell alumni and administration over the team's direction. Based on my previous tenure there, I knew that this could be a rather difficult spot to be put in."[68]

Pop informed the superintendent that he had been approached by Cornell and was considering accepting the offer. Pratt was not about to acquiesce. He responded with a letter of his own, in which he refuted all of Warner's reasons for wanting Johnson punished. He expressed regret that the situation had come to such an extreme, and how much regard he had for the man he believed was "the best coach in the country" who had "accomplished results that entitle [Warner] to greatest credit."[69]

Warner ultimately decided to return to Cornell, but soon regretted the decision. In three years, he'd be back.

SIX

Cornell
Revisited

Two thousand Cornell rooters turned out to greet Pop Warner when he arrived at Ithaca on March 3, 1904, to discuss contract terms with school officials.[1] He gave a brief speech in which he outlined his plans to overhaul the program's current structure, which gave more authority to the team captain than the coach. Warner intended to wield complete control over the team, and asked for the full support of the players, the alumni, and the fans.

After meeting with the school's administrators, Warner went back to Carlisle, where he was still under contract to coach the baseball team for one last spring. Meanwhile, there was still the awkward matter of his brother Bill, who was technically still engaged as Cornell's head football coach. Noted Carlisle historian Tom Benjey has surmised that the elder Warner used his by-now-considerable influence to resolve the issue.

"Pop understandably had misgivings about taking his brother's job," Benjey wrote, "and likely made up for it a bit by helping Bill get another job. By virtue of coaching at Carlisle for five years, Pop surely had contacts within the Indian school system, and at Sherman Institute in California in particular because Bemus Pierce coached there in 1902 and 1903." Pop, it appears, used those contacts to secure for Bill the head coaching position at Sherman for the upcoming season. Pierce, the former Carlisle star who had been serving as Sherman's head football coach, then came back to Carlisle as an assistant coach under Ed Rogers, who had been hired to replace Pop when he left for Cornell.[2]

Warner returned to Ithaca on September 1 and went immediately to work getting things in order for the beginning of camp. He tried to remain optimistic about the upcoming season in spite of the fact that he had only five lettermen returning from the previous year. "Cornell had just gone through a disastrous season," Warner recalled, "and the material in 1904 was mediocre to say the least."[3]

There was an immense amount of labor to be performed before the season-opening game on September 28, so Warner wasn't about to waste time. The coach had barely gotten his bags unpacked by the time he called his first practice on September 7. About a dozen players, mainly freshmen, reported along with assistant coaches Charles Lueder and Ralph Kent, with the returning upperclassmen scheduled to arrive on September 19, just nine days before the opener. Warner, now entering his tenth season as a head coach, was determined to have his team ready.

Pop's second go-round at Cornell began auspiciously with a 17–0 Wednesday-afternoon defeat of Colgate. Three days later, the Cornellians hosted the University of Rochester and recorded another resounding victory, 29–6. The streak continued with wins over Hobart (24–0), Hamilton (34–0), Bucknell (24–12) and Franklin & Marshall (36–5) to bring the Red Men to 6–0. Warner was undoubtedly enjoying the successful return to his old stomping grounds, but was ever mindful that his brother had guided the team to the same record the year before only to see the great start thrown away with an 0–3–1 finish. It was a scenario Pop hoped wouldn't be repeated, but with Princeton, Columbia and Penn remaining on the slate, the prospects did not appear to be in his favor.

The Princeton eleven came to town with a 6–1 record and were heavily favored, fresh off a 60–0 skunking of Lehigh. Despite their best efforts, Warner's inexperienced charges went down in an 18–6 defeat. "While I had hoped for a victory over Princeton," remarked the coach after the game, "I realize that it was too much to expect that Cornell, with practically a green team, lacking experience, and outclassed in weight, could win from last year's champions. Cornell played with a dash that was irresistible during the first part of the game, but they could not stand the pace and Princeton's bull dog spirit, determination and better endurance made her greater strength count in the end, and her victory was fairly earned. I am satisfied that every man on the team played as hard and as well as he knew how, and with the experience gained in this game and with hard and conscientious work ... the team should be a great deal stronger by Thanksgiving Day."[4]

Unfortunately for the Red Men and their fans, however, Warner's powers of prognostication proved wanting, for the loss to Princeton was just the beginning. The team lost two of its three remaining games to very nearly duplicate what had transpired a year earlier under Bill Warner's watch. Still, Pop felt his first season back at Ithaca had gone fairly well. "The Cornell football program began to slowly make some strides in the right direction," he observed. With their final record of 7–3–0, the Cornellians had finished a half-game better than they had in 1903. "However," he reasoned, "I was building for the future."[5]

The 1905 campaign followed an arc strikingly similar to those of the previous two seasons, with the club winning its first six games (5–0 versus Hamilton, 12–11 versus Colgate, 28–0 versus Hobart, 24–0 versus Bucknell, 30–0 versus Western University of Pennsylvania, and 57–0 over Haverford) before going into a tailspin and losing its final four (14–0 versus Swarthmore, 16–6 versus Princeton, 12–6 versus Columbia, and 6–5 versus Penn).

Compounding the misery of the team's late-season skid, however, was an incident that served as the backdrop to Warner's remaining time at Cornell. The flap resulted when Warner expelled popular halfback Lawrence J. Rice for "attempting to cause dissension in the team and ill-feeling between the coaches and the players." Rice, according to Warner, was "something of a hero in the minds of many and quite naturally my action embittered them and caused much trouble. I anticipated this development and was not unprepared to meet the consequences. I felt in my heart and mind that I was right. I did what any coach would do if he has 'spine,' despite the fact that it meant personal disadvantage to myself."[6]

The incident set an uncomfortable tone for the remaining year and half of Warner's tenure at the school. He later cited it as one of the main factors in his decision to leave Cornell when his contract expired at the end of the 1906 season.

In the two years since Warner left Carlisle Indian Industrial School, the institution had undergone many changes, the most significant coming in the summer following his departure, when founder and long-time superintendent Major Richard H. Pratt was relieved of his duties. Chosen to take his place was Major William A. Mercer, a career Army officer lacking in the energy, understanding and empathy for the population comprising the school's student body that exemplified Pratt's administration.[7] Those shortcomings would eventually be the undoing of the school.

Pratt, however, made one last meaningful move prior to leaving, hiring Edward Rogers, the former Carlisle star, to replace the departing coach Warner. The Carlisle players had lobbied to have one of their own at the helm, and showed their appreciation by posting an impressive 9–2–0 record. The following year, however, Mercer replaced Rogers with George Woodruff, the former Penn coach, and the team responded with a somewhat lackluster 10–4 mark. Prior to the 1906 campaign, Bemus Pierce—another Carlisle alumnus—was named to the post in what appears to have been an interim capacity. It seemed clear that Mercer had his eye on someone else to take over at the end of the season, and though Warner was under contract with Cornell through the 1906 campaign, he accepted Mercer's invitation to come down to the Carlisle campus in early September to provide instruction in the game's newly-adopted rules, including those related to the now-legal forward pass.

By this time, Warner had become a believer in the use of the forward pass. This, however, had not always been the case. In fact, Warner had initially been one of the tactic's most vehement opponents, especially after it was used successfully by the University of North Carolina in the defeat of his University of Georgia team back in 1895.[8] In the eleven years since, the rules regarding passing had evolved, and so had Warner's attitude toward them. The game that once favored bulky and aggressive behemoths employing mass momentum strategies such as the flying wedge had witnessed countless serious injuries, and even several fatalities. "There was no open play and very little variety in the attack," Warner pointed out. "Speed had little place in the order of the day. Big human 'mountains' were sought and valued by every coach whether they could navigate slowly or quickly."[9]

Shocked at reports of the carnage resulting from intercollegiate football—including several deaths in 1905—President Theodore Roosevelt demanded that the game's violence be toned down. In December of that year, the National Intercollegiate Football Conference was formed, with a seven-member sub-committee charged with developing ways to make the game safer. The flying wedge was outlawed, as were the "guards-back" and "tackles-back" formations (the former an invention, ironically, of outgoing Carlisle coach George Woodruff), in which additional linemen were placed in the backfield to assist the ball carrier. Runners would no longer be allowed to hurdle prone players. The "yards-to-go" distance for a first down was increased from five to ten. The committee also created the concept of the "neutral zone" between the opposing forward lines. Up to that point, linemen assumed positions literally nose-to-nose from each other prior to each play. Scuffling and altercations were just as likely to result as an actual offensive play. The neutral zone laid an imaginary line as wide as the length of the ball between the teams, thus eliminating contact before the snap. But perhaps the most important change brought forth was the restricted legalization of the forward pass.

"The main efforts of the football reformers has been to 'open up the game,'" observed the *New York Times*. "That is to provide for the natural elimination of the so-called mass plays and bring about a game in which speed and real skill shall supercede so far as possible mere brute strength and force of weight."

"This spelled the doom of big college supremacy on the gridiron," Warner later observed. "Coaches of the younger generation [of which he considered himself a member] were not handicapped by old customs and were quicker to adapt themselves and their teams to the new order of things than were the older and more conservative coaches of the large eastern schools. The forward pass was encouraged as the first radical step in the new direction."[10]

Warner spent a week at Carlisle, ostensibly to instruct the football team on the finer points of the new rules, with special emphasis on those related to the aerial game. "The Indians took to the new passing game very readily and made a fine showing that season," Warner observed. With their old coach providing the blueprints for their new attack, the Indians responded with a 9–3 finish.[11]

There were many who speculated, of course, that Warner's presence at the school was a sign he was going to be coming back once his contract at Cornell expired. But there was still a year remaining on his current deal, so Warner dutifully returned to Cornell to prepare his team for the upcoming campaign. Practices back at Ithaca, though, were strikingly similar to those the coach had just conducted during his brief visit to Carlisle. Footballs filled the air as players struggled to learn the proper gripping technique and throwing motion required to launch a creditable forward pass with the melon-shaped prolate spheroid in use at the time. When observers noted that what they were witnessing more closely resembled the game of basketball than football as it had been traditionally known, Warner blithely responded, "It may be basketball, but it's in the rules, so let's try it."[12]

"Undoubtedly there will be more interest in the game this year owing to the radical changes in the rules and the natural curiosity in the minds of those interested in the sport as to how the changes will affect the game," Warner told reporters covering Cornell workouts. "There are many minor changes and additions to the rules, designed to reduce the danger of injury. Penalties for intentional roughness and fouls have been increased. The rule allowing forward passing opens up a great many possibilities for new plays and there is bound to be a good deal of attention and practice devoted to acquiring cleverness in this method of advancing the ball."[13]

It is also quite possible that it was during his brief visit to the Carlisle campus that Warner first hatched the concept for what was to become his signature offensive attack—the single wing. The single wing offense is considered by many football scholars to be the genesis of the modern offense, featuring a direct snap to the tailback (or one of the other remaining backfield men) and a back stationed just outside and behind one of the ends—hence single *wing*. The object of the formation was to provide power at the point of attack. "I wish I could remember who said it," commented football historian T.J. Troup, "but the concept of the single wing is 'running a buffalo stampede through the eye of a needle.'" This is accomplished by using an unbalanced offensive line, which placed either both guards or both tackles on one side of the center. It allowed for a seemingly unending variety of options and kept the defenses on their toes in trying to guess whether a run, pass or punt was about to happen.[14]

Unfortunately, there is no definitive record of exactly when the single wing was conceived. It seems likely, however, that Warner's imagination was fired during this visit, when he was reminded what the Indian players were capable of and started to experiment with some of the myriad possibilities when he returned to Cornell. One of the reasons for the difficulty in pinpointing the date, or even the year, of its first usage is that there is no direct mention of the new formation in contemporaneous newspaper accounts. Nor did the man himself refer to it at any time during the early years of its existence. In later years, he would often recall that he came up with the single wing in 1906, but many historians place the year of its introduction at 1907, Warner's first year back at Carlisle. Without an actual name by which to call it, Walter Camp referred to this offense simply as the "Carlisle Formation." It wasn't until some time later that it came to be referred to as the single wing, differentiating it from another revolutionary formation Warner devised in 1912 incorporating two wingmen. In his 1927 book, *Football for Coaches & Players*, Warner designated the single wing "Formation A" (and the newer double wing as "Formation B").[15]

The year 1906 got off to a strange start, with the Red Men posting a 0–0 draw against Colgate on September 29. A couple of days later, Pop was contacted by family back in Springville with news that his mother was suffering from a "serious illness." He rushed home and spent an evening at her side before returning to Ithaca satisfied she was out of danger.[16]

The Cornell eleven then went on a tear, winning their next five games by a combined 165–17 to improve to 5–0–1 before their annual encounter with Princeton at New York's Polo Grounds. A throng of some 25,000 were treated to a grand display of the "modern" aerial game. "[The crowd] came to see what the new game of football was like," wrote the *New York Times*, "and it went away well satisfied. It saw dashing football, exciting and changing with an endless variety of motion, with one and then the other team monetarily in possession, each gaining slightly and then trying some new-fangled trick play that brought the ball out into the open for both to scramble for, and ended as often as not in its loss to the defenders. So in the shifting panorama luck played a considerable part, and what luck there was with Princeton." That good fortune, combined with an advantage in size and experience, spelled Cornell's doom, as Princeton walked away with a 14–5 win.

The loss was especially hard to swallow, considering it was to be the only defeat Cornell suffered all year. The Red Men won their next three (23–0 over Pittsburgh, 16–6 over Holy Cross, and 28–0 over Swarthmore) before ending the season with a 0–0 tie versus Penn.

His team's brilliant 8–1–2 record notwithstanding, Warner's relationship with the school's administrators had been irretrievably strained ever since the hullabaloo over the expulsion of Lawrence Rice the previous November. "With this incident as the keynote," he'd later recall, "the years I coached at Cornell were anything but congenial." He also noted a general disregard for sports on the part of school officials. "There was a decided lack of time for football practice, an unusually high scholarship requirement for all students, and a lack of alumni cooperation."[17]

Relief came to Warner while attending the annual Army-Navy game in Philadelphia on December 1. After spotting Carlisle's star end Albert Exendine seated on the sidelines, Warner sidled up from behind and slapped the newly-minted All-American on the back. Having heard rumors of Warner's unhappiness at Cornell, Exendine inquired if he was considering a return to Carlisle.

"You have coaches," said Warner.

"They aren't coaches," was Exendine's frank reply. He pointed out that Major Mercer was in the stands and encouraged Warner to speak with him. Sometime before the game was over, the two met and reached an accord.[18] However, in light of Warner's visit as a guest coach at the beginning of the season, and Mercer's desire to have a white man as coach and athletic director, Pop's meeting with the superintendent appears to have been little more than a formality.

Warner announced his impending departure on December 13. The president of Cornell's athletic council immediately issued a statement expressing his disappointment over the coach's decision. "I regret very much Mr. Warner's determination to accept an appointment as athletic director at Carlisle. When he returned to Cornell three years ago football was in a deplorable condition. There was not only a want of trained material but an absence of discipline and practical demoralization. His three seasons of coaching have resulted in continuous and marked progress. Our team this season was one of the very best in the country and probably the best team that ever represented Cornell. Besides developing good players Mr. Warner's entire influence has been effectively used in favor of cleanliness in play and a proper sense of the relations between sport and academic work. In baseball, Mr. Warner's success has been no less marked. The position accepted by Mr. Warner is, I understand, exceedingly advantageous to him, and one which he could not in justice to himself and his family refuse. He certainly has the best wishes of those connected with the athletic management here in his new work."[19]

Despite the public display of civility, the conditions under which Warner departed for the third, and ultimately final, time from the very place where he had learned his beloved game remained as an unpleasant memory for the rest of his life. "It seems worthy of note that in some thirty years of coaching football," he'd write in 1928, "the only place where I had unpleasant years was at my own alma mater."[20]

SEVEN

Back to Carlisle

The squad greeting Warner upon his return to Carlisle in the fall of 1907 was, in his own words, "quite good," and offered great promise for the upcoming campaign. He saw in this small but quick group the perfect opportunity to run the offense—later known as the single wing, but at this point still unnamed—that he had been refining ever since his one-week visit to the Indians' training camp the previous summer. He had some fine material to work with, led by veteran end Albert Exendine, the previous year's captain. The dashingly handsome Exendine was a freshman on Warner's 1902 squad, and had since developed into the school's best athlete, excelling in nearly every track and field event. His stellar play on the gridiron in 1906 had earned him selection to Walter Camp's All-America team. Ex had, in fact, recently graduated from Carlisle, but was allowed to remain there while he studied law at cross-town Dickinson College.[1]

Throwing the ball to Exendine—and performing all of the intricate spins, shifts and fakes called for in Warner's system—was a stellar group of backs headed by quarterback Frank Mount Pleasant. Mount Pleasant was a remarkably gifted athlete from the Tuscarora Reservation in Western New York, who at the age of 19 tipped the scales at a mere 140 pounds. His outstanding open-field running and his ability to hurl the pigskin 50 yards—with accuracy—were contrasted by his quiet off-field demeanor and extraordinary talents at the piano.[2] Warner discovered he had another fine passer—perhaps the best on the team—in Peter Hauser, a member of the Cheyenne tribe whom the coach would one day cite as the finest fullback ever to play at Carlisle.

The forward pass—the weapon that Warner predicted would revolutionize the game just the year before—was now to be a featured part of the offense he was about to unleash on out-of-step universities in 1907. Warner was light years ahead of his peers as the first coach to fully understand the game's new rules and devise ways to exploit them. With the

Carlisle Indians, he had just the vehicle through which to turn his concepts into reality on the playing field.[3]

Yet, as satisfied as Warner was with the talent that lay before him as he called his players together for the first practice of the season, he was bothered by the appearance of one young man who was there for his first tryout. The aspiring gridder was Warner's star track man, Jim Thorpe. The coach had enough football players, and certainly didn't want to risk losing Thorpe's valuable track services to injury. There was no way Warner could have known then that Thorpe's presence represented not only the future of the Carlisle football program, but also the beginning of perhaps the greatest coach/player relationship in the history of organized sport.

Thorpe's journey to Carlisle had been a long and arduous one. On the morning of May 28, 1888, he and his twin brother Charles were born to Hiram and Charlotte Thorpe in a one-room cabin just south of the town of Bellemont near the North Canadian River in the Oklahoma Territory.[4] Hiram was half Sac and Fox Indian and half Irish, and traced his lineage back to the great Sac and Fox warrior Black Hawk. He was a tall, muscular man who was known to be generous and sociable when sober, but mean and violent when not. Charlotte was of Potawotomi and Kickapoo descent, with a trace of French blood in her veins. She had received a Jesuit education and could speak three languages. At the time of their initial acquaintance, Hiram already had two wives. Polygamy, however, was an accepted part of the culture. They married and eventually produced nine children together, only four of who survived to adulthood. The home was located on a reservation, but Hiram was able to provide for his family through hard work and the good fortune of owning nearly 1,200 acres of good land abutting the river. The family grew corn, beans, hay, and squash, and raised cows, pigs and horses. They fished and hunted game big and small, and the boys were taught to use shotguns at a very early age. One of Jim's favorite activities was breaking colts.[5]

Jim and Charlie were very close and spent whatever free time they had exploring their vast spread, fishing, swimming and playing with the other children living nearby. Their competitive spirit was kept satisfied by wrestling, foot races and other sports. It was apparent early on, however, that Jim was the more athletically gifted of the two.

The boys' parents were firm believers in the value of education. In 1893, when they were just five years old, Jim and Charlie were sent to the Sac and Fox Indian Agency School, a Quaker-run boarding school near Tecumseh in the Territory, about 20 miles from the homestead. The school's mission, in addition to the obvious scholastic and religious curriculum, was to teach Indian youth vocational skills and assimilate them into white culture. This was accomplished by cropping the children's long hair, replacing their native garb with uniforms, and enforcing of a strict rule that punished children for speaking their native tongue.

Charlie was the more laid-back, adaptable twin. He had little trouble conforming to the school's precepts. Jim, on the other hand, had difficulty from the moment he arrived there. He couldn't abide by the school's regimentation and felt trapped when forced to sit in a classroom or toil in some workshop. He became a frequent runaway. Whenever he arrived home, his father would administer a beating and send Jim back.[6] This pattern repeated itself several times, eventually earning Jim the label of "incorrigible" from school staff.[7]

In May 1896, a typhoid epidemic swept through the school, and Charlie was among the dozens of students taken ill. His condition declined rapidly, and soon pneumonia set in. The family rallied around Charlie, but the boy lost his battle with the disease and passed away. The loss of his twin brother and closest companion affected Jim deeply, and is said to have made him distant and withdrawn. He refused to return to school after Charlie's death, so Hiram decided to send Jim to a school far enough away to discourage him from attempting to elope again. The Haskell Institute in Lawrence, Kansas, some 300 miles from Bellemont, was just the place.

While at Haskell, Jim was taught how to march in step and play organized sports such as baseball and the relatively new game of football, which was rapidly growing in popularity on open fields across the country. But Haskell was similar in scope to the school Jim had just left, and he quickly tired of its rules and again began running away.[8]

When Hiram was badly injured after being shot in the chest in a hunting accident, Jim made his way on foot to the Lawrence train station and hopped an empty boxcar. After traveling about 100 miles, he realized he was heading in the wrong direction. He hopped off and began following the tracks back toward Lawrence. It took two weeks on foot, but Jim finally made it home. Upon entering the family house, Jim was relieved to find his father fully recovered from his wound. Hiram, on the other hand, was furious. He applied another whipping and tried to force Jim to return to Haskell, but this time the boy wouldn't budge. Jim was now thirteen and not so easily coerced. Hiram accepted that his son possessed some of the same obstinacy that coursed though his own veins, and instead decided to put the boy to work on the farm. However, Jim suffered another setback just a short time after, when his beloved mother died from blood poisoning on November 17, 1901. Jim withdrew even further.[9]

Another incident several months later involving Hiram's violent temper brought about Jim's departure from the family farm. Jim had had enough, and this time ran away *from* home, the one place he had always longed to be. Barely in his teens and standing all of four feet, eleven inches, Jim found work in the Texas Panhandle mending fences and breaking wild horses. He refused to come home until he had saved enough money to do so unaided and be able to show his father he was now a man. When he finally returned, Jim went back to working on the farm and enrolled at the public school in nearby Garden Grove.[10]

A fateful meeting in May 1904 would alter the course of Jim's life by leading him to the school with which he would be always associated and where he became a legendary figure. On the twelfth of that month, the school was visited by a gentleman dressed in a military uniform who announced that he was there to recruit Indian children for the Carlisle Indian Industrial School in Pennsylvania. The Carlisle school was well-known and a great source of pride among Native American children across the country, as its football team had grown to national prominence in recent years. Many boys dreamed of attending the school and playing for the famous "Pop" Warner. Jim's father, who placed a high premium on education, was in full support of Jim's desire to go there. "Son," said Hiram proudly, "you are an Indian. I want you to show other races what an Indian can do."[11]

Thorpe arrived at the Carlisle school in June of 1904 as a skinny, five-foot, five-inch, 115-pound, sixteen-year-old. But after spending three grueling seasons as a hired hand on local farms as part of the school's outing program, he emerged as a sturdy young man of five-feet, ten inches and 145 pounds. Warner became aware of Thorpe in April 1907 after hearing that the 18-year-old had unofficially broken the school high-jump record of five feet, nine inches when he casually cleared the bar while wearing work overalls and a pair of borrowed gym shoes.

Jim had been crossing the track field while on his way to meet some friends for a late afternoon football game when he spotted some of the varsity track athletes practicing the high jump. He stopped momentarily to watch as each jumper cleared the bar. However, when the bar was set at five feet, nine inches, none of the jumpers was successful. Jim strode over and nonchalantly asked, "Can I give it a try?" The older fellows shared a disparaging chuckle as the bar was reset. They watched in anticipation of seeing this impudent kid fall flat on his face.

The kid set himself in position just a few feet back from the bar. He sized up its height and figured how much speed and lift he would need to clear it—the preposterous notion of coming up short never entering his mind. Jim approached the bar and jumped. At that time, the technique used in the high-jump featured a diagonal approach followed by the jumper first throwing his inside leg and then the other over the bar in a scissor-like fashion, quite different from the modern shoulders-first style popularized by Dick Fosbury in the late 1960s. With seeming ease, Jim cleared the bar and returned to earth. He stood up, brushed himself off and, without uttering a word, strode off to play football with his friends, leaving the varsity boys speechless.

The next day, classmate Harry Archenbald brought the news of the feat to the attention of Coach Warner, who then summoned Thorpe to his office to verify the account. Initially fearing he had been brought before the coach for some unwitting rules infraction, Jim was thankful to learn that Warner merely wished to discuss the astounding high jump that had the entire school abuzz. The relieved Thorpe responded, "Pop, I didn't think that very high. I think I can do better in a track suit."

"Putting my arm around his shoulder," Warner remembered, "I told Jim that we'd make sure he a got a track uniform because beginning that afternoon he would be on the Carlisle track team."[12] Warner assigned Albert Exendine to act as Thorpe's mentor as he learned the finer points of track and field events. Exendine held nearly all Carlisle records, and under his tutelage Thorpe demolished every one of those marks before the season was over.[13]

The following fall, Thorpe determined to test his mettle against the varsity squad in the more vigorous game of football. Frank Newman, one of team's assistant coaches, had encouraged Jim to try out for the team without consulting Warner. When the head man first espied Thorpe trotting onto the field in a tattered, over-sized practice uniform, he was incensed. The last thing Warner wanted to see was his star track man brutalized by a gang of gridiron toughs. After twice ordering Thorpe from the field and twice being rebuffed, the coach capitulated. Thorpe was allowed to stay, but the only action he saw was in fielding kicks at practice. It was Warner's way of making sure Jim incurred as little contact as possible. But this didn't sit well with the highly competitive Thorpe, who for two weeks continued to pester the coach for playing time before Warner finally broke. "All right," said Warner, derisively tossing a football at Thorpe. "If this is what you want, go out there and give my varsity boys a little tackling practice. And believe me, kid, that's all you'll be to them."

Thorpe proceeded to run through, around and away from the Carlisle regulars as if they were "a bunch of old maids."[14] Those who managed to get a hand on him simply bounced off. Warner couldn't believe his eyes.

Thorpe returned to where the coach was standing and handed him the ball. "I gave them some good practice, right Pop?"

One of Warner's assistants remarked, "You're supposed to let them tackle you, Jim. You weren't supposed to run through them."

Thorpe's grin soon turned into a frown. "Nobody going to tackle Jim," he said.

Warner then handed the ball back to Thorpe and said, "Well, let's see if you can do it again, kid!"

A moment later, Thorpe was tearing through the Carlisle varsity for a second time. After crossing the goal line, he returned again to where Warner and his assistants were standing, tossed Warner the pigskin and declared, "Sorry, Pop. Nobody going to tackle Jim!" After spewing a series of expletives at his defensive unit, and no doubt at himself for his lack of foresight, Warner's temper cooled with the realization of what he had just witnessed. Thorpe was an extraordinary, if raw, talent, and Pop now recognized the vast potential he possessed. As Warner later remarked, "Jim's performance at practice that afternoon was an exhibition of athletic talent that I had never before witnessed, nor was I ever to again see anything similar which might compare to it." The coach wasn't about to waste valuable time watching Thorpe languish on the junior varsity squad. Rather, he immediately assigned Thorpe to the varsity, where he could learn from the more experienced players.

There were less than two weeks left to prepare for the season opener, slated for Saturday, September 21, against Lebanon Valley College. Warner put his players through an intense regimen of conditioning exercises and drilling that included concerted attention on perfecting his revolutionary offensive system. As training camp progressed, the system began to gel. The Indians eventually developed into, Warner opined, "about as perfect a football machine as I ever sent on the field."[15]

Carlisle opened its season at home versus tiny Lebanon Valley, the small school in the heart of Pennsylvania Dutch country. With a resounding 40–0 win, Warner felt the team had "clicked into shape" and "convinced me that a big year was ahead."[16] They faced a more worthy opponent when Villanova visited the Carlisle campus the following week, but still came away with a 10–0 victory to remain undefeated.

Warner's charges had just four days to rest and prepare for their next opponent, Susquehanna, which was coming to town for a contest on Wednesday, October 2. Those four days would prove to be all the Indians needed, as they ran away with a 91–0 laugher and improved to 3–0 on the season.

Three days of rest were all the Carlisle boys were afforded as they prepared to enter the heart of their schedule. The Indians' next eight dates were daunting enough to give even the most cocksure coach—which Warner undoubtedly was—pause: Penn State, Syracuse, Bucknell, Pennsylvania, Princeton, Harvard, Minnesota and Chicago.

The team traveled to Williamsport, Pennsylvania, intent on avenging the previous season's defeat at the hands of Penn State. The State squad averaged about ten pounds per man more than their opponent, but the Indians' quickness and exacting execution of Warner's offensive scheme produced "a wealth of marvelous plays" which more than made up for their lack of girth. When the final whistle blew, Carlisle had prevailed with an impressive 18–5 win, and found themselves with a promising 4–0 record.[17]

October 12, 1907, was certainly a day to remember for Warner and the Carlisle faithful. Playing before a crowd of 12,000 at the Baseball Park in Buffalo, New York, the Indians defeated Syracuse by a 14–6 score. The team's mastery of the single wing was now in full bloom, as evidenced by the following day's observations in the *Buffalo Courier*: "Matching subtle trickery and brilliant speed against a bulldog resistance such as is seldom seen in gridiron contests, the copper-colored eleven from the Carlisle Indian school defeated Syracuse University. With all the craftiness and cunning of their race, coach Warner's protégés resorted to trick plays and fake formations at the outset."

"It was a hard game and one splendidly fought by winner and loser alike," Warner remarked after the game, while noting that all of the repetitions and drilling he had put his team through in training camp were paying dividends when it counted. "My boys bore out all that their practice led me to expect. We have a great team this year, and will show it when we stack up against the bigger elevens."

But the game was memorable for more than the victory, for it also marked the first documented game appearance of Jim Thorpe. Thorpe had spent the first four games warming the bench while starting right halfback Albert Payne carried the load (although it's very likely that Jim could have been put in at some point in the season opening whitewash of Lebanon Valley). However, after Payne was injured late in the second quarter, Jim was brought in to sub. Though no details exist as to Thorpe's overall performance, it appears he acquitted himself well enough to avoid anything more than cursory mention in the following day's papers.[18]

A relatively easy 15–0 victory over Bucknell the following week was highlighted by the first spectacular play of Thorpe's career. Sent in to receive a kickoff, Jim fielded the ball and proceeded up the field, evading tacklers along the way for what seemed to be a sure score. However, as he neared the opponent's goal line, he somehow lost control of the pigskin and fumbled. Fortunately, teammate Theodore Owl was nearby to scoop up the errant ball and carry it over for the touchdown.[19]

The defeat of Bucknell preceded what was considered by many to be the pivotal game of Carlisle's season—a contest against perennial power-house Pennsylvania at Franklin Field in Philadelphia. Prior to this matchup with Carlisle, the undefeated Quakers had outscored their opponents 179–10, and were a shoe-in to defeat the rabble visiting from the nearby Indian school. However, the Indians raced out to a 22–0 lead before the Penn men knew what had hit them. The Quakers managed to break the shutout late in the game, but the upset of the season was by then a foregone conclusion as the Indians coasted to an easy 26–10 drubbing. "The Redskins were never in danger," noted the *Buffalo Courier*. "From the second the whistle blew in the opening half they jumped into the fray with determination and simply took the heart out of the home boys. It was a case of the Indian against the white man, and the former was the superior at all departments. To the white man's credit, it must be said that he played with grit seldom seen on the gridiron, but they were outplayed and outgeneraled at the game which they themselves invented."

Now undefeated and untied after seven starts, and their explosive offense the talk of the nation, it was no longer possible for Carlisle to sneak up on an opponent. But when the Indians traveled to New York to take on Princeton at the Polo Grounds, they were greeted by an adversary of a different sort. A steady rain falling throughout the contest proved the unraveling of Carlisle's miracle season, as the Tigers handed them their first loss of the year. Since the Indians' attack was predicated on speed, shifts and misdirection, the slippery field hampered their designs all afternoon. "A rain which started as a modest drizzle and wound up as a drenching downpour robbed the contest of the spectacular features expected," wrote the *Buffalo Courier*. "It worked havoc with the Redmen's vaunted speed and lightning tricks and proved a tremendous aid to Princeton."

Relying on good old-fashioned brute strength and straight-ahead play, the Tigers ground out a 16–0 upset victory. Warner observed later that the Carlisle players never performed with their usual vigor when playing in poor weather. "Against Princeton," he recalled, "the weather was our only enemy." In discussing this phenomenon with Carlisle center Little Boy after the game, Warner learned the reason why. Explained Little Boy: "Football no good fun in mud and snow."[20]

But there may have been another factor at play in the loss—overconfidence. The defeat of Pennsylvania had instilled a sense on invincibility in the minds of the Carlisle players. This, according to Thorpe biographer Robert Wheeler, was a tendency that would haunt the Indians over the next several seasons. "This reckless tendency would prove to be a continual pitfall throughout the years, and prevented them from ever having a perfect season," Wheeler observed. "They became so emotionally keyed up for an important game that, after the victory had been achieved, the necessary unwinding process would still be evident the following Saturday."[21]

The loss to Princeton provided a dose of reality for the proud Indians, who regrouped to redeem themselves with a tough-fought 23–15 victory over hated Harvard at Cambridge. Demonstrating just what they were capable of accomplishing when they were truly focused, the Carlisle eleven provided a clinic in the use of the single wing in what the *New York Times* called "the fastest game seen in the Stadium this fall. The offense of the Indians was well nigh irresistible, and the Crimson line was completely demoralized." It was Carlisle's first defeat of Harvard after ten consecutive losses.

At Minneapolis the following week, the Indians relied on "clever trick plays and beautifully executed forward passes" to squeak past the University of Minnesota with a 12–10 victory. It was a costly win, however, as quarterback Frank Mount Pleasant—in the midst of an All-America season—was lost to a thumb injury.

The victory over Amos Alonzo Stagg's previously undefeated Chicago team in the season finale was, in Warner's estimation, "the biggest win for us that season." Stagg felt this was his best team yet, led by end Pat Page and shifty halfback Wally Steffen. But Carlisle's ends, Al Exendine and Bill Gardner, zeroed in on Steffen all afternoon, not allowing him to get to the outside, where he was most dangerous. On the other side of the ball, Stagg's strategy of holding up Carlisle's ends at the line of scrimmage was keeping Chicago close, trailing by a slim 8–4 score after three quarters. Fed up with seeing his ends getting mugged on every play, Warner devised a plan. During a break in the action, he called Exendine and Hauser to the sideline and explained what he wanted them to do. When play resumed, Hauser took the snap and Exendine, instead of charging straight ahead as he normally did, ran directly toward the sideline. Hauser dropped back to pass and, per Warner's instruction, held onto the ball a few seconds longer than usual. Exendine by this time had disappeared from the playing field. He ran behind the throng of players and spectators lined up along the bench and re-entered the gridiron about 25 yards downfield. By now, the Chicago players had forgotten about Exendine and were focused on Hauser, who was nanoseconds from being smeared. Just as he was about to be hit, he heaved the ball in Exendine's general direction. Warner, Stagg, and some 28,000 others watched in rapt anticipation as the ball soared through the clear November sky. Then the solitary figure of Exendine, sprinting toward the goal line, came into view. The ball settled into his arms at the 30-yard line, and the All-American jogged into the end zone untouched. Stagg was livid, but there was no rule at the time rendering a receiver ineligible upon leaving the field of play. Touchdown! Warner had outsmarted one of the greatest minds of the grid world. Carlisle won 18–4, spoiling the otherwise perfect season of the eventual Big Ten champions. "Few things," said Warner, "have ever given me greater satisfaction than that Chicago victory."[22]

The win gave Carlisle an overall record of 10–1. It was an impressive return for Warner, whose innovative designs allowed the Indians to outscore their opponents by a whopping 267–62! The Indians had become one of the top attractions in college football, drawing huge crowds of football devotees and curiosity seekers in every town they visited. Much of the credit for the team's surge in popularity can be ascribed to the efforts of Hugh Miller, the press agent innovatively hired by Warner to promote the team by funneling information to the biggest newspapers in the East. Warner met with Miller several times each week to discuss promotional strategies and provide information on the team and certain players. The collaboration proved wildly successful, as Carlisle reported a profit of $45,000 from ticket sales.[23]

The "Carlisle Formation," as Warner's groundbreaking offense came to be known, had the college football world abuzz. William F. Knox, head football coach at Yale, was perhaps Carlisle's biggest rooter, expressing his admiration in a post-season article for *Harper's Weekly* magazine: "There is no doubt that of all of the teams of the year the Indians are far and away ahead of every one. The great value of their pass as a scoring medium has been its great distance and accuracy. They work it beautifully. The Indians have had a harder schedule than any team in the country, and they have done marvelously well."[24]

At Carlisle, Warner had found the ideal players with which to fully develop his system—it was a perfect marriage of strategy and skill. He had at his disposal a group of young men whose athletic abilities had been developed through a "rough, hardy outdoor life that the players have been inured since the time they were born."[25] There was, Warner opined, a psychological factor involved as well. "What the Indians did have was a very real race pride and a fierce determination to show the palefaces what they could do when the odds were even. It was not that they felt any definite bitterment against the conquering white or against the government for unfair treatment, but contests between red men and white had never been waged on even terms. On the athletic field where the struggle was man to man, they felt that the Indian had his first even break, and the record proves that they took full advantage of it."[26]

While 1907 can be viewed as the year in which the Carlisle eleven "rounded into true championship form,"[27] it is amazing that the player with whom Warner is most commonly associated (Thorpe) was merely a backup on that team. "He spent a great deal of the season while sitting on the Carlisle bench," Warner remembered. "Yet it was there that he was able to learn the rules of the game. While sitting on the bench, Jim was able to observe the great kicking skills of Pete Hauser and Frank Mount Pleasant, the formidable passing abilities of Mount Pleasant, and the excellent blocking and tackling examples of Albert Exendine. Jim proved to be a fast learner.

"For Jim Thorpe," added the coach, "the 1907 season was anything but memorable."[28]

Nineteen-aught-eight was certainly going to be different.

Despite recent on-field and box-office successes, not all was on the upswing at Carlisle. On the morning of November 24, the day following the Indians' big win over Chicago, that city's *Daily Tribune* ran a scathing editorial, written by former Carlisle employee Dr. Carlos Montezuma— once one of the school's most vociferous exponents—accusing the school's football program of "professionalism." Only about a third of the team's roster, he contended, were bonafide enrollees of the school, and some not only were not students but were in actuality school employees. Montezuma's actions were made in concert with—and, it appears prompted by—fellow erstwhile staff member William G. Thompson. Both men had axes to grind after being ousted from their positions after Major Mercer took over as superintendent.[29] Professionalism was about the worst sin a college athlete or university could be accused of and, suddenly, Coach Glenn Warner and the Carlisle football team were being tested by public scrutiny. Others later charged the school with allowing players to remain on the football squad well beyond the normal four seasons (some as many as eight years), and some to play under assumed names.

Warner initiated a vigorous defense through the press: "There has been a great many stories published casting reflections upon the Indian football team, nearly all of which are untrue," he told the *New York Times*. "No one seems to understand how Carlisle could turn out such a good football team without recourse to professionalism and unfair methods. These knocks against the Carlisle team came from soreheads and hard losers, but as there seems to be no general understanding of the conditions here at Carlisle, and as so many false or misleading stories have been published, I think it advisable to nail some of the lies that have been flying around, and at the same time explain the situation in athletics at Carlisle."

To the charge of team members playing as many as eight years, Warner responded: "There are no men on the team this year who have played eight years, and there are only two who had played [as many as eight seasons] three years prior to this season." The coach confessed that there had been instances of athletes playing football for more than four seasons, but he argued that the term of enrollment at Carlisle was five years, and the players had traditionally been permitted to play as long as they were enrolled. A handful of players, such as Albert Exendine and Frank Mount Pleasant, had been allowed to remain active with the team while they were studying law at nearby Dickinson College.

"It has been said that Carlisle has no eligibility rules," said Warner, "and to a certain extent this is true. The only requirement for eligibility has been that an athlete representing Carlisle shall be a regularly enrolled student who has been admitted under the rules and requirements of the United States Indian Department. Conditions at Carlisle are so radically different from surrounding colleges and universities that there has never been the need of eligibility rules governing athletics [at the school]." Warner added, however, that Carlisle authorities were responding to this criticism and would henceforth abide by the rule limiting player eligibility to four years.

To the charge that Carlisle allowed players to compete under assumed names, Warner countered that most of the boys on the squad possessed two names—their tribal or Indian name, and the English name given them upon enrolling at the school. No efforts were ever made to deceive.[30]

There was, in fact, some truth behind Thompson and Montezuma's charges of professionalism. The accusations stemmed from the recently initiated practice of providing rewards and loans to team members with money from the Carlisle Indian School Athletic Association Fund. The association was funded mainly by the team's gate receipts, along with returns on investments made from resources in the association's account. But, as Warner pointed out in *The Arrow*, Carlisle's campus newsletter, "any surplus receipts over and above the sums necessary to maintain athletics which come into the hands of the Athletic Association are used entirely for the mental, moral and physical welfare of the school in necessary ways that are not provided by the government appropriations."[31]

The school itself benefited in multiple ways from the enormous profits earned by the football team. The athletic fund subsidized several improvements to the campus, including a new print shop and art studio, upgrades to the dining hall and dormitories, construction of a new two-story cottage for Mr. and Mrs. Warner (at a cost of $3,400), and a new hospital. In addition, the salary of the school's athletic director (Warner) was paid out of Athletic Association funds.

But the crux of Montezuma's argument centered on the preferential treatment bestowed upon the members of the school football team. Anyone close to the Carlisle campus knew the privileged life of the footballers extended far beyond what Warner referred to as "the mental, moral and physical welfare" of the regular student body, beginning with the school's new athletic dormitory. The white Victorian building, which once served as the campus infirmary, had recently been re-purposed for the exclusive use of the school's male athletes at a cost estimated between $10,000 and $13,000.[32] Some of its amenities included a wraparound porch, pool tables, a music box, and a reading room where the boys could follow their own exploits in newspapers imported from Harrisburg, Philadelphia and Boston. The most enviable features, however, were the kitchen and dining room, where the athletes found refuge from the dreadful fare served daily to the general population. The average Carlisle student received a bland breakfast of coffee and oatmeal (without sugar or milk), and an occasional meat pie with gravy. Dinners consisted of bread (without butter), vegetables, and rice with gravy. The athletes, on the other hand, dined opulently on milk, beef, potatoes and bread (with butter). For breakfast, there were stacks of flapjacks.[33]

Then there was the money. Since the establishment of the Athletic Association, a good portion of the cash the players were responsible for bringing into the school was finding its way into their own pockets. It was only fair, Warner believed, that the boys—most of whom couldn't find two pennies to rub together—should reap some financial benefit from their on-field labors. While most of the cash disbursements fell within the ten-to-twenty dollar range, others were known to have been much larger. Jim Thorpe, for example, had received a reported $500 over the two-year period.[34] While Pop initiated the system out of a sense of genuine empathy for his players, he was also fully aware of its improprieties. Though it was true that many universities were compensating their athletes in way or another, the practice at Carlisle had never been acknowledged publicly. Any player discovered to be receiving compensation for his services no longer would be considered an amateur, and thus would be ineligible to play at the college level. Whether Warner feared the inevitable scandal that discovery of the cash-reward system would bring, or he simply came to realize the system was inappropriate on several levels, the practice was abandoned after the 1908 season. The old system of rewarding lettermen with an overcoat and suit of clothes from Mose Blumenthal's store—initiated by Superintendent Pratt prior to Warner's arrival at Carlisle—was re-established.

The turbulence at Carlisle continued right through the holiday season. Just a few days after Christmas, Major Mercer announced he was stepping down from his post as commandant of the school, citing his increasing impatience with "the annoying responsibilities" of the position.[35] Since replacing founder Richard Pratt three years earlier, Mercer had proven to be an ineffectual leader overshadowed by the success and influence of his increasingly famous athletic director. He had been subjected to harsh criticism from members of the former administration (i.e. Thompson and Montezuma), and this no doubt also contributed to his desire to leave Carlisle. To replace Mercer, the Bureau of Indian Affairs appointed the first civilian superintendent—34-year-old Moses Friedman, formerly an assistant superintendent at the Haskell Institute.[36]

As the Carlisle track team gathered for the 1908 season, Warner was certainly aware of the limitless ability embodied by Thorpe. He issued a challenge, ostensibly to the squad but obviously intended to spur the monumentally proud—but sometimes lazy—Sac and Fox. "If you can clear the high jump bar at five feet, ten and a half inches, I'll take you to Philadelphia to compete in the Penn Relays."[37] The Penn Relays was a major track and field competition held at the University of Pennsylvania every April since 1895. Only the very best athletes were entered, and Warner had no doubt that Thorpe was among them. The Carlisle trackmen all gave it their best shots, but only Thorpe was able to clear the coach's dictate with a jump of five feet, eleven inches. Warner's expectations were realized when Thorpe tied for first place at the Relays with a jump of six feet, one inch—his best jump yet.

In a meet against Syracuse, Thorpe snagged five first-place ribbons (high and low hurdles, broad jump, high jump, and shot put), along with a single second-place finish (the hammer throw). At the Pennsylvania

Intercollegiate Meet at Harrisburg, Jim finished first in all five events in which he entered (high and low hurdles, hammer throw, high jump, and broad jump). At the Middle Atlantic Association Meet at Philadelphia, the final and most prestigious contest of the season, the phenom again took all five events in which he competed.[38]

Warner's growing stature in the world of college football was bringing recognition to him as one of the game's foremost thinkers. He was finding himself approached constantly by everyone from newspaper reporters to politicians to fellow coaches seeking clarification of new rules or insight into the sport's latest trends and innovations. The enterprising coach wondered if there was a way to profit from his expertise, and it turned out there was. Warner struck upon the idea of creating a football correspondence course, marketed as "Expert Football Coaching for $10," which diagrammed plays and dispensed advice on everything from strategy to protective equipment. The course, prominently advertised on the back of the annual *Spalding Official Foot Ball Guide*, proved wildly successful, as a large number of college and high school coaches and players signed up. Warner continued to publish annual supplements to the course until 1911, after which it was converted into book form.[39]

The 1908 edition of the Carlisle football team assembled for its first practice on September 1. The school's decision to comply with the rule limiting a player's eligibility to four years brought an end to the careers of such long-time stars as Exendine, Mount Pleasant, Gardner and Lubo. Some fine talent remained, including Hendricks, Payne, Little Boy, and Paul and Emil Hauser, but there was little doubt as to who the focus of this year's club was going to be. Thorpe, now a strapping 175 pounds of forged muscle, was inserted at left halfback, meaning he was now the primary ball carrier in Warner's offense. In addition to his considerable athletic prowess, Warner noted that the 20-year-old had matured into a more focused and disciplined individual over the past year in his approach to both academics and sports, and was now viewed as a leader by his teammates.[40]

The season opened on September 19 with a 53–0 undressing of Conway Hall—Dickinson College's preparatory school—followed by a 39–0 triumph over traditional patsy Lebanon Valley. Warner was expecting to make quick work of Villanova in Week 3, but midway through the game's second half he found his boys in a 0–0 deadlock. Pop had been so certain of the outcome of this contest that he held Thorpe out in order to save him for the following week's meeting with Penn State. But with the Indians holding a precarious 4–0 lead late in the game, the coach buckled and sent Jim in.

"What followed was the single most dramatic play I have ever seen in sports," recalled Chief Freeman Johnson, the Grand Sachem of the Seneca nation who was on hand to witness the game. "Jim took the very first hand-off and blasted into the line with the loudest crash I've ever heard. When he was able to continue into the backfield, I couldn't believe my eyes! He didn't use one block on his way to the goal line seventy yards away while all the time hollering, 'Out of my way! Get out of my way!'"[41]

In a single breathtaking play, Thorpe had extended Carlisle's lead to ten points and, with that, his work was done. Warner ordered Thorpe back to the bench, where he remained for the rest of the afternoon, having provided the insurance marker for a 10–0 victory.

The Indians now were in top form as they got ready to enter the heart of their schedule, with their first big test coming against Penn State. The rest Warner had given his star performer had served him well, as the Indians rolled to a surprisingly easy 12–5 win behind three Thorpe field goals.

As Carlisle prepared to take on Syracuse at the University of Buffalo the following Saturday, Warner's penchant for skullduggery was in full flower. Throughout the week, Pop was cautioning newspapermen not to expect too much from his team, as several players were suffering from serious injuries. The charade continued even as his boys took the field for their pre-game warmups, with many wearing bandages on their heads and limbs or walking with exaggerated limps. The Syracuse side of the field brimmed with confidence as they watched the poor Indians agonize through their various drills and calisthenics. At kickoff, however, the Indians were miraculously cured of their supposed infirmities and sprinted full-speed into action. The hoodwinked Orangemen were overrun as Carlisle swept to a 12–0 win, with Thorpe booting three field goals for the second straight game.[42]

Next on the docket was the University of Pennsylvania, featuring All-America halfback "Big Bill" Hollenback. Despite their undefeated record during the current season, the Quakers were seeking revenge for the 26–6 thrashing the Indians had laid on them a year earlier. The game received the usual Penn-Carlisle media buildup throughout the week, including more of Warner's disingenuous handwringing about the state of his bruised and battered squad. The Quakers, however, had learned long ago not to trust any pre-game propaganda emanating from the den of Pop Warner. "We place as much stock in the ambulance clang that comes from Carlisle," remarked one Penn player, "as we would in the story of the woman telling how old she is."[43]

The Quakers were right to ignore the sage from Carlisle, as the Indians played an inspired game and escaped with well-earned 6–6 tie. Thorpe was spectacular once again in scoring Carlisle's only touchdown on a 60-yard jaunt and then adding the extra point. The draw was to be the only blemish on Penn's otherwise perfect 11–0–1 season.

The Indians then played spoilers for another previously unbeaten team, knocking off 7–0 Navy by a score of 16–6 to remain undefeated after seven contests. But it wasn't going to get any easier as Carlisle prepared to meet Harvard, its third unbeaten opponent in as many weeks.

Crimson coach Percy Haughton had been waiting anxiously for this one. A month earlier, in fact, he had sent assistant coach Harry von Kersberg to the Carlisle-Syracuse game to scout the Indians. Von Kersberg reported that, in addition to the injury ruse, the Carlisle players had football-shaped leather patches sewn onto the fronts of their jerseys. The night before the Harvard-Carlisle tilt, Haughton ran into Warner and asked if the story he had heard about the suspiciously shaped patches was true.

"Of course," Warner replied. "There's nothing in the rules that makes it illegal for our boys to wear those things."

"Very well, Pop," said Haughton. "We'll see you tomorrow."

Just before kickoff, Haughton called Warner over to inspect the game balls. Pop was momentarily speechless when he saw that Haughton had had a dozen painted the exact color of Harvard's jerseys—crimson red. After a heated debate, Warner grudgingly acquiesced. "You win, Percy."[44]

The Carlisle players tore the patches from their sweaters, Haughton produced a brown football, and the game got under way. The heavier, more experienced Harvard boys didn't need to rely on trickery, and proved it by handing Carlisle its first defeat of the season, 17–0.

A week later, the Indians faced Western Pennsylvania (the University of Pittsburgh) on a rain-soaked field, and came away with a 6–0 victory in which Thorpe scored the game's only touchdown. The Indians then prepared for an extended trip out west that had them playing five games over a two-week stretch, beginning in Minnesota on November 21. The well rested Gophers were ready, escaping with an 11–6 upset win over the tired Carlislians, who consequently dropped to 7–2–1 on the season.

The Indians then went on a tear, beginning with a 17–0 drubbing of St. Louis University on Thanksgiving Day. Another four days found them in Lawrence, Kansas, taking on the Haskell Indian School team in a rare Monday afternoon contest. Despite arriving in an exhausted state, Warner's boys had little problem with their counterparts from Haskell, claiming a 12–0 win. But the season wasn't quite over yet as Warner, induced by a $2,500 per-game guarantee, arranged two more dates for his road-weary team.[45] Just two days after their defeat of Haskell, the Indians clobbered Nebraska 37–6, and then brought the season to a merciful end three days later with an 8–4 win at the University of Denver.

The Carlisle football team had made it through another successful season, both on the field and at the gate, with Thorpe establishing himself as one of the finest backs in the nation. So outstanding was Jim's campaign that Walter Camp recognized him with selection to the third team on his All-America squad. Thorpe's budding fame preceded the team's arrival in every city it was scheduled to play, sending ticket sales through the roof. But what Coach Warner (and Thorpe, for that matter) did not know at the time was that the budding star halfback was not going to be returning for the 1909 season. Come the following September, Warner would begin planning for life without Jim Thorpe.

The spring of 1909 saw Warner relinquish his duties as coach of the baseball team. The 30-game schedule was by this time becoming too much for Warner, who, in addition to his duties as coach of the hugely successful football program, was also charged with coaching the track team and helping organize all of the school's other athletics. Clearly, for the shrewd Warner, the track team—featuring Thorpe and long-distance star Lewis Tewanima—had overtaken the traditionally mediocre baseball team on his list of springtime priorities. Eugene Bass of Fordham University was hired to coach baseball, and Warner turned his attention to track and field.

But there was another, more practical reason for de-emphasizing baseball. Each spring at Carlisle saw the exodus of ball players to warmer southern cities where minor league and semi-pro baseball teams were readying for the upcoming season. For years, several Carlisle boys lined their pockets with cash playing ball for hire, causing Warner and the school's administrators concern over the influence the practice might have on their boys. But Warner's efforts to stem the tide failed with at least three of his athletes. When the track and field season ended, Thorpe joined up with two of his teammates, Jessie Youngdeer and Joe Libby, who had decided to head south to try to catch on with a minor league baseball team rather than spend another summer farmed out in Carlisle's brutal outing program. The trio landed in the North Carolina town of Rocky Mount, where they signed to play with that town's entry in the Eastern Carolina League. Rather than play under a *nom de plume* like other amateur players, Jim used his own name when he signed his $15-per-week contract. That season, he primarily played first base, appearing in 44 games and hitting .253 on the season. Jim also pitched, though not very well, recording nine wins and ten losses. When the season was over, he returned home to Oklahoma and lived among family and fellow members of the Sac and Fox community. He apparently had no intention of returning to Carlisle, despite the fact that he still had two years of eligibility remaining.[46]

As late August segued into early September, and with his most heralded player nowhere in sight, Warner faced the reality of starting over with an inferior squad. Some very good ball players still remained from 1908—such as brothers Paul and Emil Hauser, and guard Sampson Bird—while others, like five-foot, eleven-inch, 175-pound right tackle William "Lone Star" Dietz, were poised to move into more prominent roles after spending the previous season watching from the sidelines. The 23-year-old South Dakotan was purported to be one-quarter Sioux, but events played out later in Dietz' life would cast doubt on his claim of Native ancestry. Dietz was a multi-faceted young man who excelled not only on the gridiron and other athletic pursuits, but also as a very talented artist, being the primary illustrator for *The Carlisle Arrow* and *The Indian Craftsman*, the school's publications. Warner would put all of Dietz' talents to good use over the next few years.

The Indians breezed through the early portion of the slate with victories over Steelton (35–0), Lebanon Valley (36–0), Villanova (9–0) and Bucknell (48–6) before seeing their winning streak end with an 8–8 tie against Penn State. They rebounded to beat Syracuse (14–11), but then suffered devastating back-to-back losses against Pitt (14–3) and Penn (29–6). These marked the first consecutive defeats suffered by Carlisle since 1905, while the 29 points surrendered to Penn represented the most the team had allowed since a 29–0 loss against Harvard in 1901. Pop appeared to have his boys back on track with wins over George Washington University (9–5) and Georgetown (35–0), but the short streak was followed by a 21–8 loss to Brown at New York's Polo Grounds.

The Indians then traveled west to St. Louis, Missouri, where they were scheduled to finish the season versus that city's university team on Thanksgiving Day. This encounter was especially intriguing for Pop, since it was first time he was facing his brother Bill on the field since 1902, when Young Pop—as Bill was often called—was the head coach of the Cornell University eleven. It was the younger Warner's first season at the helm in St. Louis after serving two seasons at Colgate. Though well aware of the implications of this encounter, Bill told reporters during the week that he was putting off seeing his older brother until game time. As the teams warmed up prior to the opening kick, the two finally met at midfield to shake hands and pose for pictures.[47] But there all civility ended. The Indians apparently had been saving their finest performance of the season for the finale, running rough-shod over Young Pop's team and winning 32–0 behind Paul Hauser's three touchdowns and an 80-yard punt return by Joe Libby.

In the stands cheering his old teammates that day was one Jim Thorpe, who had ridden in all the way from Oklahoma for the event. That evening, Thorpe enjoyed a Thanksgiving feast with the team. Though he told his friends that he planned to return to Carlisle in time for the 1910 season, he was not going back just yet. When the rest of the boys boarded the train for home the next day, Thorpe was not with them, and neither was their coach. Warner had already informed the school that he was going to use the trip west as a launching point for a hunting expedition to the Oklahoma territory, which had been granted statehood just two years earlier. Since Jim was also planning to return to the Territory, Warner saw the golden opportunity that happenstance had laid before him. He extended an invitation to Jim to accompany him on the safari, which the avid hunter eagerly accepted. Over the next several days, as the two stalked prey in the vast expanse of eastern Oklahoma, the topic of Jim returning to Carlisle was most likely discussed. It is also very likely that Pop inquired of Jim what he had been doing to occupy himself since leaving Carlisle, and that Jim told the coach of his involvement with the Rocky Mount Railroaders baseball club in North Carolina. Try as he might, however, Warner could not get the enigmatic Thorpe to commit to anything more than returning in a few weeks for the school's traditional Christmas celebration.[48]

One of Warner's newcomers in 1910 was a 160-pound Sioux from Sisseton, South Dakota, named Asa Sweetcorn. Sweetcorn was a brawling, hard-drinking young man who bore a long scar across his chest that served as a warning to would-be challengers that this was a character with whom, despite his relatively small stature, one should not trifle.[49] But Sweetcorn tempered his wild side with a sense of humor. Teammate Gus Welch recalled how Sweetcorn could be seen "ripping around an end, legs and arms flying, making gestures at everybody but taking out nobody. I took him aside to find out what was going on. Slyly he whispered to me, 'Gus, that's my psychology. I keep 'em all worried and guessing and then they say, "My, what a great running guard this Sweetcorn is."'"[50]

At one practice, Sweetcorn appeared to be having trouble getting into a proper three-point stance. Warner, losing patience, approached the lineman from behind and kicked him in the backside. Sweetcorn immediately sprang up, turned face-to-face with his coach and said, "Thanks! Now I can get down. You just busted a boil that was hurting me."[51]

The football season, on the other hand, was no laughing matter as the Indians limped through their worst campaign since 1901. Predictably, they swept through the early party of their schedule, defeating Lebanon Valley (53–0), Villanova (6–0), Muhlenberg (39), Dickinson (24–0), Bucknell (39–0), and Gettysburg (29–3) before dropping three straight to Syracuse (14–0), Princeton (6–0) and Penn (17–5). The Indians then defeated Virginia (22–5), lost to Navy (6–0) and Harvard Law School (3–0), and defeated John Hopkins (12–0) before losing the season finale to Brown (15–6), leaving them with a very mediocre final mark of 8–6.

The campaign didn't reach its nadir, however, until *after* there were no games left to play. Two days removed from the season-ending loss against Brown, Warner arranged for the team to attend the annual Army-Navy game in Philadelphia. The coach directed the players to dress as if this were a business trip, so when Sweetcorn arrived at the Cumberland Valley station looking as if he had not yet recovered from a night of drunken debauchery, Warner barred him from boarding the train. Sweetcorn became so enraged he attempted to single-handedly dismantle the depot. Police were summoned and hauled Sweetcorn off to the local pokey. The episode inspired a joke that swept through both campus and town:

"Where's Sweetcorn?"

"Where he belongs."

"Where's that?"

"Sweetcorn's in the can!"[52]

Eight

Thorpe Returns

Just as he had in 1907 when he played a key role in facilitating Pop Warner's return to Carlisle, Albert Exendine was there to play a part in bringing Jim Thorpe back to the school after a two-year absence. While visiting family back home in his native Oklahoma, Exendine chanced upon Thorpe as he was making his way down Anadarko's main thoroughfare. Thorpe had been drinking, Exendine noticed, but only enough, it appeared, to put him in a convivial mood. After an exchange of salutations and a bit of small talk, Ex broached the possibility of Jim returning to Carlisle to play football.[1]

"They wouldn't want me there now," Thorpe replied.

He didn't know just how wrong he was. Talents such as Thorpe are a rarity, and without him the team had fallen from its spectacular record 11–2–1 in 1908 to 8–3–1 in 1909, and then to 8–6 in 1910. Exendine contacted Coach Warner and told him about his meeting with Thorpe and "how Jim had filled out and how he looked to me. I was really surprised at the change in him. He was as big as a mule."[2] Warner desperately wanted his All-American back, and that summer found just the thing he believed would convince him to return.

The United States team for the 1912 Summer Olympics was being pieced together, and Warner had learned that Thorpe's name was on the lists of some of the selectors. "I wrote [Jim] in the late summer and I told him he stood a good chance of being selected if he returned to Carlisle and went into hard training."[3] As far as the coach was concerned, the hard training could begin with the start of football camp the first week of September.

Thorpe returned that month and moved directly into the exclusive lodgings of the boys' athletic quarters, and subsequently back into the starting left halfback position on the football team. Occupying the backfield alongside Thorpe was an outstanding group led by quarterback Gus Welch, a five-foot, nine-inch, 162-pound Chippewa who wound up also as Jim's roommate. Halfback Alex Arcasa was a 158-pound Coleville from the state of Washington. Stancil "Possum" Powell, a North Carolina-born Cherokee, was enormous by Carlisle standards—especially for a fullback—standing five feet, ten inches in height and tipping the scale at 178 pounds.

Warner, now 40 years of age, had by this time settled into a routine of meeting every Monday morning with his scouts, D. D. Harris and Cap Craver, the latter of whom doubled as the coach's defensive assistant. The portly Warner would sit with legs splayed, elbows pointing outward with his hands on his knees, chain-smoking his beloved Turkish Trophy cigarettes while rehashing the previous week's game or planning for the next. When discussing an opponent's tendencies or featured plays, he'd ask, rhetorically, "Now, how would you break that up?"[4]

Though not a heavy drinker by any means, Warner instructed Wallace Denny—the team's athletic trainer and the coach's trusted friend—to keep a bottle of spirits handy during the nippier late autumn months, just in case. "Wally!" Pop would exclaim, "hand me my cough medicine!"[5]

After the morning meetings, Warner often headed into town to attend business—both his own and the athletic association's—at the local stocks and bonds office. Staff back at the school were instructed to tell anyone looking for the coach that he had "gone to town for a coke."[6] Evenings might find Warner huddled in his workshop. Whether he was fixing an automobile engine, devising some new piece of football equipment, or maybe carving a golf club from an old bed post, Warner never lost his penchant for tinkering. Los Angeles Times sports columnist Dick Hyland—who had ample opportunity to observe the coach while playing under him for three seasons after Warner had moved on to coach Stanford University—surmised that Warner's philosophy on life was "that a man who worked with his head for a living should work with his hands for a hobby in order to balance his life."[7]

"He was the more contemplative and deliberative mind," Allison Danzig would write of Warner many years later. "Though the roar of the crowd was music in his ears, it was not the atmosphere in which he excelled or found his métier, except as his individually fashioned machines carried out his precepts. It was behind the scenes, in the quiet of his study, that the genius of Warner found its expression. There he worked out his innovations, conceived the stratagems, and devised the departures from orthodox football that won him recognition as one of the two most fertile and original minds football has known, the other being [Amos Alonzo] Stagg's."[8]

With that "fertile and original mind" working in perfect synchronicity with Thorpe's vast talent, Carlisle tore through its first eight games, knocking off Lebanon Valley (53–0), Muhlenberg (32–0), Dickinson (17–0), Mount St. Mary's (46–5), Georgetown (28–5), Pittsburgh (17–0), Lafayette (19–0) and Penn (16–0) in succession. The week leading up to the traditional Harvard encounter in Game 9 received its usual hype, stirred to a fever pitch by Crimson Coach Percy Haughton, who winked that he was considering using his scrub team against the Indians and saving his starters for their upcoming faceoffs with Dartmouth and Yale.

Warner wasn't sure Thorpe could even dress for the game until almost kickoff. All week long Jim had been using crutches to hobble around campus. Pop retreated to his workshop and fashioned a cast to stabilize Thorpe's leg in hopes that he might heal in time to play at least some of the game. The cast ultimately worked well enough to allow Thorpe to play with a heavy wrap on his leg, but his playing time was going to be limited. "Because of these injuries," Warner recalled, "and also because I knew that Harvard expected Jim to carry the ball on every play, I switched the plan of attack, and used him mostly as interference through the entire first half."

Thorpe also toughed out field goals of 13 and 43 yards that allowed Carlisle to escape the first half with just a three-point deficit. Early in the second, the Indians sprang a series of reverses that left the boys in crimson grasping at—and gasping for—air, and led to Thorpe's third field goal and a 15–9 lead.

Haughton had been true to his word, playing his reserve team throughout the first half. "Late in the second half when every Carlisle man was out on his feet," Warner recollected several years later, "[Haughton] sent in his regulars, all fresh and rampant. Thorpe had the heart of a lion. Although every movement must have been an agony, not once did he take time out. It was a bitterly fought game with Haughton throwing in that brand-new team in the last quarter while we were compelled to hold our original line-up, and as Jim saw the day going against us, he forgot his wrenched leg and sprained ankle and called for the ball. And how the Indian did run! After the game one of the Harvard men told me that trying to tackle the big Indian was like trying to stop a steam engine."[9]

Warner remembered it as one the greatest games Thorpe ever played, as big Jim's heroic efforts propelled the Indians to an 18–15 upset victory. The team was welcomed back at campus by a large crowd of students and townspeople, who treated their local heroes to a celebratory parade through the town while the school band performed rousing renditions of the school fight song and other popular numbers. "Between the victory over Harvard and the parade," Warner wrote, "this was one weekend that the Indian boys at Carlisle would long remember."[10]

But the Carlislians suffered a huge letdown a week later, losing 12–11 to a vastly inferior squad from Syracuse. Held at Syracuse's Archbold Stadium, the game was played in frigid and muddy conditions, which ultimately slowed the Indians' speed-based attack. As far as the coach was concerned, however, the team had lost because of a smug sense of invincibility adopted after its victory over powerful Harvard. "As often happens to other excellent teams," he opined, "the game would be lost by the Indians because they underrated their opponent, and lost through overconfidence."[11]

Despite avenging the collapse at Syracuse with wins over Johns Hopkins (29–6) and Brown (12–6) to bring the season to a close with an outstanding 11–1 record, that single defeat is most likely what cost Carlisle recognition as the top team in the nation.[12] Still, it had been one of the finest campaigns in school history, and Thorpe had performed spectacularly throughout, earning selection as a first-team All-America from Walter Camp.

With the gridiron season now over, Warner focused his energies on preparing Thorpe for the following summer's Olympiad. Though the football All-American was undoubtedly the star of the track squad, fellow Carlislian Lewis Tewanima was by no means any less skilled in his chosen discipline, and was sure to make the U.S. team as well. Warner, in fact, felt Tewanima was the best long-distance runner in the country.[13]

The two were entered in several meets during the winter track season, and dominated their respective events each time. When the spring season arrived, they continued to prepare and work their way into world-class condition. "Since these two boys were students of the Indian school and therefore wards of the government, I was detailed by the superintendent to accompany them on their trip to Stockholm for the Olympic Games."[14] This assignment carried with it the responsibility of acting not only as Thorpe and Tewanima's coach, but also as their chaperone.

Warner found himself, at times, becoming frustrated with Thorpe, who seemed decidedly indifferent about the prospect of representing his country on the world stage. "What's the use of bothering with all this stuff?" Thorpe once asked. "There's nothing in it." Once, while riding the train from a meet back to the Carlisle campus, Warner spotted Thorpe making his way through the cars puffing away on a stogie. After enduring the coach's remonstrations, Thorpe replied, "Shucks, Pop, I'm through with track. It's me for baseball."

"Pulling him down beside me," Warner recalled, "I pointed out the duty he owed to his school and to his race. After a while he heaved a deep sigh and groaned, 'Oh, all right, but I'd rather play baseball.'"[15]

Carlisle's final meet that season was scheduled against Lafayette in Easton, Pennsylvania. Warner made the bold move of bringing just eight athletes along for the meet, while the Lafayette contingent comprised nearly 50. After counting the sparse Indian delegation as it prepared for the meet, the Lafayette coach pulled Warner aside and asked where the rest of his team was.

"Right here," Warner replied.

"You'd better call off the meet," warned the Lafayette coach. "We have a squad of fifty. No sense in making a farce out of things."

"We'll try to make a contest out of it," said Warner.

They did. Carlisle won in a rout, 71–41, with Thorpe taking first place in six events. In the 440 Yard Dash, Thorpe, Tewanima and a third Carlisle runner finished 1–2–3.[16]

According to local legend, Thorpe accompanied Pop during a brief visit to the coach's hometown of Springville, New York, in early June. The two stayed at the East Main Street home of Pop's parents, and Thorpe spent several days working out on a horse track. "Jim would jog or run next to the horses my uncle was training on the Dygert Track," explained Pete Dygert, the current owner of the property. "[Thorpe] had unnatural speed. More importantly, he had great endurance to keep pace with the horses and sulkies at slower speeds."

Longtime residents recalled for many years afterward the sight of Warner and his prize pupil tooling around the quiet little village. "[Thorpe] hung around with my uncle Leon Dygert and they caroused together in the evenings and had a great time. They were approximately the same age and build. I was told they boxed together, but usually saved their best for evening matches against others. I was told they did so, bare-fisted and my grandmother would be very upset over the swollen faces and black eyes."[17]

The U.S. Olympic team, consisting of 164 athletes, along with myriad coaches and dignitaries, set sail from New York aboard the S.S. *Finland* on June 14. Accounts vary as to Jim's intensity of training during the voyage, with some supposed eyewitnesses asserting that he did little more than lie in a hammock while his teammates ran laps on the ship's deck. There were others, though, who insisted he was a regular participant in team workouts. After reaching Sweden, the entire squad stayed at a private facility outside Stockholm where everyone, including Thorpe, worked out every day leading up to the games.[18]

Jim's first event for the Pentathlon was the Broad Jump, which he won with a leap of 23 feet, two and seven-tenths inches. He also took first place in the 200 Meter Run (22.9 seconds), the 1,500 Meter Run (four minutes, 40.8 seconds), and the Discus Throw (116 feet, eight and 4/10 inches). He placed third in the Javelin Throw (153 feet, two and nineteen-twentieths inches), but it didn't matter, as he won the gold easily. The Decathlon was not scheduled for another six days, so in the interim, Jim joined Pop in watching Tewanima snag a silver medal in the 10,000 Meter Run.

In the Decathlon, Thorpe won four events including the 1,500 Meter Run (four minutes, 40.1 seconds), 110 Meter High Hurdles (15.6 seconds), High Jump (six feet, one and six-tenths inches), Shot Put (42 feet, five and nine-tenths inches), took third in four events (Broad Jump, Pole Vault, Discus Throw, 100 Meter Run), and fourth in the two remaining events (400 Meter Run and Javelin Throw). His point total of 8,124.96 stood as the Olympic high-water mark for 16 years.

On July 15, the closing day of the Olympiad, Thorpe was brought before Sweden's King Gustav V for the presentation of his gold medals. As he laid a laurel wreath on Thorpe's brow, the king proclaimed, "You, sir, are the greatest athlete in the world."[19]

Pop, along with Lewis Tewanima (center) and Jim Thorpe (right), being honored by the Carlisle Indian School upon their triumphant return from the 1912 Olympic Games. August 16, 1812. (From the Cumberland County Historical Society, Carlisle, Pennsylvania.)

Thorpe's reply, according to eyewitnesses, was modest and simple: "Thanks, King."

Upon returning to the United States, the members of the American team were honored with a parade down Fifth Avenue in New York City, which was attended by a crowd estimated at over one million. The star attraction, of course, was Thorpe, who was transported alone in an open car, followed by a second automobile carrying the trophies he had received from the king of Sweden and the czar of Russia. On August 16, the citizens of Carlisle honored their three famous world travelers with an extravagant celebration attended by some 15,000 revelers. Several VIPs gave speeches, including Superintendent Friedman, whose remarks included a recitation of a congratulatory letter to Thorpe written by President William H. Taft. Friedman made a point of lavishing praise upon Warner, declaring him the nation's foremost athletic coach, and asserting that the marvelous

The 1912 Carlisle football team. Front row (L to R): George Vetterneck, Roy Large, Alex Arcasa. Middle Row: Pete Calac, Joe Bergie, Joel Wheelock, Stancil Powell, Joe Guyon, Elmer Busch. Back Row: Charles Williams, Gus Welch, Jim Thorpe, Pop Warner, Robert Hill, William Garlow. (From the Cumberland County Historical Society, Carlisle, Pennsylvania.)

achievements of the two Indian athletes would not have been possible without him.

"It was a day," Warner wrote many years later, "that I will always remember."[20]

Some of the new faces joining the Carlisle football team in 1912 included two men relegated to the line despite possessing talent enough to star in the backfield, were it not for the fact that Warner had his stellar quartet of Thorpe, Welch, Arcasa and Powell returning. Twenty-year-old Pete Calac was a five-foot, ten-inch, 185-pound Mission Indian from California. "I had never played football before [coming to Carlisle]," Calac recalled. "I was pretty husky for a kid and they took an interest in me. One person in particular took special notice of me and taught me the fundamentals of the game. His name was Jim Thorpe. I became a substitute very quickly and eventually got into quite a few games that year."[21]

Joe Guyon was a 19-year old Chippewa from Minnesota who presented the perfect physical specimen. The physician conducting Guyon's initial medical examination at the school described the boy as "a picture of health ... splendidly developed."[22] Both boys would play significant roles with the team over the next couple of seasons, with Guyon taking over at left tackle and Calac filling in at the right tackle spot vacated by Lone Star Dietz when his playing career ended at the conclusion of the 1911 schedule. Dietz, whom Warner considered a "coach on the field" when he played, had recently been hired as an assistant on Pop's staff.[23]

Carlisle opened the season with perhaps the strongest team it had ever fielded, and scored four straight victories over patsies Albright (50–7), Lebanon Valley (45–0), Dickinson (34–0) and Villanova (65–0), before being embarrassed in a scoreless draw against Washington & Jefferson, another traditionally weak team.

As the train carrying the disheartened Indians made its way back to Carlisle following the W&J debacle, it was necessary for the team to disembark in Pittsburgh to transfer cars. The three-hour stopover afforded several of the boys—Thorpe included—ample opportunity to patronize a local watering hole. Within an hour, word got back to Warner that some of his players were in town kicking up a ruckus. Thorpe proved the most belligerent, requiring Warner to physically "escort" him back to the depot and later onto the train that was to convey the team the rest of the way home. The story that hit the papers the next day exaggerated the encounter between Thorpe and his coach, suggesting that the two had actually come to blows, a charge which Warner categorically denied. There may not have been a physical altercation, but Warner was irritated enough to threaten his best player with expulsion.

"When Thorpe violated the training rules," Warner later remembered, "I felt it my duty as a matter of discipline to drop him from the football team unless he apologized to his teammates and promised to obey the rules in the future. 'Thorpe,' I said, 'you've got to behave yourself. You owe it to the public as well as to your school. The Olympic games have made you a public character, and you've got to shoulder the responsibility.' I emphasized how he had gotten the worst of the publicity at Pittsburgh, when I was credited erroneously with having cleaned up the world famous athlete in a fist fight. He was very penitent and called all the boys together and apologized for his actions on that trip. From that time on he trained faithfully and no fault could be found with his behavior the rest of the time he was at the school."[24]

The Indians took out their frustrations from the Washington & Jefferson tie by clobbering Syracuse—the team that had spoiled their undefeated season the year before—by a score of 33–0, followed by drubbings of Pitt (45–8) and Georgetown (34–20).

The day after their defeat of Georgetown, the Indians boarded a train and headed north—way north—for a hastily arranged contest with a team from Toronto University scheduled for the day after that (Monday). The first half of the contest was played under American Intercollegiate rules, and Carlisle stormed to a 44–0 lead by intermission. Canadian rules were enforced in the second half, and this resulted in Toronto's only score when Thorpe failed to return a punt out of his own end zone, giving the Canadians a one-point rouge.[25] The Indians departed the Great White North with a 49–1 triumph, and a tidy $3,000 profit for the Athletic Association.[26] The following Saturday, they extended their string of victories to five with a 34–14 rout of Lehigh.

For some time, Warner had been devising a new offensive formation that was intended to take his signature single wing to another level. The concept, he explained, was to carry the idea of placing one of the halfbacks in a position just outside and a step behind one of the offensive ends (as in the single wing formation) "a step further by placing both halfbacks in position close to the line and wide enough to outflank the defensive tackles."[27] Where the single wing emphasized power at the point of attack, this new concept—which also featured wider spacing between the offensive linemen—was more about spreading the field and expanding opportunity. Considered by many historians to be the progenitor of the modern shot-

Pop with his starting backfield, 1912: (L to R): Gus Welch, Alex Arcasa, Pop, Stancil Powell, Jim Thorpe. (From the Cumberland County Historical Society, Carlisle, Pennsylvania.)

gun formation, the double wing (as it became known) gave the Indians a dizzying multiplicity of play options that could be run to either side of the field at any point along the offensive line, and literally doubled the possibilities presented by the old single wing.[28] He had been introducing the squad to its various aspects at practices throughout the season, but was looking for just the right time to use it in a game. Just as he had shown impeccable timing when he sprang the new three-point stance on unsuspecting Columbia back in 1899, Warner identified the perfect moment to unveil his latest innovation—Carlisle's upcoming encounter with Army scheduled for November 9.[29]

"[Warner] has prepared several spectacular football evolutions for the delectation of the Cadets," wrote a *New York Times* reporter after observing a Carlisle practice that week. "These plays were run over this evening. Probably the forward pass, which received close attention this afternoon, will be used, and there is sure to be more kicking than usual in the Army game."

Army had a strong team led by captain/tackle Leland Devore (first-team All-America, 1911), and an aggressive, over-achieving halfback/linebacker named Dwight D. Eisenhower. They came in to this weekend with a record of three wins and one loss (to Yale), but were nevertheless favored to crush the diminutive Indian squad from Pennsylvania's Cumberland Valley.

This was not the first meeting between Carlisle and Army. The two combatants had met once before—back in 1905 during George Woodruff's tenure as the Indians' head coach—with the Indians claiming a 6–5 victory. There were no players left from the 1905 squad, of course, so Warner, mistaking that his team might be in need of a little motivation, came up with some words of inspiration he hoped might provide the impetus for victory. As the Indians stirred in the clubhouse prior to heading out for the pre-game festivities at Cullum Field, Pop delivered an impassioned pep talk more in keeping with the tradition later forged by Knute Rockne than he himself was known for, filled with images of Indian War battlefields and forefathers brutally murdered by ruthless American soldiers.

"He was really excited," Pete Calac remembered. "He stood at one end of the locker room facing the team who were standing on the benches, and he began to pace back and forth and then up and down the aisle between the men to give them individual instructions. By golly, I didn't think we had any chance against Army that year. They were very big, much bigger than we were. They thought we would be a pushover."[30]

The West Pointers, however, were in for the game of their lives.

The Indians won the coin toss and opened their first offensive series configured in Warner's new formation, and immediately began chewing off big chunks of yardage. "The shifting, puzzling, and dazzling attack of the Carlisle Indians had the Cadets bordering on a panic," wrote a *New York Tribune* reporter. "After a few minutes of play none of the Army men seemed to know just where the ball was going or who had it." Arcasa for fifteen ... Thorpe for fifteen ... Powell for seven ... Thorpe for twenty. But when Thorpe fumbled at the Army 15—his only mistake of the day—the drive stalled. Army recovered and eventually drew first blood when halfback Leland Hobbs scored from four yards out to give his team a 6–0 lead. The Indians stormed right back, tying the game a few minutes later when Joe Bergie thundered over from the West Point six. They seized the lead when Thorpe kicked the extra point, and never looked back.

The Cadets had been reading about Thorpe's heroics all season long and seemed hell-bent on knocking the All-American out of the contest, as if the very outcome depended on it. They nearly succeeded early in the second half when Eisenhower and fellow linebacker Charles Benedict slammed into Thorpe with a classic high-low tackle, which left the star halfback lying on the ground with an injured left shoulder. After several minutes, one of the officials announced that it was time to resume play. Army captain Devore rejoined, "Nell's bells, Mr. Referee, we don't stand on technicalities at West Point. Give him all the time he wants."[31] The Indians didn't take well to the remark, and began running most of their plays directly at the six-foot, four-inch, 225-pound tackle. It wasn't long before Devore was losing his cool and began looking for someone on whom he could take out his frustrations. After one play, as Joe Guyon lay prostrate on the frozen turf, Devore sidled up and brought his foot down square in the middle of the Chippewa's back. The referee had no choice but to toss Devore from the game. The Cadets never regained their composure. The Indians continued to pour it on, with Arcasa scoring three touchdowns in a 27–6 romp.

Despite being held without a touchdown (though he did kick three extra points), Thorpe played what many historians consider to be a career-defining game. "Standing out resplendent in a galaxy of Indian stars was Jim Thorpe," blared the *New York Times*. "The big Indian Captain added more lustre to his already brilliant record, and at times the game itself was almost forgotten while the spectators gazed on Thorpe, the individual, to wonder at his prowess. To recount his notable performances in the complete overthrow of the Cadets would leave little space for other notable points of the conflict. He simply ran wild, while the Cadets tried in vain to stop his progress. It was like trying to clutch a shadow."

Predictably, the victory over Army had sapped the Indians of their vigor, and they came out flat the following Saturday against an unusually weak Penn squad (which had already lost four games on the season) and fell, 34–26. "One of the touchdowns which Pennsylvania made was on a long pass," Warner remembered. "I thought Thorpe could have knocked down the pass if he had tried. After the game I asked him about this and he said, 'Oh yes, sure I could have knocked that down. I didn't think the receiver could go to it. I saw him running down there and the ball coming but I didn't think it was possible for him to reach the ball.' That showed the one weak trait in Thorpe's character which is a dangerous trait in any football player ... he was inclined to be careless."[32]

As careless as he was against Penn, Thorpe was nothing short of spectacular in the next two games, his last as a collegian. In the first, Thorpe scored all of Carlisle's points in leading the team to a 30–24 victory over Springfield YMCA. In the finale, played in a blinding snowstorm at Brown University on Thanksgiving Day, Thorpe scored three more touchdowns (giving him 25 on the season) and added two conversions in a 32–0 blowout.

The trip to Brown, despite the victory and the Olympian's Herculean performance, proved an injurious one for both Thorpe and Warner. During the week leading up to the game, the coach had taken the team to Worcester, Massachusetts, to prepare. Among the on-lookers at one of the Carlisle practices was a minor-league baseball manager named Charley Clancy, who was in town visiting relatives. As the players jogged past, Clancy turned to the person standing next to him and casually mentioned that he knew Thorpe from his days playing baseball in the Eastern Carolina circuit. It just so happened that the person with whom Clancy shared this revelation was a reporter from the Worcester *Telegram*. When the reporter returned to the *Telegram* offices, he relayed the intelligence to the paper's editor, Roy Ruggles Johnson. Intrigued, Johnson cracked open a copy of the *Reach Baseball Guide* and there within its pages found Thorpe posing with his fellow Rocky Mount Railroaders in a team photo.[33]

On January 22, 1913, the paper dropped the bombshell: Jim Thorpe was no amateur. His pay-for-play baseball career was fully exposed, and the story spread like wildfire. Thorpe initially denied the story, while Warner and Superintendent Friedman pleaded ignorance. The Amateur Athletic Union immediately initiated an investigation.

When Thorpe played baseball for pay, he did so under his own name, not considering that it might one day cost him his status as an amateur. A return to Carlisle at the time he signed on with Rocky Mount was uncertain, and the Olympics were not even a thought. Warner, on the other hand, armed with a law degree and having by now been involved in college-level sports for a full two decades, undoubtedly possessed a full understanding of the differences between amateur and professional athletics. Not only had Warner turned a blind eye to Thorpe's baseball career, he was almost solely responsible for launching Jim on his Olympic Odyssey.

"At best, Jim held only a nebulous conception of the meaning of amateurism," Thorpe biographer Robert Wheeler observed, "but those individuals under whose jurisdiction he was permitted to compete at Stockholm knew full well what he was doing." First among those individuals, not only in Wheeler's eyes but those of other historians—as well many of as Thorpe's descendants—was Carlisle's famed football coach. While there is no direct evidence to prove that Warner knew of Thorpe's involvement in minor league baseball, it is highly doubtful that he did not. "It is difficult to imagine," Wheeler continued, "that Warner, who helped develop the youngster into a man of national renown in the world of football and amateur athletics, was not sufficiently curious to keep tabs on his prize pupil. Considering the countless hours spent together and the confidence existing between them, could Thorpe have left Carlisle for two full years and Warner not have known where he had been?"

"I never made any secret about it," said Thorpe. "I often told the boys, with the coaches listening, about things that happened while I was at Rocky Mount."[34]

Warner and Friedman advised Thorpe to throw himself on the mercy of the investigative committee. Pop helped Jim write a letter explaining his actions and declaring that the coach and superintendent had no prior knowledge of his participation in pay-for-play baseball. One supposed eye-witness, a school employee, later claimed that Warner actually wrote out the letter's contents and had Jim copy it onto a separate sheet of paper.[35]

"I hope I will be partly excused by the fact that I was simply an Indian schoolboy and I did not know all about such things," Thorpe's letter read. "In fact I did not know I was doing wrong because I was doing what I knew several other college men had done except that they did not use their own names."[36]

Yet, when the committee published its decision on January 27, 1913, the coach emerged virtually unscathed. Thorpe, however, was not so lucky. Warner the gambler had played the odds that the committee would have sympathy on the poor, unsophisticated Indian boy and all would be well. He lost. Though Pop himself had been absolved, Thorpe was ordered to return his medals, and his Olympic records were to be stricken from the books.

The public response to the committee's findings leaned in Thorpe's favor. Many saw the hypocrisy in the AAU's interpretation of professionalism, given the fact that many collegians were receiving cash and other incentives to play at their respective universities, and that those same universities were making millions on the backs of these so-called amateur athletes.

With Thorpe now officially declared a professional, he began to think seriously about a career in the big leagues. "When it became known Jim had played professional baseball and that he was no longer an amateur," Warner recalled, "he was immediately in great demand by different managers of the big league teams of the country. They figured that since he was a great athlete, he would likely develop into a star baseball player."

Jim asked Pop for his assistance in negotiating with the numerous baseball executives who were expressing their eagerness to sign him. Warner sent telegrams to every major league club notifying them that Jim's services were available to the highest bidder.

"He was about to sign with the Cincinnati Reds," Warner remembered, "when my old friend John McGraw of the Giants phoned to tell me that if Thorpe was going to play professional baseball, he was in the market. I told him Cincinnati was bidding high and in characteristic McGraw language he offered to double. The next day [February 1, 1913] I took Thorpe over to [New York City] where he signed with the Giants."[37]

Thorpe's deal was reported to have been for a staggering $6,000 per season (approximately $141,500 in 2013 dollars) with a $500 signing bonus—the highest fee ever paid to a rookie ballplayer to that point. Warner was reported to have received a commission of $2,500 for his services. However, after seeing the report published in the *New York Sun*, he fired off a letter to McGraw asking the Giant skipper to issue "an authoritative denial." Warner insisted there was "not an iota of truth in the story, and that the assistance he gave Thorpe was inspired solely by his desire to advance Thorpe's interest."[38] Paid or not, by representing Thorpe in these negotiations, Pop was pioneering the art of sports agency—several decades before the profession would become an integral part of the sports landscape.

The 1913 season was going to be another difficult one for Warner, for not only was he losing the cornerstone of his offense, he was losing virtually three-fourths of his starting backfield since Arcasa and Powell had also reached the end of their terms. Fortunately, Carlisle had two excellent backfield candidates waiting in the wings in tackles Calac and Guyon, although shifting them off the line would create two other openings that were not going to be easy to fill. But Warner was prepared to meet the challenge, and still game enough to roll up his sleeves and personally demonstrate how he expected his men to play a position, if need be.

"Warner is a big man and always keeps himself in condition good enough to be able to demonstrate a point himself," wrote an *Outing* magazine reporter after observing a Carlisle practice session. "From the start of a recent season, it was apparent that there was something wrong with the candidate who was best equipped physically for a certain position. He quickly mastered the theory of correctly handling the position, but in actual competition he couldn't put it into effect. Finally Warner came to the conclusion that his failure was one of courage rather than lack of football sense. That afternoon [Warner] donned a playing uniform and took the opposing line position for the scrub eleven. The battle of the tackles was the feature of the week's scrimmage. The Indian was forced to fight his hardest for sheer self-preservation. The incident is typical of Warner's attitude toward his team. He critically surveys a candidate, makes a mental estimate of what his efficiency should be, and then proceeds to make him into the playing unit, supplying all essentials, even a fighting spirit, if that is needed."[39]

Given the circumstances under which the team was beginning the new campaign, it would have been perfectly understandable if Warner had needed to inject some fighting spirit into his players. The 1913 Indians, however, proved every bit as plucky—and nearly as talented—as the previous year's squad, sweeping aside Albright (26–0), Lebanon Valley (26–0), West Virginia Wesleyan (25–0) and Lehigh (21–7) and Cornell (7–0) en route to a 5–0 start. The team then suffered its usual mid-season slump in losing to Pitt (12–6) and tying Penn (7–7) before bouncing back with victories over Georgetown (34–0) and Johns Hopkins (61–0).

After nine games, the Indians stood at 7–1–1, with an undefeated Dartmouth eleven up next. Even though the boys from New Hampshire were slightly favored, Warner felt confident that a Carlisle victory was in the offing. Warner, still unable to resist the lure of an honest wager, staked $300 on a Carlisle victory. With odds at five-to-three, Warner stood to collect $500 if the Indians won. But when the Indians trotted into the clubhouse at intermission trailing by three points, Pop was compelled to resort to an unorthodox—and ultimately controversial—motivational ploy. He ordered the doors closed and instructed the boys to gather around him. "If each of you wants to earn five dollars apiece to have a little fun when we stop off in New York on the trip home," he announced, "all you have to do is win this game."[40]

The proposition worked like a charm. The Indians came out smoking and rallied to win, 35–10. But the incident, while arguably providing the impetus for victory, had a negative long-term effect. Discontent had been boiling under the surface all season as some of the boys harbored resentment toward Warner and Superintendent Friedman for how they had allowed their friend Thorpe to be disgraced in the Olympic scandal. By the time of the Dartmouth game, several of the players were displaying open hostility toward their coach. That same month, nearly 300 Carlisle

students, led by Thorpe's close friend—and Warner's star quarterback—
Gus Welch, sent a petition to the secretary of the interior, calling for an
investigation into the conditions and management of the school. At season's end, Warner and the school would be embroiled in their third serious
controversy in six years.

The Indians finished out the year with wins over Syracuse (35–27)
and Brown (13–0). Whatever hard feelings the players might have had
toward Warner certainly were not evident on the playing field, for the 10–
1–1 mark stands as one of the greatest seasons in the school's history, and
was the fourth time in Warner's tenure that Carlisle finished with just a
single loss. The *Newark Evening News* ranked the Indians the third-best
team in the nation. Both halfback Joe Guyon (with 20 touchdowns, nine
conversions and a field goal) and guard Elmer Busch earned second-team
All-America recognition from Walter Camp.

In response to the petition submitted by the Carlisle students, a four-
man Congressional committee commenced an investigation in early 1914.
Several school employees and students (including athletes) were interviewed. Inspectors found the school run down and many of the children
expressing enmity toward Warner and Friedman. The students complained about the food and bedding, and the uneven manner in which
discipline, including corporal punishment and hard labor, was used as a
consequence for misbehavior. Welch testified that his coach was "a man
with no principle," while other players testified that he often insulted and
swore at them. Some reported seeing Warner selling game tickets in hotel
lobbies and pocketing the money, and recounted his offer to reward them
with a cut of his bet winnings from the Dartmouth game.

A thorough audit of the Athletic Association's finances was conducted, and no evidence of misappropriation was found. The athletic
director (Warner) was criticized for what were described as "irregularities"
in paying publicists Hugh Miller and E. L. Martin for "boosting the athletics" at Carlisle, but what the committee seemed to overlook—or at least
failed to acknowledge—was the fact that money spent publicizing the
football team resulted in enormous returns in the form of gate receipts.
Those funds ultimately had subsidized nearly every physical improvement
made to the campus over the previous several years.[41]

The committee found fault with Warner for profiting from an
arrangement between the school and the Springville Canning Company,
a vegetable-packing concern based in Warner's hometown and in which

he held a large financial interest. "The Springfield [*sic*] Canning Company received various large checks for canned goods," the report stated. "Note the extravagant expense bills paid to Glenn S. Warner, amounting in some instances to over $1,500 for a single trip." Warner defended the arrangement, testifying that it allowed the school to purchase its produce at "jobbers' [wholesale] prices," and that any profit made was in turn used to acquire athletic equipment they couldn't get through official channels.[42]

Ultimately, the investigation uncovered no evidence of criminal wrongdoing on Warner's part. Still, his credibility among the players had been irreparably damaged, and the committee noted in its final report that Warner's presence at the school had a "demoralizing" effect and recommended that he resign. Superintendent Friedman was charged with embezzlement and was forced out in September 1914, but was eventually cleared. Siceni J. Nori, Friedman's chief clerk and a Carlisle graduate, pled guilty to misappropriation of funds and destroying evidence, and served time in prison.

Warner chose to ignore the committee's recommendation that he resign and stayed on for one more campaign—altogether his thirteenth at Carlisle. Given the circumstances, however, there was no way it could have gone well. Athletics were de-emphasized as a result of the hearings, meaning there was substantially less money available for equipment, travel and other expenses needed to run a first-class football program. The lavish dorm and dining privileges enjoyed by the male athletes were also shut down. Warner's two best players, Guyon and Welch, refused to return to the team, while the rest of the squad had lost respect for its coach and spirit for the school. Indeed, as Warner conceded years later, "My last season at the Carlisle Indian School proved to be a disastrous one."[43]

After opening the campaign with unimpressive wins over Albright (20–0), Lebanon Valley (7–0) and West Virginia Wesleyan (6–0), the Indians suffered back-to-back losses to Lehigh (21–6) and Cornell (21–0). Their performance to this point was a big drop from the previous season, when they burst from the gate with a 5–0 start while outscoring their opponents 105–7. By comparison, the 1914 team, playing against the same five opponents, stood at 3–2 and was being outscored 39–42. It didn't get any better when the Indians traveled to Pittsburgh in Week Six and were defeated, 10–3.

Despite the fact that he had stubbornly refused to resign following the recent Congressional investigation, word on the street had it that

Warner was not likely to remain at Carlisle beyond the end of the current football season. Pitt officials, aware of Warner's indisposition, took advantage of his presence in their city and arranged a meeting with the embattled coach. "After the game," Warner recalled, "the University of Pittsburgh management asked me if I would come to Pittsburgh. Because of the conditions at Carlisle, I was very glad of this opportunity."[44]

Although he did not sign right away, rumors of his impending departure were soon making the rounds. In early November, the *Pittsburgh Gazette* reported that the coach had "definitely decided to sever his connection with the government school at Carlisle." The *Gazette* named Pittsburgh and the University of Minnesota as the chief suitors of Warner's services, with the former likely to be the winner. Sure enough, Warner signed a three-year contract—for a reported $7,000 per season—with the western Pennsylvania school on November 11.[45]

Meanwhile the Carlisle football team continued to stumble through its worst season in a dozen years, losing to Penn (7–0) and Syracuse (24–3) and tying Holy Cross (0–0) to bring their record to 3–5–1 with a trip to Chicago and its first-ever meeting with upstart Notre Dame due up next.

The University of Notre Dame football team had burst into national prominence a year earlier when they stunned Army with a 35–13 drubbing that featured a heavy dose of long forward passes between quarterback Charles "Gus" Dorais and his ends, Fred Gushurst and Knute Rockne. Although forward passing was legalized in 1906 and had since that time been used to great success by several schools—most notably Warner's Carlisle Indians—the Army-Notre Dame tilt is often credited with being the first major collegiate contest in which a team's entire game plan relied heavily on the tactic. Rockne, the recipient of one of Dorais' three touchdown throws that day, was no longer on the roster, having graduated the previous spring. He was still on the Notre Dame sideline, however, serving the first year of what was to become a legendary coaching career as an assistant under current head man Jesse Harper.

Carlisle was bolstered by the return of Gus Welch, who had continued attending classes on campus while preparing to enter Dickinson Law School. It was a heroic effort on Welch's part, but it nearly cost him his life. Late in the game, the out-of-shape quarterback suffered a fractured skull and cheekbone after receiving a knee to the face while tackling fullback Ray Eichenlaub. The play was merely a microcosm of the entire game, as the boys from South Bend ran roughshod over the demoralized Indians in a 48–6 rout.

The Indians ran out the string by going 2–3 in their last five games,

Pop Warner (at left, in hat) instructs his football players at Carlisle practice, 1913. Standing (L to R): Joe Bergie, Elmer Busch, Pete Gaddy. Kneeling or in position: Joe Guyon, William Garlow, Bruce Goesback, Pete Calac. (From the Cumberland County Historical Society, Carlisle, Pennsylvania.)

leaving them with their worst record (5–9–1) since 1901. For the first time in recent memory, the team failed to appear on any meaningful post-season power rankings, and not a single player was selected All-America.

The disastrous campaign signaled an ignominious end to Carlisle's days of gridiron glory. Although the school continued to field teams through 1917, it never again enjoyed the remarkable success it had achieved during Warner's tenure. In September 1918, the Carlisle Indian Industrial School experiment was discontinued and the school re-purposed as a hospital for wounded soldiers returning from World War I battlefields.

The school gave Warner a grand going-away banquet on February 25, 1915. His time at Carlisle had had more than its share of highs to go along with a handful of lows—of heady accomplishments and rocking controversy. His teams were victorious in 114 of the 164 games they played (a winning percentage of 69.5), and he was responsible for developing nearly a dozen players into All-Americans. And though his reputation was set back by the Thorpe scandal and the Congressional investigations that came a year later, those controversies were quick to fade from the public consciousness.

Greater successes at Pittsburgh—and later Stanford—would solidify Warner's place among the pantheon of the era's coaching giants that included such names as Stagg, Heisman, Yost and Haughton. Still, for many—including the coach himself—the Warner name was destined to forever be associated first and foremost with Carlisle. Later in life, when he was asked to recount his illustrious career in various newspaper and magazine series, the majority of Warner's musings focused on his time at the Indian school. "The experiences that stand out most vividly in my memory," he'd write, "are those connected with the Indian lads."[46]

NINE

Pittsburgh

Pop Warner arrived at the University of Pittsburgh on September 1, 1915, after spending a restful summer back home in Western New York. A week later, he assembled the football team at Camp Hamilton, a remote facility in the town of Windber, Pennsylvania, nestled in the Allegheny foothills, which Pitt had been using for its training camps for the past two years. It didn't take Warner long to recognize that this squad was a major upgrade from the one he had taken to camp at Carlisle a year earlier.

"When I took the Pitt squad to Windber," said Warner, "I found that I had many strong natural players who knew more football than one generally sees in a college eleven. This was a new experience for me and it enabled me to get off to a flying start. I knew after one week at Windber that we would have a great team, because the boys are crazy over the game."[1] This was in stark contrast to the players normally coming out for the teams at Carlisle, most of whom had never played organized ball or had proper training in the game's fundamentals. The Panther players were, in general, possessed of a different pedigree—bigger and stronger physically, and much better trained.

They were also high-spirited. In just the first few days at Windber, Pop recalled seeing as many as a dozen fistfights, some of which devolved into all-out melees. He finally held a meeting and let the players know in no uncertain terms that fighting was not allowed—in practices or in games. "A few of the players tried to test me on this subject, but I quickly set them straight on any confusion that they might have had regarding this rule."

There were several players also who liked to sneak out after curfew and visit the local nightspots. Warner was, at first, fairly successful in nabbing the perpetrators as they tried to sneak back into camp in the wee hours of the morning, and he always made them regret their misdeeds at the next morning's practice. But some of the boys soon learned that if they stopped just outside of camp and listened very carefully, they could

Pop Warner, head football coach at the University of Pittsburgh, late 1910s. (Courtesy Pitt Athletics.)

hear some very loud, distinctive snoring, signaling their coach was fast asleep and it was safe to return. But Warner was no fool. He caught on quickly and soon devised a plan to turn the tables on the transgressors. On one of the final nights of camp, Warner pretended to be sleeping, even conjuring up a thunderous snore to complete the ruse. When the players, upon hearing the coach's throaty siren call, tried to enter camp, he was lying in wait. "After a good chewing out that night, I held off punishing them at practice the next morning. My message had been sent and was well received. These guys knew who was in charge of the Pitt team now."[2]

The Blue and Gold had enjoyed a fine campaign in 1914 under the guidance of former Princeton great Joe Duff, finishing with eight wins against a single loss. Duff left behind an exceptionally talented group to the incoming coach, including center Bob Peck (Pitt's first-ever All-America selection in 1914), along with tackle Claude "Tiny" Thornhill, end Pat Herron, and halfback Andy Hastings (all of whom would at one time receive All-America honors). Among the outstanding players joining the team this season were end Clifford "Doc" Carlson, guard John "Jock" Sutherland, fullback George "Tank" McLaren and guard Herb Sies, bringing the total number of current or future All-Americans on the '15 Panthers to eight!

The Panthers opened the Warner era with a 32–0 pasting of Westminster College, and after drubbing Navy a week later with the worst defeat in its history (47–12), the media were already declaring this Pitt team one of the finest elevens ever assembled. "Football experts who witnessed the contest," wrote the *Pittsburgh Press*, "are ready tonight to give Glenn Warner credit for producing an engine of destruction rarely equaled."

Warner was not inclined to disagree. "I have coached several teams that I thought pretty well of," he commented, "but none of them compares to the Pitt team this year. It is the best all-around aggregation I have seen in years, and I don't think there is a team in the country which can beat us."[3]

Warner's boys then backed up their coach's boast by crushing his former school, Carlisle, in a game so one-sided (45–0) that Warner mercifully used his scrub team throughout the second half. They then laid waste to Penn (14–7), Allegheny (42–7), Washington & Jefferson (19–0), and Carnegie Tech (28–0) to remain undefeated after seven games.

The season finale had Pitt facing its cross-state rivals at Penn State on Thanksgiving Day. The Panthers, of course, were looking to finish their year unbeaten and untied, while the Nittany Lions, at 7–1 against a much weaker schedule, were playing for little more than a dubious claim to the state championship. It wasn't even close. Pitt registered its third straight shutout to capture a 20–0 victory, the state title, and the undefeated season. It was Warner's first unblemished finish since his University of Georgia team went 4–0 back in 1896.

At season's end, there was some dispute over which school should be crowned national champion. Most experts agreed it was between the two best teams in the East—Pitt and Cornell University—both of which had finished the season without a loss. (Warner later recalled sending a telegram to Al Sharpe, Cornell's head football coach, challenging them to a one-game playoff to settle the matter. The offer was rebuffed.[4]) The issue would not be put to rest officially until 1933, when noted football historian Parke Davis retroactively declared Pitt to be 1915 champions.[5]

The Warner family was deeply saddened by the passing of Adaline, Pop's mother, on January 12, 1916. Pop's parents had returned to Springville after spending three years in Texas in the early 1890s, and had continued reside in the house his father built while Pop was still a school boy. Accounts suggest that Adaline had been in failing health since their return to the area, but a recent downturn left her on death's door for several days. Fortunately for Pop, he was able to be home with his family at the time of her death.

Nineteen-fifteen was indeed the finest season Warner had ever experienced as a head football coach, with his team finishing undefeated and several of his players being selected as All-Americans. But as good as the Panthers were '15, they were going to be even better a year later. "The Panthers that year," he'd recall, "were composed of as fine a bunch of football players as I have ever seen together."[6] Without question, the 1916 Pitt Panthers were one of the finest football combinations ever put together. Propelled by Warner's offensive system, the team was poised to steamroll its way through another stellar campaign and an unqualified national championship.

Warner had the good fortune of having 17 lettermen from the '15 squad returning, including nine starters and eight Walter Camp All-America selections, led by center Bob Peck, whom the team elected its captain for the coming fall. He considered Peck to be the greatest center he ever coached, calling him "the most accurate and dependable passer I have ever known. In spite of his light weight [175 pounds], Bob was a power on the offense, while his defensive play was something to marvel at, for he possessed ... uncanny ability to anticipate the strategy of opponents."[7]

The Panthers kicked off their season with the traditional warmup contest versus Westminster College and won easily, 57–0. A week later, they visited Annapolis to face the Midshipmen and were very nearly upset. Several Pitt fumbles kept the Middies in the game, but two missed extra-point attempts spelled Navy's doom, allowing the Panthers to escape with a narrow 20–19 win. It was the last time the Panthers faltered for the rest of the year.

When Pitt traveled to Syracuse to play the Orangemen the following Saturday, there were a couple of special guests in attendance. Warner's recently widowed father, now 76 years of age, rode the train from Springville to see his famous son's team in action. Also present among the orange throng was Walter Camp, "Dean of American Football," who was making the rounds checking out candidates for his All-America team.

Neither left Archbold Stadium disappointed, for what Messrs. Warner and Camp witnessed was a singular exhibition of straight-ahead football predicated on the ball-carrying of Pitt's fine backfield men, who out-rushed their orange counterparts by 200 yards (329–29). Pop attributed his team's success to its commitment to a straight-ahead ground game. With center Bob Peck and the Panther phalanx blowing Syracuse's hefty defenders off the line, Tank McLaren and his backfield mates ground out chunks of yardage almost at will.[8]

"Pitt students, alumni and admirers were unbounded in their enthusiasm last night when the joyful news of the victory was spread about," proclaimed the *Pittsburgh Press*. "On every tongue Glenn Warner's praises are being sung." Most prominent among them were those of Pitt officials whose responsibility it was to ensure its football team continued its winning ways, and thereby continued generating those huge gate receipts. Recognizing that they had in their midst the man who was at that time the top mind in the game, those officials approached Warner with an offer to tack an additional three years onto his original contract. The coach affixed his signature to the new deal on October 25, ensuring he would remain with the Blue and Gold through the 1920 season.[9]

Three days later, Warner led the powerful Panthers onto the muddy turf of Forbes Field to face the University of Pennsylvania, who at 3–1 was still entertaining thoughts of a national championship. But the Pitt machine put an end to the Quakers' titular aspirations with a convincing 20–0 victory in front of an assemblage of 32,000 rooters.

Pitt improved to 7–0 on the season with wins over Allegheny (46–0), Washington & Jefferson (37–0) and Carnegie Tech (14–6), giving them 15 straight victories since Warner took over as coach. All that was left for the Panthers was the traditional Turkey Day tilt with Penn State. Warner, sensing his players were becoming a bit too self-satisfied with their accomplishments, employed a bit of psychology to ensure over-confidence would not stand in the way of a second-straight undefeated season. During the week, Pop admonished the players for their cockiness and proclaimed that this attitude was going to cost them the game and their perfect record. When his declaration was met with a chorus of hearty disapproval, the coach took the charade a step further by betting each man five dollars they would lose.[10]

Whether his charges needed the extra incentive is debatable, but the bet was nevertheless one Warner was more than happy to pay off. The result was a 31–0 blowout victory, another undefeated season, a five-dollar augmentation to each player's wallet, and nearly unanimous recognition as the top team in the nation.

At the conclusion of the 1915 season, Warner had proclaimed the Panthers to be the best team he ever coached. He was now inclined to change his mind. A quick comparison of the Pitt teams of 1915 and '16 shows why: Despite both squads finishing 8–0 against very similar opposition, the latter outscored its opponents 255–25, just a shade better in both points scored and allowed by the former (247–26). Additionally, the '16 Panthers faced more winning teams than they had the previous year.

"The Pittsburgh team of 1916 was considered for many years as the best of all time," Pop observed. "No doubt there have been better teams in later years because football standards of play have improved so much since then. But that team was the best I ever coached."[11]

A terrible war had been raging on the European continent since 1914, but for two-and-a-half years the United States had managed to stay out of it. Everything changed in early 1917 after German U-boats sank seven American ships in the North Atlantic and then attempted to establish a military alliance with Mexico against the U.S. On April 6, Congress declared war against the German empire, and suddenly the conflict in Europe was transformed into a world war. By the time it was over in November 1919, approximately 4 million Americans had served in the U.S. military in some capacity.

A large number of the men enlisting in the armed forces were college-age football players, leaving some universities without enough bodies to field a team. The Big Three of Harvard, Princeton and Yale all played abbreviated schedules, while several schools had no choice but to suspend football operations for the year. The University of Pittsburgh was one of the few schools not badly affected by the martial fever sweeping the country. Though he had lost three of his All-America players to graduation, Coach Warner still had eight veterans returning from the previous year's undefeated squad, which augured well for another fine season for the 1917 Panthers. The team gained additional fame that year as the "Fighting Dentists" because several of its members, including Katy Easterday, Skip Gougler, Tank McLaren, Jake Stahl and Jock Sutherland, were studying dentistry.[12]

The Panthers opened the campaign with wins over West Virginia (14–9), Bethany (40–0) and Lehigh (41–0) before facing their first real competition when Buck O'Neill's Syracuse Orangemen came to town in Week 4. But the Panthers easily swept the New Yorkers aside too, with McLaren rushing for three touchdowns—including a school-record 91-yard romp—to lead his team to a 28–0 win.

With Pitt's uninterrupted string of dominance now at 20 games over two-and-a-half seasons under Pop Warner, some doubters began looking for signs that the team might finally be ready to stumble. Penn, at 3–1 and with the state title as an added incentive, seemed like a good candidate to knock mighty Pitt from the ranks of the unbeaten. This, however, was not going to be the week. Some sloppy play early on allowed the Quakers to draw first blood, but the resilient Panthers roared back with two unanswered touchdowns and won, 14–6. They continued their triumphant ways with defeats of Westminster (25–0), Washington & Jefferson (13–10) and Carnegie Tech (27–0).

Pitt's traditional Thanksgiving-Day tilt with Penn State and an exhibition contest against an aggregation of military "all-stars" remained to be played, but that didn't stop several newspapers from prematurely proclaiming the 8–0 Panthers the top team in the East, and clamoring for a game between them and the top southern team, Georgia Tech (also 8–0), to decide a national champion. The American Red Cross proposed having the teams face each other in a benefit game on November 24, with the winner taking the title and the proceeds going to support the war effort.[13] But since the Panthers already had the two other games scheduled on November 29 and December 1, that would have forced them to play four times in 15 days, so Warner declined. Warner and Georgia Tech's coach, John Heisman, went to great lengths in trying to arrange a game, but there were too many conflicts, with end-of-the-semester school work and travel being limited by the war effort preventing the contest from taking place. The two legends agreed to have their teams meet the following fall to settle the matter.

The Panthers brought the season to a close with a 28–6 trouncing of Penn State on Thanksgiving Day, and a 30–0 win two days later in an exhibition game against a team made up of soldiers from Camp Lee, Virginia. For the third straight year, the Panthers were undefeated and untied, but the national championship was awarded to Heisman's Georgia Tech team. The Golden Tornado matched Pitt's final regular-season mark of nine wins and no losses, but outscored its opponents by a whopping 491–17, as opposed to the Panthers' aggregate 230–31.

As the fall of 1918 approached, the United States was still embroiled in the war that had severely limited the play of university football the year before. Yet another national emergency in the form of an influenza epidemic was now resulting in implementation of quarantines that forced the cancellation of even more of this year's college football season. The University of Pittsburgh jettisoned its entire October slate and played an abbreviated schedule of five games, all within the month of November. Even the usual pre-season camp at Windber was canceled. Despite the concomitant shortage of manpower experienced on universities across the nation, the Panthers had the good fortune of acquiring two future All-Americans in halfback Tommy Davies and center Herb Stein.

The season opened with a 34–0 defeat of Washington & Jefferson, followed by a 37–0 drubbing of Penn, bringing Pitt to 28 consecutive wins under Warner. Next up, however, was John Heisman's Georgia Tech machine, which itself hadn't lost in 33 straight games!

This was the one so many had been waiting for—Heisman and Warner—arguably the two greatest coaches of the day—were finally going to face each other for the first time in two decades. Warner's celebrated single wing offense was going up against Heisman's famed "jump shift."[14] The host city of Pittsburgh was stirred into a frenzy throughout the week as boosters took to the streets to get an early start on the celebration of their team's all-but-certain triumph. Betting was heavy, with gamblers finding odds on a Pitt victory ranging anywhere from 10-to-7 to 10-to-4.[15]

A hardy crowd of 39,000 shivering souls braved the frigid temperatures and blowing winds at Forbes Field that Saturday for the chance to witness a bit of football history. A fairly large segment of the assemblage were Georgia Tech devotees, many of whom came into town aboard the same train carrying Heisman's fabled eleven, who were fresh off a 128–0 skunking of North Carolina State (their third 100-point outing on the season, by the way).

"The southerners came to Pittsburgh with a beating of drums and a great blare of trumpets," Warner recalled. "They brought their band with them, together with a large delegation of rooters, and they fully expected to clean up on Pittsburgh."[16]

As the combatants stirred in their respective dressing rooms before the game, Heisman launched into a spirited pep talk that could be heard clearly on the other side of the thin walls separating the teams. Once he realized what he was hearing, Warner instructed his players to put their ears to the paneling and pay close attention. Heisman tarried on, waxing poetic about the heroic feats—and selfless deaths—of ancient Greek soldiers. The Pitt boys were spellbound. When Heisman finished his grandiloquent oratory, Warner turned to his team and said, "OK, boys. You heard that. Go out there and tear 'em up!"[17]

And tear 'em up they did, as Pitt stopped the mighty Golden Tornado with a resounding 32–0 defeat, and in the process reaffirmed its claim as the best team in the nation. "The University of Pittsburgh football team," wrote the *New York Times*, "settled the question of intersectional rivalry very decisively today when it put down to defeat the great scoring machine of Georgia Tech. The famous jump shift was shown here for the first time, and it took the Pitt players just about ten seconds to get on it and smother it so deep that Johnny Heisman could almost be heard groaning from his place on the sidelines."

Five days later, Warner's boys played their usual Thanksgiving Day game against Penn State, and despite being scored upon for the first time all year, the Panthers won easily, 28–6. This was supposed to have been the final game of Pitt's season, but when Warner received a telegram containing a challenge from an all-star aggregation of Naval Reservists stationed at Cleveland, Ohio, he couldn't resist. It was a decision he would long regret.

The game was played before an enthusiastic crowd of 15,000 at League Park in Cleveland. The Panthers took the opening kickoff and marched right down the field, with Tank McLaren carrying it over from the one to give Pitt the game's first lead. The extra-point attempt by Davies failed, so the score stood at 6–0. The Reserves managed to pull within three in the second quarter with a 40-yard field goal, but Pitt came right back, driving all the way to the Reserves' one-foot mark when the timer inexplicably blew the whistle ending the half ("inexplicable" because only nine minutes and 45 seconds of the 15-minute period had elapsed). Outrage overtook the Pittsburgh side of the field, but Warner and his players eventually cooled and repaired to the locker room for intermission. There was no more scoring until the fourth quarter, when Pitt halfback Katy Easterday extended his team's lead to six points with a 20-yard field goal. But then, something strange happened. According to the Pittsburgh faithful, time slowed down to the point where it seemed the game was never going to end. After what felt like an eternity, the Reserves were awarded possession of the ball on a disputed play at the Pitt 35. From there, they were able to drive to a touchdown that tied the game at nine apiece. After the extra point that gave the Reserves a one-point lead, the final whistle blew, ending the fourth quarter—some 26 minutes after it started! Final score: Cleveland Naval Reservists 10, Pitt 9. The Panthers' winning streak under Warner was finally over after 29 games.[18]

Warner never accepted the defeat as legitimate. He continued to argue its validity for years afterward. "We got rooked out of a victory," Pop declared angrily in an interview 30 years after the fact. He was never able to reconcile how the second quarter could be stopped when his team was in possession at the one-yard line with more than five minutes remaining, or how the fourth quarter was allowed to continue more than eleven minutes beyond regulation and then be declared over once the Reserves had scored the go-ahead points. "That was the rawest bit of officiating I ever saw."[19]

If Warner was looking for sympathy, he wasn't going get any from those who had fallen victim to his streak of perfection over the preceding three-plus seasons. "'Haw, haw, haw,' is the jeering resonance of the entire athletic world," the *Washington Times* mocked. "This makes every team that has met Pittsburgh in the past four years roar with delight. It was all right when Pitt was winning. Warner would growl at all complaints and chuckle quietly to himself. Now the shoe is on the other foot. The whole sport world is laughing at Warner, for nobody believes the officials were crooked or that the Naval Reserves did to Pitt any more than Pitt has been doing to others for years."

Despite the loss, Pittsburgh's performance over the course of the abbreviated 1918 campaign was good enough that the team is generally recognized today as that year's national champion. Still, as far as Warner was concerned, the Panthers' otherwise successful season always bore the stain of that single defeat, and remained a bitter memory for the rest of his days.

The conflict in Europe was nearly at an end by the time the 1919 season arrived, and the influenza pandemic that had brought the North American continent—and indeed the entire world—to its knees over the preceding year and a half had all but subsided. Still, this campaign was going to be more challenging for Warner and the Panthers than either of the previous two. Pittsburgh had been one of the few university teams whose roster had not been either partially or totally decimated by wartime enlistments, but that was about to change. Attrition of a different kind— that of graduation—had visited the campus in the spring of 1919, leaving the Blue and Gold roster seriously lacking in experience as it prepared to enter its fifth season under Coach Warner. Of the 43 men he had coming out for this year's squad, only nine possessed actual game experience, and three of those had been absent the previous fall while serving overseas.

"The coming season will be an unusual one in many ways and the Panther rooters are not too optimistic as to the outcome," the *New York Times* observed. "The material is the poorest in years, with few tried performers available, and the schedule is the hardest Pitt ever arranged. While the return of Hastings, DeHart and Morrow from the service bolstered up the back field considerably, the line material is very green and Warner will have to do a lot of figuring in order to prepare a defense which will take care of the opposition. It is generally felt that Warner has one of the biggest jobs on his hands that he ever tackled to shape a team, and if he can come through with even a fairly successful team he will have accomplished a real feat. The Panthers haven't lost a college game since the Cornellian took charge here four years ago."

If the Panthers were a weaker team, however, it wasn't detectable when they kicked off the season with a 33–0 defeat of Geneva College, and then followed it up with a 34–13 win over West Virginia. But cold reality set in when they traveled to central New York in Week 3 to take on the 2–0 Orangemen of Syracuse University.

Fifteen-thousand rooters turned out for what most figured to be a routine win for the visiting Panthers, but when the final whistle blew, it was the host city of Syracuse that was celebrating perhaps the greatest upset in its school's history. "There were few Orange supporters who had looked for a victory," wrote the *New York Times*. "Thousands of dollars went begging at odds of 2-to-1 on Pittsburgh before the teams trotted on the field. One man from Pittsburgh with twenty-six $1,000 bills could not get the money covered, and he is a happy individual tonight."

Syracuse took the game's first lead with a 30-yard field goal early in the opening period and never looked back. Buck O'Neill's boys were able to cross the Pitt goal line in the first, second and fourth quarters in handing the Panthers a 24–3 defeat, their first regular-season loss since November 1914, the year before Warner took over as coach.

Having his string of consecutive victories end after 31 games was more than the Old Fox could bear. Instead of returning to Pittsburgh with his players as he normally would, Warner decided to disembark as the team train passed through Springville on its way back to western Pennsylvania. When the coach finally returned to campus after taking a few days to decompress, his players would have preferred that his arrival had been indefinitely postponed. "Pop was in no hurry about getting his men out on the field," reported the *Pittsburgh Gazette Times.* "It was the first chance he had for a heart-to-heart talk with the team since the Salt City disaster, and he was in perfect voice. Warner does not mince words on such occasions, and the chances are, some of his charges would have welcomed a chance to crawl into a hole and hide before he was through with them."

The tongue-lashing served its purpose, as the Panthers rebounded to defeat Georgia Tech the following week, 16–6. The Panthers then knocked off Lehigh (14–0) and squeaked by Washington & Jefferson (7–6) to bring them to 5–1 on the season.

Prior to leaving for Philadelphia, where they were scheduled to face Penn in Week 6, Warner learned that he would be doing so without his two star halfbacks, Jimmy DeHart and Tommy Davies, both of whom were sidelined by injuries. Even worse, DeHart's badly sprained ankle was expected to keep him out of action for the balance of the season. Without the two big guns, the Panthers' offense was able to muster only a single field goal, and left the City of Brotherly Love with a devastating 3–3 tie.

A 17–7 victory over Carnegie Tech improved Pitt's record to 6–1–1, leaving them with a very slim outside shot at the national title. But Warner suffered another setback during the week leading up to the big game when he was notified that he would be without the services of another one of his best players—quarterback Jim Morrow—who was being suspended for academic reasons.[20] It was just another blow for the Panthers, who were already going to be without DeHart due to injury.

The Nittany Lions were coached by Hugo Bezdek, who had earned Warner's contempt through his practice of pulling his team's bench right up to the sideline during games, where he would sit with the water bucket between his legs and instruct players as they stood on the field during timeouts. This was at a time when coaches were not allowed to direct their teams' activities during the course of the game. Warner, the man who made his reputation coming up with new ways to circumvent rules he deemed inconvenient—and quite likely a bit jealous that he himself hadn't devised this ingenious ploy—formulated a plan of his own to thwart his Penn State counterpart. The night before the game, Pop and several of his players visited Forbes Field and nailed the visitor's benches to four six-foot posts located a good 20 yards from the playing field. While the Pitt side of the field had a good chuckle watching Bezdek and his staff turn purple struggling vainly to free the benches from their moorings, the State side got the last laugh with a convincing 20–0 victory, their first over Pitt in the Warner era.[21]

With the loss, the Panthers fell to 6–2–1. Despite the comparatively mediocre record, the university rewarded Warner with another contract extension, this one to run through the 1923 season. With an overall record of 35–2–1 in regular-season games in his first five years at the school, he'd certainly earned it.

By 1920, college football was becoming big business, second only to major league baseball in popularity among spectator sports. Warner had been at the vanguard of famous coaches who midwifed the game from its embryonic stages of mass momentum plays and grid-lined fields to the multi-million-dollar behemoth football had become. During Warner's early years of coaching, crowds might have counted less than one thousand, or perhaps as high as three or four thousand. It was now commonplace to read reports of stadiums jammed in excess of 40- or 50-thousand fans—sometimes more!

Despite Pitt's relatively lackluster performance in 1919, Warner was still at the top of his game as the decade that came to be known as the "Roaring Twenties" dawned. The Panthers ultimately had won 92 percent of their starts during Warner's five seasons, placing him among the upper echelon in the profession that was slowly being overrun by a younger generation of coaches that included Knute Rockne of Notre Dame and Andy Smith at the University of California. If the 1920 season was to provide any indication, Pop's place among them was more than secure.

After bursting from the gate with cakewalk wins over Geneva (47–0) and West Virginia (34–14), the Panthers let their guard down in Week 3 and were tied by a tough Syracuse team, 7–7. They bounced back into the win column the following Saturday with a hard-fought 10–3 victory over Georgia Tech.

The days leading up to Pitt's Week 5 contest with Lafayette received plenty of newspaper coverage, since it was going to be the first meeting between Warner and one his former star players, who was now head man at the Easton, Pennsylvania-based school. "The Eastonians are coached by Dr. John B. (Jock) Sutherland," the *Pittsburgh Gazette Times* observed, "one of the greatest lineman the local school ever turned out and one of Pop Warner's best pupils. While Sutherland was playing here he was studying every chance he got, not only in the school room, but on the gridiron.

He picked up a lot of dental knowledge and a lot of football knowledge at the same time. He made good last season, and was re-engaged. He is making good again this season. But his supreme test comes next Saturday, when he stacks his charges up against the 'Old Master,' the man who taught him all the football strategy he knows."

Sutherland's boys put up a strong fight, but the Panthers ultimately prevailed for a 14–0 victory on the heels of Tom Davies' touchdown runs of 49 and 26 yards. After the game, the teacher paid the student a visit in the Lafayette locker room. Though his Panthers had emerged triumphant, Warner recognized that the man known affectionately to all who knew him as "the Scot" was in the process of building a formidable team. "Lafayette has a wonderful line," Pop told Sutherland. "It is the best I have seen. Jock, I'll make a deal with you. Give me your wonderful line and I'll give you my backfield and in addition throw in several other players."[22]

The Panthers then faced the University of Pennsylvania, which was now being coached by Warner's long-time rival John Heisman. Davies was again spectacular, returning a kickoff 96 yards for one score and an interception 65 yards for another to lead Pitt to a 27–21 win. The following Saturday, the Panthers knocked off Washington & Jefferson by a 7–0 score to improve to 6–0–1, keeping their very dim title hopes alive for at least on more week.

The Panthers hosted Hugo Bezdek and the Penn State eleven in the season finale on Thanksgiving Day. Neither team was able to generate offensive sparks on the muddy field, resulting in a scoreless draw. State fans accused Warner of soaking the turf with a fire hose prior to the game as a means of slowing down the Nittany Lions' speedy rushing attack. It was a maneuver the Old Fox was certainly not above employing, and one that would not have surprised anyone who knew of the mutual dislike between the two coaches. Warner, of course, dismissed the accusations as little more than sour grapes.[23]

The tie left the Blue and Gold with a final record of 6–0–2, giving Warner his fourth, and ultimately last, unbeaten year at Pittsburgh. Those two ties, however, cost him what would have been his fourth national championship, as the Panthers were bested by California and Notre Dame (both 9–0), Harvard (8–0–1), and Princeton (6–0–1).

The Pittsburgh Panthers had enjoyed six outstanding seasons since Pop Warner came aboard in 1915, going undefeated four times and having an unprecedented number of players selected as All-Americans. It was a testament to Warner's abilities that the string of successful campaigns continued as long as it had. By the same token, such heady success couldn't be expected to last forever, and for the Panthers of the University of Pittsburgh and their fans, the 1921 season would be when things started to change.

After defeating Geneva 28–0 in the season opener, the Panthers lost to Jock Sutherland's boys from Lafayette, 6–0. It was a tough loss for Warner to swallow, but some tried to find a silver lining in the fact that Lafayette's coaching staff was composed solely of men who had spent their apprenticeships in the Warner workshop.

"While yesterday's game was a defeat for Pitt," observed the *New York Times*, "it was a triumph for the Warner system, for Lafayette is coached by Sutherland, Gougler and Seidel, three stars who learned the game under the 'Old Fox' at the University of Pittsburgh." It's highly doubtful the intensely competitive Warner would have found solace in that little tidbit—he'd most certainly rather have had the win.

The Panthers then went on a tear, knocking off West Virginia (21–13), Cincinnati (21–14), Syracuse (35–0) and Penn (28–0), to improve to 5–1 before suffering consecutive losses to Nebraska (10–0) and Washington & Jefferson (7–0). They brought the season to a merciful close on Thanksgiving Day with a scoreless draw against Penn State.

It had been a disappointing campaign for the Panthers—the 5–3–1 record easily the worst in the Warner era, while the late-season losses to Nebraska and W&J represented the first consecutive defeats suffered by Pitt since 1912. Warner accepted much of the responsibility for his team's poor showing. "I may say that I am to blame more than anyone else," he told reporters. "I realize I have become a little careless. We have been winning all along since I came to Pittsburgh. I have not maintained the same discipline and training as in the past. I have been inclined to let the loose ends take care of themselves, to permit players considerable freedom off the field. But, believe me, I am going to get down to brass tacks next year and it will be a different story."[24]

Pop looked back on the '21 season as a pivotal one for himself. Since his arrival in 1915, the Panthers had been one of the most dominant teams in the nation. However, new powers like Notre Dame, Lafayette and the University of California were encroaching upon the rarified turf normally occupied by teams like Pitt, Georgia Tech, Harvard and Penn. While Warner publicly shouldered much of the blame for his team's less-than-spectacular finish in 1921, he was privately questioning Pittsburgh's long-term commitment to remaining competitive, which to his thinking included building a much-needed modern stadium and continuing to recruit top-level talent for the football squad. Around this same time, Warner began receiving correspondence from a school which seemed solidly committed to elevating its hitherto mediocre football team into that exclusive upper echelon.

As perhaps the most famous football coach in the country, it was inevitable that Warner was going to receive offers from other schools, but whenever he did, he always dismissed them without much thought. By this time, however, Pop was a man of 50 years, and a series of letters from one school in particular—California-based Stanford University—managed to seize his interest. Stanford was hoping to lure Warner out to the West Coast to turn its fledgling team into a powerhouse like the one he had built at Pittsburgh and fill the school's new 60,000-seat stadium with paying customers. The author of those missives, Leland Cutler—a prominent member of Stanford's Board of Athletic Control—finally caught up with Warner by phone and gave the coach a brief synopsis of his grand scheme. Warner was intrigued, and asked Cutler to come to Pittsburgh to discuss the proposal further. Cutler flew to the Steel City and the two enjoyed a working dinner at the Pittsburgh Athletic Club. Cutler presented Warner with Stanford's financial package and strategic plan for transforming the school's football team into a winner. There was no doubting Stanford officials were determined about the future and direction of their football team, and that their offer to Warner was a serious one.

There was, however, at least one very large catch—Warner still had two years remaining on his contract with Pittsburgh, and he advised Cutler he felt honor-bound to fulfill it. It was at this point, according to Warner, that Cutler offered a bold proposal. He suggested that if Pitt insisted on Warner honoring his contract, he could send a couple of his assistants as advance men for those two seasons. They could install the coach's system preparatory to the man himself coming out to California once his current contract expired.

Pop was initially stunned by Cutler's suggestion, but then he thought back to the time when he coached simultaneously at Iowa and Georgia in the mid-to-late 1890s. Maybe it wasn't such a crazy notion after all. As his new friend continued the sales pitch, Warner felt himself warming up to the idea. Before the evening was through, Cutler had Warner's firm handshake, signifying an accord.[25]

Stanford University in Palo Alto, California, was founded in 1891 by

Leland Stanford, former U.S. Senator and Governor of California. Stanford and his wife sought to establish a school in honor of their son, Leland, Jr., who had died as a result of typhoid fever in 1884 at the age of 15. Leland, Sr., who had amassed a large fortune as a railroad executive, endowed $5 million toward the establishment of the school with the stipulation that it would carry their son's name, hence the institution's full title is Leland Stanford Junior University.

Stanford fielded its first football team the same year as its founding. They were skunked 49–0 by the University of Michigan in the very first Rose Bowl Game in 1902. Because of concerns over the violence of the game during the early part of the century, football was replaced by rugby in 1906, and would stay sidelined until the final months of World War I. The school athletics department joined the Pacific Coast Conference (today the Pacific 12, or "Pac–12," Conference) in 1918, and revived its football program the following fall under head coach Bob Evans. The team enjoyed moderate success over the next couple of seasons, but never finished better than second in the conference, and was never able to defeat its arch-nemesis, the University of California Golden Bears, who compiled a record of 42–13–3—and two undefeated campaigns—from 1916–1921 under coach Andy Smith. Bringing in Pop Warner represented Stanford's first step toward respectability and overcoming the dominance of Smith's so-called "Wonder Team."

While Warner had not been actively pursuing a new job, the thought had clearly entered his mind at some point. He'd write years later of at least two prominent factors playing into his decision, one of which reveals at least some degree of premeditation. "I thought the opportunity for success was greater [at Stanford]," he confessed, adding, "I felt my health would be better on the Pacific coast. Weather conditions at Pittsburgh during the football season are rather disagreeable, and much of the late season work had to be done upon a field which was ankle deep in mud. At the close of every season I would be in poor physical condition, twice being rendered incapable of coaching while I recuperated in a hospital. Doctors advised me that the climate of the Pacific coast would be much better for a man of my age and in the work in which I was engaged."[26]

His mind made up, all that was left now was for Warner to travel out to California to meet with Stanford officials and hammer out the minute details of his contract. In mid–January, Pop made the trip and met with several of the school's power brokers, including Cutler, university president Ray Lyman Wilbur, athletic board president Dr. T. M. Williams, and athletic director Walter Powell. Even in that day and age before the advent of the internet and 24-hour sports networks, news of Warner's presence on campus spread like wildfire.

"When the New Year opened," wrote the *Berkeley Daily Gazette*, "word came from Stanford that the Cards were on the market for a new coach. Now Warner comes to the coast as a guest of the Stanford athletic board of control and in all probability will consider a job as Stanford coach for 1924. If Warner does come to Stanford it will be a mighty big boost to for Pacific Coast football. Warner is classed as one of the best coaches in the country ... and he will have plenty of good material to work with at Stanford. The Cardinals have plenty of good men, but they have never had the man who could produce a good team. With Warner things would be different. He would be under a long-term contract and could be largely independent."

On February 1, the school went public with the announcement that Warner had signed a deal to act as advisory coach of the football team for the next two seasons, and become head coach in 1924 when his contract at Pittsburgh ended. Figuring that Pitt would most likely refuse a request to cancel the remainder of Warner's pact, Warner took Cutler's advice and sent two of his most trusted men out to Stanford to install his system. "I was asked to recommend coaches for carrying on the preliminary work," he recalled. "Andy Kerr, freshman coach at the University of Pittsburgh for several years, was a football student of unusual merit, and upon my suggestion he was secured as a coach at Stanford for two years starting in 1922. Tiny Thornhill, old Pitt tackle, who had been assisting [Charley] Moran at Center College, was selected as assistant to Kerr."[27] Warner also asked Wallace Denny, his trusted athletic trainer and friend at Carlisle, to be part of the advance team.

Warner's contract provided a retainer salary of $3,000 and a $2,500 expense account for his two seasons as advisory coach, with a raise in salary to $7,500 (and the same $2,500 expense account) once he settled in as head man, along with a clause that called for an additional $2,500 if Stanford made it to the Rose Bowl.[28] The contract also included an agreement whereby Warner would come out to Stanford the next two springs to conduct off-season training camps. Since the two universities were more than 2,000 miles apart and not on each other's schedules—and the Panthers did not partake in spring training—the arrangement received grudging consent from Pitt.

Warner held his first spring camp at Stanford in late April 1922. Accompanying him out to the coast was trusted assistant Tiny Thornhill.

Some 90 candidates turned out for what proved to be a very spirited camp. "Intensive work is going on," the San Jose *Evening News* observed, "as the veteran Pitt coach is installing the famous 'Warner system' from the ground up. The players are enthusiastic about the work, and even the veteran members of last year's varsity declare they have learned more football under Warner and Thornhill than they ever knew before."

Warner was back at the helm when the Pitt gridders returned to Camp Hamilton on September 5. Controversy surrounding his decision to sign with Stanford lingered—including questions of whether he was going to be able to devote all of his energies toward developing winners at Pittsburgh during the next two seasons—but the no-nonsense coach did not allow any of the clamor to disturb the team's training routine, resulting in a smoothly run camp for the 33 candidates present. But when the Panthers stumbled out of the gate by going 1–2 in their first three games, the naysayers were out in full force, shouting, "Told you so!"

As Warner prepared his charges for the Week 4 contest with Syracuse and struggled to put the team's disappointing start behind them, he began to notice some physical ailments that eventually became serious enough to warrant a visit with a doctor. On Friday, October 20, Pop was admitted to the hospital for what was initially thought to be mumps, but was later discovered to be a weird combination of ailments including rheumatism, bronchitis, hives, and ptomaine (food) poisoning. He'd recover all right, but it was going to take a few days. In the meantime, his team had a game to play, so the Panthers left for Syracuse without him, leaving assistant coach Alex Stevenson in charge. No problem—Pop's game plan was already in place. The Panthers won 21–14. Their coach was released three days later and went right back to work.[29]

The Panthers did not falter the rest of the regular season, defeating Bucknell (7–0), Geneva (62–0), Penn (7–6), Washington & Jefferson (19–0), and Penn State (14–0) to finish their slate with a record of 7–2, an improvement over the previous year's mark (5–3–1), but still below the standard Pitt fans had come to expect from their team.

The Thanksgiving Day tilt with Penn State normally signaled the end of the season for the Panthers, but not this year. Warner had arranged for his team to gather one more time for a trip out to the West Coast to face the Stanford Cardinals. He saw the trip as an opportunity to assess the progress being made by assistants Kerr and Thornhill, and evaluate the talent of the Stanford players in game conditions. For Pitt fans, however, the contest afforded the chance to vent their resentment toward the school that had filched their team's coach, and hopefully claim whatever bragging rights there were at stake between the two schools.

The Redshirts were never really in it, as the Panthers built a 16–0 lead before surrendering a single fourth-quarter touchdown en route to an easy win. In their next-day reports of the game, West Coast writers couldn't resist taking jibes at the peculiar coaching arrangement between the two universities. "Coach Glenn Warner's Pittsburgh Panthers," quipped the *Berkeley Daily Gazette*, "handed Coach Glenn Warner's Stanford Cardinals a 16–7 defeat at Stanford Stadium Saturday, but displayed to the five or six thousand hardy souls who occupied a tiny section of the stands a pure exhibition of Atlantic seaboard football."

Warner recalled being impressed with Stanford's performance, remarking that the team had "improved noticeably" since his visit the previous spring, and that Kerr and Thornhill had "done an excellent job in preparing them fundamentally."[30] The showing bolstered Warner's confidence that a strong, well-trained team would be waiting for him when he arrived for good in 1924.

Pop dutifully returned to Pittsburgh for the start of the 1923 training camp, intent on honoring the last year of his contract with the school. Though his intentions were noble, the results were no better than the previous year's—in fact, they were worse. After opening the campaign with victories over Bucknell (21–0) and Lafayette (7–0), they lost four straight (13–7 to West Virginia, 3–0 versus Syracuse, 7–2 against Carnegie Tech, and 6–0 versus Penn), the longest losing streak in Warner's nine years with the team. They managed to halt the skid with a 13–7 win over Grove City, but at 3–4, the season was already a total loss.

Next up for the Panthers were the Presidents of Washington & Jefferson, a game that was to mark the last meeting between Warner and fellow legend John Heisman. The Presidents were off to a 5–0–1 start in Heisman's first year with the team, and were heavily favored to win this one. Warner, of course, wanted nothing more than to redeem this dreadful campaign by upsetting the long-time rival he'd first faced some 28 years earlier as a rookie coach guiding the University of Georgia eleven against Heisman's Auburn team. Things did not look good for Pitt in the early going, however, as W&J staked a 6–3 lead by the end of the first half. But the Panthers roared back in the second half, scoring ten unanswered points to eke out a 13–6 surprise win.

"There were cheers for 'Pop' Warner," wrote the *Pittsburgh Press*. "Those yells must have gone deep to the heart of the 'Old Fox' of Pitt, game through a sad last season at the school for which he did so much. This game meant all to the old warrior."

The Panthers' usual season-ender against Penn State was always a top draw, but with this being Warner's valedictory game, interest was through the roof. The stadium's 30,000 seats were sold out well over a week in advance. Graduate manager Ernest Couzens, whose job it was to oversee the sale and distribution of tickets, was reported to have required a cordon of police surrounding his office to keep the crush of ticket-starved fans from breaking down the doors.

The school and followers of the football team were pulling out all the stops to give Warner a going-away party that was sure to be remembered for years to come. Prior to kickoff, the Panther mascot presented Warner with a diamond scarf pin, a token of affection from the student body. In the stands, fans held up large gold-and-blue placards that spelled out "Pop."

Once the game got underway, however, it looked as though Bezdek's boys were well on their way toward wrecking Pop's celebration after staking an early 3–0 lead on a first-quarter field goal. But the Panthers were not about to let one of their coach's most detested rivals get the better of him that day. Just as they had against Washington & Jefferson the week before, the Panthers fought back, scoring two touchdowns in the second quarter and another in the third to claim a 20–3 victory.

The win allowed the Panthers to finish 5–4, one game above .500 but still the worst final record the team had experienced during Warner's reign. Despite the disappointing season and the unpopular manner in which he was taking his leave from Pitt, Warner was doing so on good terms. Unlike his departures from Cornell and Carlisle, where some hard feelings lingered as he closed the doors behind himself, Pop's exit from the University of Pittsburgh was met with sentimentality on his part and expressions of affection from the Pitt community.

"My nine years' service at Pittsburgh had been very pleasant," he'd recall, "and was made so because I had the support of the alumni and student body, and I was blessed with very loyal and efficient assistants in Floyd Rose and Alex Stephenson. I acquired a great many loyal friends while I was associated with the University of Pittsburgh and will always look back with a great deal of pleasure upon the nine seasons I spent there."[31]

Herb McCracken, who played three seasons at Pitt under Warner, recalled, "You had such great respect for Pop Warner that you wanted to give him the best you had on every play. He was warm, affectionate, but aloof to the extent that you respected him for what he knew. We played for Pop because we held him in such high respect."[32]

Ralph S. Davis, sports columnist for the *Pittsburgh Press*, spoke for a large segment of the community when he wrote: "It is with genuine regret that thousands of football lovers in this city mark his going. He placed Pitt in the front football rank. He is a genuine gridiron wizard. Pitt will miss him beyond question, for his equal is hard to find. And as he goes to Stanford next fall, he will take with him the best wishes of all who have thoroughly enjoyed football as played by the teams he has coached."

To replace their departing coach, the University of Pittsburgh hired Jock Sutherland, Pop's former pupil who had been enjoying great success as the head man at Lafayette, compiling a record of 33–8–2 in five years with the Leopards. Pop was, of course, very pleased with the choice, considering Sutherland to be not only a good friend, but also an outstanding coach who would carry on in the best Warner tradition. He would indeed, for over the next 15 seasons as the Panther's head coach, the Scot—utilizing his mentor's signature single and double wings as his primary offensive attack—posted a record of 111–20–12 while claiming five national championships.

TEN

Stanford

Warner recalled feeling extremely calm as he relaxed on the train carrying him out to California and Stanford University. His advance team of Andy Kerr and Tiny Thornhill had done a splendid job of laying the groundwork and installing his system. All that was left was for the master himself to add the final touches necessary to transform the team into a "slashing, hard-hitting outfit that could unleash at will the much-noted firepower of my single-wing and double-wing offenses."[1]

His first squad at Stanford consisted of several players who were on the cusp of breaking out as stars, including a stellar pair of ends in Jim Lawson and Ted Shipkey. Lawson would receive All-America honors at the end of the season, and Shipkey two years later. Halfback Norm Cleaveland had gained fame recently as a member of the United States' rugby team that won the gold medal at the 1924 Summer Olympics in Paris. But the team's best player was one whose name was destined to become, along with Jim Thorpe's, one of the two most frequently associated with Pop Warner—fullback Ernie Nevers.

Nevers was born in Willow River, Minnesota, on June 11, 1903. His family moved several times while he was still a youngster, eventually settling in the city of Superior, Wisconsin, on the shore of the Great Lake bearing the same name. As an above-average sized 14-year-old sophomore at Superior Central High School, Ernie tried out for the football team for the first time. He was originally played at tackle and made a mark for himself excelling on the defensive side of the ball. That same year (1917), the Superior Central Vikings won the Wisconsin state championship, outscoring their opponents 427–7. Nevers proved to be a versatile high school athlete, standing out also in baseball, basketball and track. But just as Nevers was about to enter his senior year, the family relocated to Santa Rosa, California. The sport of football had just been adopted by his new school and Ernie, according to legend, seemed to know more about the sport than his coach. He took control of the offense, designed the team's plays, and installed himself at the fullback position. The team went on to win its conference championship, and suddenly every recruiter on the West Coast had his sights set on the Hollywood-handsome lad.

Desiring to remain as close to home as possible, Ernie enrolled at Santa Rosa Junior College and helped organize that school's first football team. A year later, the six-foot, 200-pounder transferred to Stanford University in Santa Clara County. The story was told that Nevers chose Stanford after being abducted by a group of Cardinal fans who had spotted him in nearby Berkeley—home city of the University of California—and held him captive until it was too late to enroll in classes at Cal. By that time, if he was still looking to enter college, he had no choice but to enroll at Stanford. Nevers later debunked the myth, revealing that although he initially preferred Cal, he instead chose Stanford because he feared the Golden Bears would have had him line up as a tackle. He was eager to show what he could do with the pigskin in his hands.[2]

Whatever the reasons behind his decision, it turned out to be a good one for Nevers and everyone associated with Stanford, fans included. Coaches Kerr and Thornhill had spent their first season at Stanford installing Warner's system, which included heavy reliance on the double wing formation, meaning that Nevers, as the fullback, was going to be the primary ball carrier and passer when he joined the varsity squad as a sophomore in 1923. All he did that year was lead Stanford to a 7–2 finish and earn third-team All-America honors from Walter Camp. Warner had every reason to expect big things from Nevers in '24. Unfortunately, the man teammates had taken to calling "Big Dog" suffered a broken left ankle in a pre-season scrimmage game against a team composed of sailors from a nearby Navy base, and was going to miss a sizeable chunk of the upcoming season.

It didn't appear the Cardinal eleven were missing a beat, though, when they presented their new coach with a 20–6 opening-day triumph over Occidental College, amassing 455 yards of total offense in the process while yielding just 48 to their hapless opponent. They then defeated a strong aggregation from the Olympic Club of San Francisco (7–0) and the University of Oregon (28–13) at home before traveling up to Portland, Oregon, to face the University of Idaho.

Idaho was designated to wear their white jerseys in this contest, but, through some mix-up, had only their red jerseys available. When informed of his opponent's wardrobe gaffe, however, Pop was prepared. Having learned a hard lesson when his Cornell squad failed to bring a backup set

Pop with trusted assistant Andy Kerr, circa 1924. (Courtesy of Stanford University Archives.)

of clothes when they faced Penn in a bitterly cold and wet afternoon back in 1898, Warner always had his equipment manager pack two sets of uniforms for all road games. The Stanford boys donned their white jerseys and hit the field, but it didn't matter very long as both teams found themselves caked with mud caused by heavy rains. Neither team seemed able to mount a credible offense in the quagmire until Stanford managed a late field goal to take a 3–0 lead that held as the final score.

Santa Clara was up next, but with the University of Southern California scheduled for the following week, Warner decided to hold his starters out and save them for the tougher Trojans. Stanford's second-stringers had no trouble with Santa Clara, registering a 20–0 victory. Warner's ploy, however, went for naught as USC cancelled at the last minute. Stanford was able to arrange a substitute game with the University of Utah and won easily, 30–0, to improve to 6–0 on the season—their best start since 1905 (8–0).

The November 15 contest against Montana marked Nevers' much-anticipated return to the Stanford lineup. He managed to play only about three minutes, however, before having his other (right) ankle wrenched in a pileup. When Nevers attempted to punt the ball on the next play, his ankle snapped and he had to be carried from the field. Even without the

Big Dog, the Cardinals won easily, 41–3, but Nevers was going to be laid up for several more weeks.

After seven games, the Cardinals were perched atop the Pacific Coast Conference with a perfect record, but they were scheduled to face Andy Smith's University of California machine, which, though seeded second in the conference at 7–0–1, had still not lost a conference game since 1919. Nevertheless, the Golden Bears were taking every measure they could—both on the field and off—to improve their chances for victory. On Thursday, Cal officials came forward with their contention that Stanford's star halfback Norm Cleaveland should be disqualified from playing in the game due to the fact that he had appeared briefly in one game while still a sophomore in 1921, meaning that 1923 was in actuality his senior season. Warner felt Cal's maneuver was dastardly, but the protest was upheld, leaving Stanford to face its archrival without its two best backfield men.[3]

It was a thriller, and though his team did not win, Warner proclaimed this—with some measure of hyperbole, no doubt—to be his greatest day in football. "I'll never forget that game. Few people, if any, gave us a chance to down the Bears or even come close." Cal was indeed in control of the proceedings for the better part of three quarters. When the Golden Bears staked a 20–6 lead late in the third period, a large number of fans began making their way toward the exits. "The crowd of 77,000 thought it was hopeless and many left. But they missed one of the great comebacks of football." In the fourth quarter, reserve halfback Ed Walker hit Ted Shipkey in the end zone with a 38-yard strike, closing the gap to 20–13. Moments later, with time running out, Walker became the unlikely hero when he connected with Murray Cuddeback for an 81-yard catch-and-run to daylight to even things up at 20 apiece. "It wasn't a victory," Pop declared, "but I've treasured that 20–20 tie more than any other game in my 46 years of coaching."[4]

While Warner might have been guilty of a slight bit of exaggeration, there's no denying the game's importance in terms of its ultimate meaning (as well as the effect it had on the man's wallet). The tie improved Stanford to 8–0–1 on the season, while Cal found itself a game behind with a mark of 7–0–2. By finishing with the best record in the conference, Stanford had earned the right to play in the annual Rose Bowl game in Pasadena, California, on January 1. And by earning the Rose Bowl berth, Warner pocketed a tidy $2,500 bonus.

At the time, the team representing the West (usually the Pacific Coast Conference winner) was afforded the privilege of choosing its opponent in the big game. Warner invited the undefeated Fighting Irish of Notre

Dame, which featured the legendary "Four Horsemen" backfield of Jim Crowley, Don Miller, Elmer Layden and Harry Stuhldreher. They were coached by one of the biggest legends of all time in Knute Rockne. This game would have it all: Warner's vaunted single and double wing formations going up against Rockne's fashionable "box shift" ... the most famous backfield ever assembled ... the best from the West versus the best from the East, both unbeaten ... the winner likely to be named national champion. It was sure to be spectacular on the field and lucrative at the box office. Rockne wasted little time in accepting the challenge.[5]

Ten days before the game, doctors removed the cast from Ernie Nevers' right ankle. After walking on crutches for five days, he was finally allowed to run. Warner wanted desperately to have his stud fullback on the field for the Rose Bowl, but felt Nevers' leg needed some support and protection, as the Irish were sure to target the lame limb. He asked the team's physicians to construct a brace for Nevers' leg, but the endeavor proved unsuccessful after several attempts. Finally Warner, recalling the day when he made his living as a tinsmith, decided to try his hand. He invited Nevers to his workshop one evening and started tinkering. The coach fashioned a piece of aluminum, lined it with rubber from a tire's inner tube and taped it snugly to Nevers' lower leg, from upper calf down around the ankle and to the arch of his foot. Ernie gave it a tentative thumbs-up, but wanted to try it out at practice the next day. After a few more adjustments, he declared the brace acceptable and agreed to wear it in the game.

Because of the distance between the two schools, there was very little information upon which either coach could prepare a defense. Warner tried to get some intelligence on Rockne's tendencies, but ultimately decided to just play the game using the same strategies that got the Cards to the big game in the first place. "To my way of thinking," said Warner, "scouting the opponent as a means of winning ball games is greatly overrated by most coaches. It is my experience that these detailed scout reports are entirely too voluminous to be really helpful. The match was unanticipated and we had no opportunity to scout Notre Dame. So I wrote to a friend who coached an Eastern team that played the South Bend boys. He sent me the entire season's reports made by his scouts on Notre Dame's games. It was a regular five-foot shelf and by the time I waded through it I was lost in a maze of detail. So we just went down to Pasadena and played football."[6]

Over 53,000 fans baked in the sweltering 90-degree heat for the privilege of witnessing the intersectional battle of the undefeateds, and what they saw has gone down as a classic in the annals of college football history. Stanford took the game's first lead on a 27-yard field goal by Murray Cuddeback after the Stanford defense forced a Notre Dame fumble deep in its own territory. The Irish fired back in the second quarter when Elmer Layden slammed over from three yards out, making it 7–3 Notre Dame. Layden widened the Irish lead to 13–3 midway through the quarter when he snatched a Stanford pass and sprinted 78 yards for a score. Early in the third, Notre Dame's Ed Hunsinger recovered a muffed punt return on Stanford's 20-yard line and returned it for a touchdown, giving the Irish a commanding 20–3 lead. But the oppressive temperature began to wear on the boys from back east, while Nevers, well acclimated to the California heat, seemed to gain strength. Late in the third, Nevers picked off an ill-advised Stuhldreher aerial, leading to a seven-yard scoring pass from Ed Walker to Shipkey, and pulling Stanford to within ten points. The Cards seemed to be on the brink of a rally when a fourth-quarter drive brought them to the Notre Dame two-yard line. But the Notre Dame defense stiffened, repulsing Stanford's best efforts on the first three downs. On fourth, Nevers went straight at the Notre Dame defensive front and appeared to have crossed the goal line before being thrown back. The Stanford sideline erupted with cheers as head linesman Walter Eckersall raised his hands to signal the marker. Referee Ed Thorp, however, disagreed and overruled Eckersall, and awarded possession to Notre Dame. Backed up against their own goal line, the Irish had no choice but to punt the ball back to Stanford, giving the Cards another golden opportunity to close the gap. With the ball on the Notre Dame 40, however, Nevers threw a pass into the flat that Layden saw coming a mile away. This time, the Irish fullback raced 65 yards for the score, giving Notre Dame a 27–10 lead. The game ended moments later with the score intact.

Regardless of the 17-point margin of victory, the contest was much closer than it appeared. Many eyewitnesses in fact believed that Stanford was the better team that day. While Notre Dame's Layden was brilliant on the defensive side of the ball, Nevers had played all 60 minutes of the game, carrying the pigskin 34 times for 114 yards, more than all Four Horsemen combined. It was turnovers that cost Stanford the game and, ultimately, Warner his fourth national championship.

"By all rules of football mathematics," observed an *Associated Press* reporter, "Stanford should have won. Coach Glenn Warner's men gained 164 yards from scrimmage; Knute Rockne's swift South Benders gained 134. The Cardinals registered 17 first downs; Notre Dame made 7 ... but one mistake may wreck a ton of statistics, and there were several Stanford mistakes. Notre Dame took advantage of all of them and won."[7]

Warner knew it, too. "In the game," he'd write, "Ernie smashed the

Seven Mules [Notre Dame's forward line] for gains on every buck, and slowed the Four Horsemen to a walk. It is not often that I wolf over losing a game, but if I sit back on my haunches now and split the air with a wail it is because Nevers deserved a victory that afternoon. Time after time he carried the ball the length of the field, alternating terrific bucks with savage end runs, only to have his efforts brought to naught by poor field generalship. Twice, for instance, when Notre Dame's goal was menaced, the quarterback called for a pass out into the flat zone, where it could not be covered, and twice Layden intercepted and raced away for touchdowns."[8]

In a heartfelt letter to Warner the next day, Stanford president Ray Lyman Wilbur offered words of consolation, along with his opinion on referee Thorp's call on the Cardinals' disputed fourth-quarter touchdown. "I have rarely before seen a game which I felt so little reconciled itself with the score. It seemed to me that the Stanford team, except in a very few instances, played in a remarkably brilliant manner. I should have been better contented if that six inches could have been on the other side of the goal line so that the score could have been at least 20–17."[9]

The victory allowed Notre Dame to claim the championship, and solidified Rockne's place among the Roaring Twenties' athletic iconography populated by Babe Ruth, Jack Dempsey and Bobby Jones, surpassing the likes of Warner, Amos Alonzo Stagg and John Heisman in popularity among fans of the gridiron sport. Warner, whose place in the sporting world was already set, was forced to return to the drawing board, content with the knowledge that he was—hopefully—going to have Nevers for the entirety of the 1925 season.

The Stanford football team of 1925 had the good fortune of having on its roster the player many felt was the best in the country in Ernie Nevers, but not much else. There were only four other players with more than one year of varsity experience returning from the previous year. Several of the younger players who had been developed under the Warner system by Andy Kerr and Tiny Thornhill were now ready to take their places among the first-stringers, but just how much their inexperience would affect the team's overall performance was cause for concern.

Adding to Coach Warner's unease was Nevers' performance in the classroom. A dislike for schoolwork was another trait the Big Dog shared with Jim Thorpe, and if Stanford's high academic standards were not met, a player could find himself disqualified from participating in athletics. Just a few years earlier, Warner's Pittsburgh Panthers had lost two of their top players (Jim Morrow and Jim DeHart) as a result of poor grades, and the coach did not relish the thought of losing Nevers for even a single down.

"Nevers kept me on tenterhooks every season," Pop recalled. "While possessing a fine mind, he disliked the grind of study, and examinations were even harder on me than him."[10] Fortunately for all concerned, Ernie, while not necessarily a diligent student, never allowed his grades to fall below acceptable standards.

It didn't take long for the Cards' inexperience to show, as the San Francisco Olympic Club prevailed for a surprising 9–0 opening-day win in what was supposed to be little more than a non-conference test run for the Redshirts. They bounced back a week later to defeat Santa Clara, 20–3, and then knocked off Occidental, 28–0 (with Nevers gaining 100 yards on 19 carries and scoring two touchdowns).

Stanford then faced Howard Jones' University of Southern California Trojans before 80,000 at the Los Angeles Coliseum. This game received a great amount of pre-game hype due to the last-minute cancellation of

Pop with his star fullback, Ernie Nevers, 1925. (Courtesy of Stanford University Archives.)

the previous year's meeting between these two teams. After jumping out to a 13–0 by the end of the first half, the Cards let up in the second, surrendering nine unanswered points before regrouping to blunt the Trojan rally and escape with a narrow 13–9 win.

The University of Oregon eleven visited Palo Alto a week later. Pop was obviously taking this opponent lightly, opening the game with his second-stringers. But when the halftime scoreboard read Cards 14, Ducks 13, the coach ordered his first stringers to take the field for the third-quarter kickoff. The Stanford starters scored three second-half touchdowns to secure a 35–13 victory. The Cards then played host to another Oregon-based team, this time an aggregation from the Oregon Agricultural College (today known as Oregon State). In the Redshirts' 26–10 win, Nevers carried the ball 24 times for 126 yards and two scores, and was directly responsible for making 10 of Stanford's 21 first downs.

The Cards were still in contention for first place in the conference when they traveled to Seattle to take on the University of Washington. But Warner's boys came out flat and allowed the Huskies to outplay them on a muddy field and claim a 13–0 victory and, ultimately, the conference title.

Stanford then met up with the eleven from the University of California—Southern Branch (now known as UCLA). Warner and several of his first-stringers skipped this contest, instead taking in the California-Washington game in anticipation of the following week's matchup with the boys from Berkeley. With Kerr and Thornhill in charge, and only two starters playing, the Cards still managed an 82–0 skunking.

Any meeting with the Golden Bears was big as far as the Stanford faithful were concerned, but this season's finale carried even greater significance due to the fact that it was going to be Ernie Nevers' last as a collegian. An over-capacity crowd of 72,000 jammed into Stanford Stadium, and were treated to one of the most exciting games in Cardinal history.

The Cards snatched the game's initial lead when halfback Mike Murphy scored on a short run early in the opening frame. Moments later, George Bogue added another touchdown on a reverse, and the first period ended with the Cards ahead 13–0. Nevers scored Stanford's third marker early in the second, increasing the lead to 20–0. Cal seized the momentum in the third quarter and eventually managed crack the goose egg, making it 20–7. But Nevers provided his team with some cushion when he scored his second touchdown on a short run in the final frame, putting Stanford up, 27–7. The Bears managed one last score late in the game, but the Cards repulsed the Cal rally and held on for a historic win. The Redshirts had finally stemmed the tide of consecutive losses to Andy Smith's Wonder

Team at six. Nevers was spectacular in his swan song, handling the ball on all but three offensive plays, racking up 117 yards on the ground and scoring two of Stanford's touchdowns. "The game was a dazzling array of 'Pop' Warner's plays perfectly executed for two quarters, a great deal of Captain Ernie Nevers, of a green Stanford line which outplayed and out-guessed its more experienced opponents, and much of a portly gentleman who sat on the Stanford bench and smoked cigarettes incessantly (while across the field Coach Andy Smith of the Bears all but drowned himself in his own waterbucket)."[11]

Even though the Cards had not won their conference championship, the team had, over the course of Warner's first two seasons in charge, accomplished nearly everything school officials had desired when they first conceived the idea of bringing him to Stanford back in the fall of 1921. The Cards had won the conference and made it to the Rose Bowl in 1924, and had finally gotten off the schneid by knocking off the California Golden Bears in '25. And though Warner was losing his best player to graduation, there were even greater achievements looming in Stanford's not-too-distant future.

Stanford's football season was barely over when Pop attended a dinner on December 1 in New York City with several other famous coaches, including Tad Jones of Yale, Fielding Yost of Michigan and Knute Rockne of Notre Dame. The group, formed in 1924 as the Intersectional Board of Football Coaches, had gathered in the Big Apple for the purpose of select-ing an All-America team. A reporter present at the event asked Warner to name the greatest football player he had ever seen. Warner replied frankly: "Ernie Nevers, Stanford fullback, is the greatest player I ever have seen, and I have coached Jim Thorpe and seen Willie Heston of Michigan in action many times. Nevers has no weakness so far as I can see. He does every-thing." Warner went on to criticize Thorpe for his carelessness, citing the 1912 game against Penn in which Thorpe failed to make the effort to knock down a pass that resulted in a Quaker touchdown.[12] Though he had been put on the spot, Warner answered candidly. What might have made his response seem strange, however, was an article appearing in that same month's issue of *Athlete and Sportsman* magazine in which Warner named Thorpe as the all-time best.

"'Thorpe was the greatest football player, bar none, that I ever saw in action," he said. "He was a born football player. He knew everything that a football player could be taught and then he could execute the play better than the coach ever dreamed of." Warner's comments on Thorpe, it should be noted, were actually made the previous February, prior to Nevers' fabulous season of 1925. It was a question that would dog Warner for the rest of his life, and though he almost always named Nevers first, he would often qualify the answer by adding that Thorpe was the best halfback and Nevers the best fullback.[13]

The 1926 season was going to be a test for Pop Warner. His Stanford Cardinals had been one of the best teams in all of college football the year before, but he was going to be losing not only his best player to graduation, he was also losing trusted assistant Andy Kerr, who had accepted the head-coaching position at Washington & Jefferson College. To replace Kerr, Warner hired Chuck Winterburn, who, having played halfback for the Old Fox for three seasons at Pitt, was well-versed in the Warner system. Replacing Ernie Nevers, however, was not going to be so easy. Pop had senior George Bogue and couple of talented undergrad backs in Dick Hyland and Clifford "Biff" Hoffman, but whether they could fill Nevers' huge cleats remained to be seen.

The Cards opened the campaign with a bizarre arrangement in which they played two games in a single afternoon. Warner saw the two scheduled opponents as warmup fodder for the rest of the season, so playing them back-to-back would allow him to observe all 51 of his players in action on one day. The Redshirts faced Fresno State in the first game and won easily, 44–7. In the second game, they met up with California Tech and eked out a 13–6 win.

The season-opening twin wins were merely the beginning of a monster season for Stanford, as they dominated the conference by rolling through the next seven games (19–0 over Occidental, 7–3 over the San Francisco Olympic Club, 33–9 against Nevada, 29–12 versus Oregon, 13–12 over USC, 33–14 over Santa Clara, and 29–10 over Washington) for a brilliant 9–0 start. USC was still in the hunt, however, sitting a game behind with a record of 7–1. The Cardinals had only to defeat or tie an uncharacteristically weak Cal team in the regular-season finale to clinch the conference title and earn their second Rose Bowl appearance in three years under Warner.

The Golden Bears were reeling at 3–5 in their first year without Andy Smith, who had passed away suddenly from pneumonia the preceding January, and were therefore no longer the formidable—or despised—opponent they once were. So the only surprise in the Cardinals' defeat of the Bears was the 41–6 final score.

The University of Alabama, the top team in the Southern Conference at 9–0, was invited to face Stanford in the Rose Bowl. The Crimson Tide had won the game the year before, and were looking to become the first team to win in consecutive years. With a crowd of 68,000 on hand, Stanford took the game's first lead on a first-quarter strike from George Bogue to Ed Walker. That was all of the scoring until the waning moments of the fourth, when Alabama blocked a Stanford punt to set up a short touchdown run, pulling the Tide to within a point. Stanford still had a chance to win, but would have to block the point-after attempt to clinch it. But Alabama hurried into formation before the Cardinals could get set, and Herschel Caldwell's kick was true. The game ended moments later deadlocked at seven apiece, the last tie in Rose Bowl history.

Once again, Warner's team had won the statistical battle but walked away from the big game without the victory. The Cardinals' 350 rushing yards were 233 better than the Tide's 117, and they also held the advantage in first downs (12–6). "The result of that game was a keen disappointment to the followers of Stanford," he recalled, "for the coast boys after having the game pretty well in hand were tied when victory seemed assured. I believe also that if in the Alabama game the southern boys had been leading up to the last few minutes of play and Stanford had come up from behind, the Cardinal supporters would have left the field in a cheerful mood. It is not how you start but how you finish that counts in football."[14]

Even with the Rose Bowl tie, Stanford was recognized as the top team in the nation with its outstanding 10–0–1 overall record, and was awarded the Rissman National Trophy (given to the national champions from 1926 to 1930, and retroactively back to 1924). It was Pop's fourth, and ultimately last, national championship.

Warner's base pay of $7,500 as head football coach at Stanford was indeed handsome. Earning the approximate equivalent of $101,000 in 2013, Warner was pulling down more than the highest paid professor at the school. There were critics who moralized that mere coaches should not earn such exorbitant salaries, but the truth was that Warner was not even the highest paid coach in the game at that time. Notre Dame's Knute Rockne was said to be earning $10,000 per season.[15] John Heisman's contract at Rice Institute was reported to be worth $9,000.[16]

Like those other coaches, Warner continued to seek other means of income while banking his hefty university remuneration. While at Carlisle, for example, Pop had invested in several lucrative ventures (including the

Pop and Tibb Warner at home in Palo Alto, California, 1927. (From the Concord Historical Society, Inc., Concord, New York.)

Springville Canning Company), and created another source of revenue by developing a correspondence course for football coaches. In 1912, he had the entire four years' worth of lessons bound and sold the collection as a book, eventually selling all 10,000 copies printed. Warner also sold several of his inventions to the Spalding sporting goods company.

NOTRE DAME CATHEDRAL
PARIS, FRANCE – AUG. 1928

KNUTE ROCKNE'S
OLYMPIC GAMES TOUR.

Reminder of a
great trip and
Christmas greetings

Christy Walsh

PHOTO
KEYSTONE
PARIS

Pop Warner (right) attending the 1928 Olympic Games in Amsterdam. With him are his friends Knute Rockne (left) and Christy Walsh. Behind them stands Notre Dame Cathedral. (From the Concord Historical Society, Inc., Concord, New York.)

Being considered one of the country's most recognizable authorities on football, Warner was frequently asked by newspaper and magazine editors to write about, or give his opinion on, some aspect of the game. A few years earlier, Warner had become acquainted with an ambitious young lawyer named Christy Walsh, who was carving out a niche for himself as a sports agent and promoter representing such luminaries as Babe Ruth, Ty Cobb and John McGraw. Walsh started out ghost-writing stories for show biz folks, the types whose stories and opinions were eagerly sought by besotted fans but who had little time or inkling to actually sit down at a typewriter and write them themselves. He eventually transferred his focus to sports figures—baseball, in particular—and struck gold when he snatched the Sultan of Swat as one of his first clients.

Walsh was extremely ambitious and, by dint of furious enterprise, developed his newly forged trade into a full-time business, building a highly successful syndicate of scribes to act as ghost writers for some of professional baseball's biggest names. Among those who moonlighted for Walsh were such famed sportswriters as Damon Runyon, Frank Menke, and Ford Frick (who later became commissioner of Major League Baseball). Walsh brokered deals with players whereby they agreed to allow their names to be used for syndicated news stories and biographical features. These pieces were often partly made up and almost always hyperbolized, but they proved wildly popular with readers. Walsh was able to add Warner's name to his stable and soon Pop's "columns" began appearing in newspapers across the country. Though most of the stories spewing forth from the Walsh syndicate were ghostwritten, it appears that much of the writing attributed to Warner was in fact—to some degree—his own. It is obvious from reading the content of his other published works (the correspondence course, his books and other articles) that Warner was erudite and articulate, and more than capable of rendering a compelling and well-written article if asked to do so. Between 1927 and '28, Warner authored, or at least partly contributed to, a 60-part autobiographical series for Walsh called "My Life in Football" (later renamed "My Forty Years in Football").

Warner's second book, titled *Football for Coaches & Players*, was published by arrangement with Stanford University Press in late summer of 1927, just in time for football season when interest would be at its highest. The 225-page opus expanded upon his 1912 manual, Warner noted in the book's preface, "with the idea of making this work a complete text on football for the use of coaches and players." Pop offered his readers instruction on the fundamentals of passing, kicking, tackling, and the basics of each position on the field. He provided tips on proper diet, sleeping habits and physical conditioning for players, how to plan the weekly practice routine, and treat football-related injuries. Warner also included sketches depicting proper techniques and diagrams of his signature plays and formations.

William "Lone Star" Dietz, Warner's former tackle at Carlisle who had been coaching Stanford's freshman football team, was employed to sketch the illustrations and play diagrams.

"Pop's latest literary effort," wrote the *Pittsburgh Press'* Ralph Davis in his review of the book, "is a distinct contribution to the various paper pamphlets and books on the great autumn sport which have always been numerous but the value of many could be easily questioned. Football for Coaches and Players is well worth reading by spectators as well as directors and participants."[17]

Warner arranged for Stanford to open the 1927 campaign the same way the team had in '26, with a Saturday twin bill that allowed the coach to observe every one of his players in action in a single afternoon. The Cardinals dumped Fresno State, 33–0, in the opener, and then squeaked by the San Francisco Olympic Club, 7–6, in the closer.

The Cards ran into trouble in Week 2, however, losing 16–0 to St. Mary's College of California. Stanford had never lost to St. Mary's before, but the Gaels took advantage of several Cardinal mistakes and held on for the upset win. "The St. Mary's defeat was not surprising," Warner rationalized. "Both teams fought hard and seemed to be evenly matched but Stanford's fumbles were frequent and costly and St. Mary's scored 16 points to Stanford's nothing although making but two first downs."[18]

The Redshirts were not down long, defeating Nevada (20–2), tying USC (13–13), then beating Oregon State (20–6) and the University of Oregon (19–0) to improve to 5–1–1 after seven games. They then traveled to Seattle to face the University of Washington on a muddy gridiron. The field was so bad that Stanford supporters suspected the conditions had been augmented by use of a fire hose. "Every time our halfbacks tried to run, they fell on their faces," recalled Stanford captain Hal McCreery. "Biff [Hoffman], who had to grip the ball to throw it, might as well have been trying to grab a piece of quicksilver. At halftime, we were behind seven to nothing." But the Old Fox, proving his powers of improvisation were just as strong as ever, came up with a solution. "In the dressing room, Pop went over to Biff and said, 'Show me how you grip the ball.' Then he got a thumbtack and taped it to the inside of Biff's index finger so the point just stuck out of the tape. That thumbtack did it. Biff, who could throw the ball farther than any man I ever saw, just reared back and dropped it in Dick Hyland's arms twice in the second half and we won the game."[19]

The 6–1–1 Cardinals returned to Palo Alto to face perennial patsy Santa Clara. Confident his team was in good hands with his assistants in charge, Warner decided to skip the game and instead head over to Berkeley and scout the California-Washington game. Though Pop had left the team to be coached by assistants before, he never lived to regret the decision the way he did after finding out the Cardinals had been embarrassed (13–6) by such an inferior foe, and, in the process, put their conference title hopes in serious doubt.

"Santa Clara had not made a very good record and was not supposed to be in Stanford's class," Warner recalled. "The result of the game showed how important is the proper mental attitude on the part of football players. I did not anticipate that we would have any trouble with this game and I went to Berkeley and the Stanford team was left in the hands of my assistants. Stanford started with the second team which played on even terms in the first half. In the second half the Stanford varsity took the field and they were beaten by Santa Clara. The score in the first half was 6 to 6 and Santa Clara added seven points to that score when the varsity went in against them. After Santa Clara scored their touchdown on the varsity in the second half the Stanford players became panic-stricken and demoralized in their desperate efforts to overcome their opponent's lead. They realized too late that games cannot by won on reputation."[20]

The Cardinals found themselves in a must-win situation when they faced Cal in the regular season closer. To ensure victory, Pop was pulling out all the stops, mixing in a few long-forgotten plays with some new ones created just for this occasion.

"Coach 'Pop' Warner and his fighting Reds visited the gridiron graveyard and dug up plays buried years ago which they used against the Bears with success," noted the *Berkeley Gazette*. "The Statue of Liberty and the guard-around play were among those used and they brought the fans to their feet just as they did in the old days." But those old chestnuts weren't all, as Warner devised a new "series" play that he planned to use after the Cards had successfully run the Statue of Liberty.[21] With the score tied at seven apiece midway through the third, Stanford found itself with a first down at Cal's 13-yard line. Fullback Biff Hoffman called the Statue of Liberty to Robert Sims, who picked up eight yards to set up a second-and-two at the five. This was the perfect time to run Pop's new play. After taking the snap from center, Hoffman feigned as if he were running the statue again. But instead of transfering the ball to another back as he had on the

Opposite: **Pop confers with Biff Hoffman, Stanford captain, 1928. (Courtesy of Stanford University Archives.)**

previous play, Hoffman pulled it down, tucked it behind his back, and beat a path around the opposite end. Cal defenders were completely duped and wound up chasing the other man running in the opposite direction. Hoffman ran unmolested for the touchdown, giving the Cards a 13–7 lead.

Warner's new play—the very first "bootleg"—had worked as well as he could have hoped, and the Cards held on for the win, improving their record to 7–2–1. It appeared, however, that defeating Cal might not be enough, for at the same time Stanford was beating the Bears, USC was busy destroying Washington State—27–0—to improve to 7–0–1, and apparently clinch first place in the conference. But Stanford's two losses had been suffered at the hands of non-conference opponents (St. Mary's and Santa Clara). Within the conference Stanford and USC both stood at 4–0–1, so it was left to the Rose Bowl committee to decide which was going to represent the Pacific Coast Conference in the big game. Wanting the team they felt that figured to be the biggest draw, the committee picked Stanford.

This year's game set the Cardinals against Warner's old team, the Pittsburgh Panthers, who were coming to Pasadena at 8–0–1. With the match up of Warner and his former assistant coach, Jock Sutherland, the game was easily the most hyped of the entire college football season. "Newspaper writers tried to make a big deal about the 'Old Master' and the 'Young Pupil' coaching against one another," Pop recalled. "But I knew Sutherland was one of the most talented young and upcoming coaches in the country. So I didn't buy into the psychological trap that was being set for me."[22]

Stanford's offense spent the better part of the first two quarters in Pitt territory, but was unable to put any points on the board, and the teams repaired to their dressing rooms locked in a 0–0 stalemate. Pitt took advantage of a rare Stanford mistake early in the third quarter, scoring the game's first points when Jim Hagan recovered a Cardinal fumble and returned it 20 yards for a touchdown. But the point-after attempt was blocked, leaving the Panthers with a tenuous 6–0 advantage. Later in the same quarter, Stanford took the lead when Frank Wilton recovered a teammate's fumble and sprinted the remaining five yards for the score. Biff Hoffman's conversion attempt was good, putting Stanford up by one. The Cardinals dominated the fourth quarter and eked out a 7–6 victory.

After three invitations to the Tournament of Roses, Pop Warner was finally taking home the bouquet. Making it all the more savory was the fact that it had come at the expense of his former team. As expected, newspapers played up the mentor/protégé angle, the *United Press* reporting

the game as "a victory for western football over eastern, a triumph of
teacher over student, an exciting, freakish affair with the result in doubt
until the final scrimmage."[23]

Despite the Rose Bowl victory, Stanford's overall record of eight wins,
two losses and one tie was not good enough to earn Warner his fifth
national title. This year's Rissman Trophy was awarded to Bob Zuppke's
University of Illinois machine, which finished the year at 7–0–1.

Pop Warner's teams had been wildly successful in recent years using
his "B" (or double wing) formation, but as the 1928 season rolled around,
the Old Fox decided it was time for a change and devised a variation to
the standard B in order to best utilize the talent he had at hand. This mod-
ification featured two fullbacks (Biff Hoffman and Chuck Smalling) placed
at different distances behind the offensive linemen and having different
responsibilities. The deeper set fullback (Hoffman) stood about six yards
behind the center and was expected to be the team's best all-around athlete. The second fullback (Smalling) was set about three yards in back of
the line and to the right of the deep full back. This man was expected to
be the more powerful runner.

For the third straight year, Warner arranged for the Cardinals to open
with a doubleheader—only this time, the Redshirts were shocked by an
all-star aggregation from the San Francisco Young Men's Institute, losing
7–0. They bounced back to win the second game against West Coast Army
(21–8), but irreparable damage had already been done to Stanford's season.
Warner was now conceding that playing two games in one afternoon was
not such a brilliant idea after all, and the practice was hereafter abandoned.
The loss suffered at the hands of YMI was the first sign that this was not
going to be Stanford's year, for a week later the Cards suffered another
setback by losing to the San Francisco Olympic Club, 12–6. They appeared
to have turned things around by winning their next four (Oregon, 26–12,
UCLA, 45–7, Idaho, 47–0, and Fresno State, 47–0), but then were
defeated by USC, 10–0.

The Cardinals stood at a mediocre 5–3 with Santa Clara due up next.
The Broncos had upset the Cards with a 13–6 stunner in 1927 while Warner
was off scouting another game. He was determined that there would be
no repeat. After a bit of soul searching, he arrived at the conclusion that
the new twist on the B formation he had implemented at the start of the
campaign had not turned out to be the next best thing. He decided to revert
to his bread and butter A formation (or, as most followers of the game

knew it, the single wing). With the back-to-basics approach, Stanford avenged the previous season's shocker by skunking the Broncos, 31–0.

Among the crowd of rooters present at the Stanford-Santa Clara contest were Herbert Hoover—the former secretary of commerce who just four days earlier had been elected the nation's 31st president—and his wife, Lou. Hoover was a Stanford alumnus (class of 1895) and former student manager of the school's baseball and football teams, as well as a longtime friend of university president Ray Lyman Wilbur. It is likely Hoover and Wilbur discussed more than old times and football during this visit, for just a few months later, Hoover tapped Wilbur for the cabinet position of secretary of the interior, which office Wilbur subsequently held for the entirety of Hoover's presidency.

Stanford then defeated Washington (12–0) and tied California (13–13) to improve to 7–3–1, but those three losses were the most suffered by the Cardinals during the Warner era, and ultimately cost them a third straight conference title. But there was still one more game on Stanford's slate, as Warner had arranged for his boys to travel east and face the powerhouse Army team at New York's Yankee Stadium.

This was to be the first time the Stanford eleven ventured beyond the Rockies for a game, and Pop wanted nothing more than to make a good showing in his return to the East Coast. The Cadets were a strong team, sitting at 8–1, and were favored by most of the big-name New York reporters, but once the game got underway, the 86,000-plus in attendance were almost immediately disabused of the notion of Army's superiority. The Cardinals dominated right from the get-go, playing an aggressive game and employing an array of trick plays and forward passes from the double wing that completely bamboozled the unsuspecting West Pointers. By the time it was over, Stanford had gained 322 yards of total offense while holding Army to a mere 113, and picked up 26 first downs while yielding eight in scoring a convincing 26–0 victory.

"No man with a fluid ounce of pity in his soul can relish the task of setting down in type what Mr. Warner's team did to the Army," wrote *Pittsburgh Press* columnist Joe Williams of the New Year's Day massacre, while noting that at least 16 Cadets were sent to the infirmary that afternoon. "Those white-shirted giants from the Golden Gate rolled over the Cadets in unending waves of force and destruction. After each fresh charge there would be Army men scattered around the landscape of the Yankee ball yard in sundry patterns of disfiguration."

Warner was ecstatic. His return east had been resoundingly triumphant, and the double wing offense that the Cardinals employed so skillfully in the destruction of the boys from West Point was the talk of the football world. To the large number of coaches watching the display from the bleachers, most of whom were still adhering to either the single wing or the Notre Dame shift, it was a revelation. When Warner attended the American Football Coaches Association convention in New Orleans a month later, he was met by a swarm of fellow coaches seeking to learn his "new" system—the very same one his Carlisle Indians had unleashed on this same Army team back in 1912. Over the next couple of seasons, the B formation—or variations of it—would become the predominant offensive attack in the nation.[24]

The huge victory helped succor the sting of the down year his team had just gone through. While 8–3–1 might have been a banner year for most teams, it was below the standards Warner had established since moving to the West Coast. But with at least a dozen lettermen slated to return for the next season, there was reason for optimism.

Indeed, 1929 opened with great promise, as the Cardinals knocked off West Coast Army (45–0), the Olympic Club of San Francisco (6–0), Oregon (33–7), UCLA (57–0) and Oregon State (40–7) to start the season at 5–0 for the first time in three years. They ran into trouble in Week 6, however, losing for the third straight time to Howard Jones' tough Southern California Trojans (7–0). The Cards rebounded to win their next two over California Tech (39–0) and Washington (6–0) to improve to 7–1, but then lost a close one to Santa Clara (13–7).

Sitting at 7–2, Stanford still had an outside chance at the conference title, but their next opponent—the University of California—was also in the hunt, and undefeated. The game was sure to be a pitched battle between old rivals, and was sold out well in advance. Warner, seeking to provide some inspiration, presented his players with brand new uniforms—white jerseys with red trim and red pants with white stripes—just for the occasion. The ploy worked. The inspired Cardinals lost the coin toss but forced California to fumble on its opening drive. Six plays later, Lud Frentrup scored to give the Cards the game's first lead. The Golden Bears scored later in the quarter, but the failed extra-point attempt left them trailing by one, 7–6. That was as close as they were going to get. Stanford pierced California's goal line in the second and third quarters, securing a 21–6 victory.

The vanquishing of Cal left a three-way tie for first place in the conference, since USC had beaten Stanford, and Cal had defeated USC. The Rose Bowl committee ultimately selected USC to represent the conference in the big game, so Warner went ahead with scheduling a game with Army for December 28 at Stanford Stadium. The Cadets were still licking the wounds left when the Cardinals ran roughshod over them at Yankee Stadium the year before. So bent on redemption was General Douglas MacArthur, the former superintendent at West Point, that he was reported to have "ordered" Army coach Biff Jones to win this game. It seems, however, that Warner and his troops did not learn of Dugout Doug's orders until it was too late. The Stanford defense never allowed Chris Cagle, Army's star half-back, to break loose, holding the All-American to just 48 yards on 11 carries. On the other side of the ball, fullback Chuck Smalling picked up 113 rushing yards and three touchdowns to lead the Redshirts to a 34–13 win.[25]

"The cagey tactics of Glenn Warner, the wiliest old fox in football, and the powerful running drive of his Stanford football team were too much for Biff Jones' hard bitten Army Cadets here today," wrote the *Pittsburgh Gazette*. "Pop's formations are somewhat like those he used to show at Pittsburgh, but the actual working of his old favorite plays has been changed considerably, and after today's display it can hardly be said that his shifting has turned out badly."

Stanford's record of 9–2–0 was good enough only for a second-place finish in the conference, just a single game behind 10–2–0 USC.

As Stanford's spring camp of 1930 ushered in Warner's 36th year as a coach, he and Notre Dame's Knute Rockne were still the two most recognizable names in the world of college football. Though not yet 60 years of age, Warner had already attained living legend status among followers of the grid sport. The demand for his expertise that began with his early successes at Cornell and Carlisle had not ceased—it had, if anything, increased. Warner had responded to the earliest requests by establishing a correspondence course and writing books on coaching, and, more recently, conducting popular football clinics with his friend Rockne. He also was very generous in helping other coaches who requested to observe his practices first-hand. As far back as 1902 he had allowed his brother Bill, then captain of the Cornell football team, to attend workouts at Carlisle, and had since allowed several other head men to attend his team's practices.

He never worried that giving his secrets away would come back to haunt him. In the preface of his 1927 book, Warner wrote, "Several coaches with whom I have talked regarding the publishing of this book have expressed the thought that I would probably not want to publish many inside facts, especially regarding the plays which I myself have been, and am still, using. They will no doubt be rather surprised and perhaps incredulous when I state that this book outlines the exact methods I have been using myself, and contains plays all of which I have been using in recent years or am using now ... I have no fear of lessening my efficiency as a coach by giving to other coaches the methods, tactics, and plays which I have employed."

Pop, in fact, seemed to derive a certain odd satisfaction from imparting his secrets to opposing coaches and then turning around and beating their teams with the very same plays he had been so generous in sharing. One of his favorite stories centered on the time he gave an assistant coach from the University of Pennsylvania a complete tutorial on the Warner system a week before their teams were scheduled to meet, even drawing diagrams for the coach to take back to Penn practices for reference. But when the Quakers met up with Warner's Panthers the following Saturday, they found they still had much to learn as the Pitt boys laid a 20–0 thrashing on them.[26]

It appeared Pop had found a couple of new suckers during this spring's camp when he deigned to allow Ross MacKechnie and Lou Hammack—coaches of the West Coast Army football team—to attend Stanford's spring camp to learn directly from the master. By the time they were through, the two were so thoroughly sold on the Warner System that they decided then and there to make it WCA's modus operandi for the upcoming season. They were convinced that their decision was the right one when the Cadets opened their campaign on September 13 with a victory over the San Francisco Olympic Club. But when they traveled to Palo Alto a week later for the Cardinals' season opener, things were drastically different. Even after having been granted access to the den of the Old Fox himself, the Cadets never stood a chance. Final score: Stanford 32, West Coast Army 0.

Warner may have shared many of the secrets of his success with MacKechnie and Hammack, but he wasn't about to give away his entire playbook. Behind the closed door of his office, Pop had been stealthily devising a new formation, designated formation C (in keeping with the alphabetical nomenclature established with his A and B formations). This new configuration featured a balanced offensive line (unlike its predecessors) and ends split wide to augment the passing game. The halfbacks were positioned about a yard back and just outside the offensive tackles.[27] With the addition of about 50 plays that could be run from the C formation, the Cardinals had a seemingly endless arsenal from which to choose. With this expanded playbook, the Cards seemed almost unstoppable as they tore through their next five games, defeating the San Francisco Olympic Club (18–0) and Santa Clara (20–0), tying Minnesota (0–0) and beating Oregon State (13–7) to arrive at 5–0–1, with hated USC set to visit Palo Alto in Week 7.

The Trojans, of course, had been dominating the series in recent years, going 2–0–1 in the teams' last three contests, and were a three-point favorite to win again. Warner knew his men were going to be keyed up to the point of distraction, so he arranged to have the team spend the night before the game in an out-of-town hotel to help them relax. It didn't help. The Trojans imposed their will on the Cardinals throughout the contest, posting a 41–12 victory that ultimately cost Stanford any hope for a conference title.

The Cardinals rebounded to beat UCLA (20–0), Washington (25–7), and California Tech (57–7). Warner's boys kept the string alive by skunking California, 41–0, which represented the largest margin of victory recorded by either team in the long history of the rivalry.

Stanford brought its season to a close a week later by wrecking Dartmouth's perfect record with a 14–7 drubbing at Palo Alto. It must have seemed weird to Warner, since this was the first year in recent memory in which Stanford didn't finish with either a bowl game, an extended trip east, or a long wait prior to playing the season finale.

Knute Rockne's accomplishments as head coach at Notre Dame (five seasons undefeated and three national championships) brought him acclaim that surpassed even that of his friend and colleague Pop Warner. Like his Stanford counterpart, Rockne enjoyed many lucrative perks resulting from his team's success, including invitations for speaking engagements, conducting football clinics, product endorsements, book deals, and more. But confirmation of Rockne's preeminence among his peers came in early 1931 when he received an offer from Universal Pictures to star in a motion picture—tentatively titled *Bucky of Notre Dame*—based on the story of Paul "Bucky" O'Connor, the scrub halfback who filled in with the starters in the 1930 season finale and sparked a huge victory for the Irish over USC. Though no one knew it at the time, that was the last game in which Rockne's redoubtable shadow would pace a Notre Dame sideline.

Rockne arranged to fly out to the West Coast at the end of March to meet with studio executives and hammer out the details of the film. He wired ahead to Pop that he was coming west, and the two made plans to

One way for famous coaches such as Pop Warner and Knute Rockne to earn a little money on the side was by through endorsement deals such as this one. This ad for football equipment bearing Pop's name appeared in magazines in 1928. (Courtesy Alan V. Manchester, Springville, New York.)

get together with another friend, Bill Ingram, the head football coach at Navy, for a "quiet reunion." On March 31, Warner and Ingram boarded a plane in San Francisco with plans to welcome their friend when he arrived at Grand Central Airport in Glendale, California. Upon disembarking, the two were met instead by a group of reporters who relayed the stunning news that their now legendary friend had been killed in a plane crash that morning while en route to the coast. Somewhere over the farmlands of Kansas, they were told, Rockne's plane lost a wing and went into a spin before finally slamming to earth in a wheatfield in the small town of Bazaar, killing the coach, his five fellow travelers and two flight staff.

Warner was stunned. He had known Rockne since their first encounter as Carlisle head coach and Notre Dame assistant back in 1914, and considered Knute to be one of his closest friends. "He was the greatest figure in football today," said Warner, still trembling after taking a moment to compose himself. "One man with no enemies. The greatest friend of all his players and he did a lot for them, but he did an awful lot more for the game."[28]

Rockne was the first American cultural icon whose death was spread with the lightning speed offered by such modern methods as radio and the home telephone. His fame transcended the sports world, as evidenced by the outpouring of affection expressed in the thousands of telegrams and letters received from all walks of life. Former presidents, Hollywood stars, foreign dignitaries, and countless everyday folks sent their condolences to the Rockne family. President Herbert Hoover went so far as to describe Rockne's death as a national disaster. For a generation of Americans, this was the first time in their lives when they could later recall exactly where they were and what they were doing when they heard the news of the passing of a famous person—as so many today can still recall where they were when they heard about the deaths of John F. Kennedy or John Lennon.[29]

"No one ever asked me to pick the greatest football coach of all time," Pop would later write, "but if I were asked I would unhesitatingly name Rockne. No man ever had a stronger or more magnetic personality. No man has ever had greater ability to transform that magnetism into football results. It is my contention that, with such power as a coach and such personality, Knute Rockne would have been just as successful with the punt formation system the single wingback system, or the tiddlywinks system as he was with the Notre Dame system."[30]

The Stanford footballers entered 1931 with a new mascot after a unanimous vote by the Executive Committee for the Associated Students,

Pop Warner (standing to the left with back to camera) presides over team exercises, 1931. Assistant coach Tiny Thornhill stands at center in the foreground. (Courtesy of Stanford University Archives.)

which took place in late November, 1930, changed the nickname of the school's athletic teams from Cardinals to Indians. Though the true reasons for the name change are lost to history, it was justified since the Indian had—according to Stanford's official history—long been a part of the school's athletic tradition.[31]

The newly-minted Indians opened the campaign with a resounding 46–0 win over West Coast Army, then tied San Francisco's Olympic Club (0–0), defeated Santa Clara (6–0), Minnesota (13–0) and Oregon State (25–7), tied Washington (0–0), and beat UCLA (12–6) for a 5–0–2 start— the furthest they had gone into a campaign without losing a game since 1926, their last undefeated season. But just as they had the last two years, the Trojans of Southern California were coming along just in time to derail Stanford's great start.

Defeating USC had become a near-obsession for Warner. He spent much of the previous half-year distracted with thoughts of how he could finally break the string of dominance Howard Jones was holding over him. He thought he had found the solution with a radical defense designed to contain the Trojans' potent ground game. Warner's idea had Stanford's defensive ends lining up approximately 15 yards outside the defensive tackles, and charging in along the line of scrimmage toward the interior of the line as the quarterback barked out the signals. The idea was for the ends to enter the backfield with a full head of steam just as the ball was snapped and disrupt the play before it could have a chance to unfold. Unfortunately for the Indians, Howard Jones, like Warner, had a few tricks of his own up his sleeves.

The Trojans had been using a pre-snap shift in which the offensive linemen positioned themselves a full yard off the line of scrimmage and then shifted forward as the signals were called out. Jones added a new wrinkle for this game by instructing his quarterback to call the signals using an erratic cadence. This resulted in a disruption of the defensive ends' timing, causing Stanford to be flagged several times for offside. Although losing 19–0 was an improvement over the 29-point loss the Indians suffered at the Trojans' hands the previous year, it ultimately extended Stanford's string of futility against USC to five straight games (four losses and a tie), and severely strained the patience of many of the team's followers, including a good number of influential alumni. Stanford had not won its conference since 1927, and there was some grumbling that perhaps the game was passing the team's aging coach by.

The Indians regrouped to defeat Nevada (26–0), but then lost a close one to the University of California (6–0), before bringing the season to a merciful end with a 32–6 defeat of Dartmouth. The Indians' final record of 7–2–2 was disappointing, however, when considering the team's 5–0–2 start.

The early 1930s were, in Warner's words, "tumultuous times" for universities in the Pacific Coast Conference. This was especially so at Stanford, where those whose interests were primarily athletic found themselves at odds with faculty and the administration over the school's direction. Prior to accepting the post as secretary of the interior under President Hoover in 1929, Stanford president Ray Lyman Wilbur had proposed eliminating the freshman and sophomore classes and re-focusing the school's mission to becoming a "graduate-level superpower." With the proliferation of junior colleges throughout the state, Dr. Wilbur believed Stanford could jettison the two initial grades and simply recruit the best the junior schools had to offer for its upper level classes. Although Dr. Wilbur's idea was ultimately rejected, recruiters from other Pacific Coast universities advised prospective enrollees that Stanford was expected to drop its freshman and sophomore classes within the next couple of years. Many football players took the bait and signed elsewhere. As a result, Warner found his roster more wanting in talent with each passing year and, as a result, it became harder and harder to keep pace with the rest of the teams in the conference.

Whatever the reasons for Stanford's recent turn of football fortunes, neither boosters nor alumni were happy. "The enthusiasm and the spirit of the average college student body is such that it will not stand for having its team defeated year after year by any outstanding rivals," Warner observed. "If those in charge of athletics do not find some way to win their share of games, the student body and alumni soon brings about a change in the administration. It is one of the unfortunate developments of college athletics that the teams which have overstepped the bounds of propriety in the gathering of material have often been the greatest drawing cards."[32]

Yet despite growing anti–Warner sentiment among followers of the Stanford football team, the administration offered the coach a five-year extension to his existing contract in February 1932, increasing his base salary to $15,000 per season (approximately $260,000 in today's dollars).[33] The Indians might not have claimed a conference title in five years, but their overall record of 65–13–7 was better than any other PCC member over that same period—except, of course, USC (73–12–2).

If Warner's detractors needed convincing that his creative juices were still flowing, his supporters could have pointed to the coach's latest innovation—improvements to football "shoulder protectors"—which was filed with the U.S. Patent Office on April 8. The invention, designated U.S. Patent Number 1,887,473 when it was issued the following November, improved protection and range of motion for the wearer.

As usual, Stanford got off to a fast start in 1932, defeating the San Francisco Olympic Club (6–0), the University of San Francisco (20–7), Oregon State (27–0), Santa Clara (14–0) and West Coast Army (26–0) to begin the campaign at 5–0. But fans were reserved in their enthusiasm, since the Indians were slated to face mighty Southern Cal in Week 6. Since both teams were coming in undefeated, prognosticators generally agreed that this game would ultimately decide which was to going to be taking home the Pacific Coast Conference pennant. The Trojans had had the Indians' number in recent years, of course, having won the last four meetings between the clubs. This year's USC team was considered to be the strongest yet, with a string of victories stretching back 14 games.

While discussing the upcoming contest with reporters at a mid-week practice session, USC coach Howard Jones suggested that the Indians had been flouting the in-motion rule by not having their motion man stop for a full second prior to the snap. He told them he was going to insist that game officials time Stanford's backs with a stopwatch. When told of Jones' contention, Warner cracked that he had no quarrel so long as the officials made sure the Trojans were positioning seven men on the line of scrimmage, an obvious reference to the pre-snap shift Jones' boys had been using in riding herd over opposing teams for the past couple of years.[34]

The Indians gave the Trojans a momentary scare when they marched all the way to the USC 5-yard line on their first offensive series, but ultimately came up empty when the Trojan defense stiffened. It was all Southern Cal from then on, with the Trojans taking to the air for two touchdowns and winning 13–0.

The USC game was just the beginning of a downward turn that saw the Indians drop their next two, 13–6 to UCLA and 18–13 to Washington, and fall to 5–3 on the year. It seemed a mid-season lull was becoming an annual tradition for the Indians, but losing three straight was the final straw for many of the team's followers who had not already turned coat on the venerable coach.

With the weak California Aggies coming to town in Week 9, it was a good time for Warner to duck out for a few days and scout the Cal-Idaho game being played the same day at Berkeley. With his assistant coaches in charge, the Indians cruised to a 59–0 win. Pop returned in time for Stanford's final conference game against the California Golden Bears, who, like the Indians, were in the midst of a mediocre season, coming into the weekend with the same record of six wins and three losses. With little on the line other than pride, it's not surprising this game ended in a scoreless tie.

For the fifth straight year, Stanford—with a record of 1–3–1 within the conference—was not going to be playing in the Rose Bowl. That left Warner free to accept an invitation to bring the Indians up to western Pennsylvania to take on Jock Sutherland's undefeated Pitt Panthers. With everything that was going on, it was good the Indians were going to be a long way from home for the final game of their season. It was a very close game, but the Panthers kept their streak alive with a 7–0 triumph to improve to 8–0–2. Their superb season would come to an inglorious end with a 35–0 shellacking at the hands of USC in the Rose Bowl.

With the defeat, the Indians fell to 6–4–1, the most losses the team had suffered in Warner's nine seasons at Stanford. Bill Corbus, the Indians' outstanding guard, was a near consensus first-team All-America selection (thus earning the distinction of being the last player coached by Warner to be so honored).

Warner's return to the Steel City was significant for more than the game that was played that afternoon. A few weeks earlier, Warner had received a telegram from Philadelphia businessman Charles G. Erny—who also happened to be a member of the board of trustees at Temple University—inviting the legendary coach to meet while he was in Pittsburgh for this contest. Warner had met Erny the year before during a stopover in Philly on his way back from the Stanford-Dartmouth game, and was treated to a tour of Temple's new $450,000 football facility. Warner agreed to meet again, but asked Erny to come by his hotel room the evening following the game.

As the two relaxed in front of the fireplace and puffed away at fine cigars, Erny gave Warner a brief history of the university and its athletic programs. It wasn't long before he came to the purpose of the meeting, inquiring of Warner if he might be interested in coming back east to take charge of the Temple football team. It all sounded familiar to Pop, for it was little more than a decade earlier that he had been wooed in a similar fashion by Leland Cutler of Stanford. Erny capped his pitch with a stunning offer of a five-year guaranteed contract worth $100,000. Pop rose from his chair, walked across the room and stared out the window. A thousand things went through his mind, not the least of which was that it had not even been a full year since he agreed to a five-year extension to his pact with Stanford. On the other hand, there was the negative sentiment pervading the Stanford campus over this year's team's lackluster performance and recent inability to beat USC. This opportunity could very well be his last chance to restore whatever luster his reputation had lost. He wondered, though, if at his age (61) he still had the energy to take over another fledgling football team and transform it into a winner. What about the autumn climate back east? Could his health hold up against the blustery, cold conditions of late fall in eastern Pennsylvania? But after weighing in the significant financial setbacks he had suffered as a result of the stock market crash of 1929 and the ensuing Great Depression, Pop concluded this was an offer he simply couldn't refuse. Without further deliberation, he turned back toward Erny, extended his hand, and accepted.[35]

Pop tendered his resignation from Stanford on December 5, and the response was almost instantaneous as reporters descended upon the Warner home in search of answers. "I believe this to be a wonderful opportunity and I am satisfied I am bettering my position," he told them. "After all, nine years is enough for a coach to stay in one place. I was at Pittsburgh that long. Every move I've made has been an advancement."[36]

Later that evening, a group of more than 80 of his players marched to Warner's house and pleaded with him to stay. "We didn't play very well for you this season, Pop," said center Bill Bates, acting as spokesman for the group. "Come back next year and we'll show you. We'll fight down every team on the coast for you if you'll stay."[37]

Their pleas brought tears to Warner's eyes. "I appreciate it boys," he said, "but I can't do it. I have signed the contract and it's too late."[38] Pop encouraged the boys to carry on and continue playing as hard for their new coach as they always had for him. He then invited them all in for a snack, which sent his wife, Tibb, into a bit of a panic. Mrs. Warner, however, was accustomed to having groups of football players coming around, and somehow managed to provide enough cookies, sandwiches, coffee and tea for the whole gang.[39]

Some players felt their loyalty belonged more to their coach than their school. Fullback Bobby Grayson, tackle Bob Reynolds and halfback Frank Alustiza all announced their desire to transfer to Temple so they could continue to play for Pop. Though none actually transferred from Stanford, the gesture itself was indicative of the affection the players had for the Old Fox.[40]

"Glenn Warner was not the magnetic, vibrant personality that was Knute Rockne," Allison Danzig observed. "He was not a dominant, forceful leader of men, as was Rockne, though he could win their affection and loyalty as could few others. This was demonstrated at Carlisle, again at Pittsburgh and once again when, upon his signing a contract to go to Temple University, eighty-two members of his Stanford squad called on him and begged him, with tears in their eyes, to tear up the contract, declaring they would fight their hearts out for him if he stayed."[41]

Such deep feelings were not limited to the boys wearing Stanford uniforms. Leland Cutler, the Stanford Board of Trustees member who spearheaded the recruiting campaign that had brought Warner to the school, wrote, "I am shocked at news of your leaving Stanford and genuinely regret your decision. Quite aside from the fact that in my opinion you are the greatest football coach in America, you are also a great gentleman, having been a big factor at Stanford in developing Stanford men along right lines. Wish that you had talked to me before deciding because I could have convinced you that Stanford wanted you and would have a place for you always. Good luck, Pop."[42]

There was plenty of speculation surrounding Warner's decision to

**Pop Warner showing off one of his masterpieces, Palo Alto, California, 1932.
(From the Concord Historical Society, Inc., Concord, New York.)**

leave after honoring only one year of the five-year contract extension he signed just 11 months earlier. While most papers published stories claiming Warner was feeling the heat from alumni who were less than happy with Stanford's recent on-field performance, one reporter from United Press defended the coach against such charges, writing, "It has been said orally and in newspaper columns that Howard Jones, of Southern California, really ran Pop off the Coast. Supporters of this claim point to the fact that for five consecutive years the Trojans have won from the Indians. No doubt these beatings did nettle Pop, who isn't hard to nettle and who likes his team to win. These losses did cause discomfort among certain of the Stanford old grads and Warner claimed it was the criticism of these alumni that led him to make a change. Our own hunch is that Warner liked the salary Temple offered and that neither alumni critics nor Howard Jones had much to do with his decision."[43]

No matter the reasons, Warner was moving on and was now focused on the task that lay ahead, which began with assembling his staff. Desiring to surround himself with men familiar with his famous system, Pop hired Fred Swan—who had played tackle for him at Stanford and more recently served as freshman coach at Wisconsin—to coach the line. Chuck Winterburn, who had been serving Pop as an assistant at Stanford for the past seven seasons, was going along as his backfield coach. Also joining the staff at Temple was Wallace Denny, Warner's trusted friend who had served under him as athletic trainer at both Carlisle and Stanford. Heinie Miller, the former Penn All-American who had been head man at Temple for the past eight years (guiding the Owls to an aggregate 50–15–8 record), was retained as an assistant coach and scout.

ELEVEN

Temple

For the past nine years, Pop and Tibb Warner had been living the snowbird life, spending the late summer and fall seasons in sunny California and the late spring and early summer months back home in Springville, where Pop continued to own the East Main Street home his father had built back in the 1880s. The move to Temple would make it much easier for the couple to visit friends and family back home more frequently. Both still had relatives living in the vicinity, and the familiar surroundings seemed to have a rejuvenating effect on the coach whenever they returned.

Warm summer evenings might find Pop engaged in a game of cards, whether contract bridge or perhaps poker. On summer days, anyone attempting to locate the Old Fox would do well to look first at the Springville Country Club, which the coach helped found in the early 1920s. An avid golfer and renowned crafter of hand-made clubs, Warner had served as president of a group that purchased a parcel of land from the old Buffalo, Rochester & Pittsburgh Railroad just south of the village with the idea of turning it into a park for family picnics, entertainment and sports such as tennis and golf. Warner, along with longtime friend and fellow golf enthusiast Dr. Ralph B. Waite, laid out the initial nine-hole course. Approximately 200 shares of stock were sold at $50 apiece. Over time, golf became the primary focus of the venture. Club members fortunate enough to have played rounds with Warner recalled for years afterward how in the middle of a game he might suddenly trail off under the shade of a nearby tree, pull out a piece of paper and begin sketching out a football play or formation. Indeed, even when he was away from the playing field, the coach's mind was never far from the game.[1]

He was never very far from the game physically, either. Several weeks of every summer found Warner living out of a suitcase. Whether in a far-off town lending his expertise and prestige to a football clinic or giving a speech in front of some fraternal organization or youth group, Pop seemed to have a hard time turning down any request for a personal appearance.

Temple was a second-tier football power at the time of Warner's arrival, having posted respectable records of 8–1–1 and 5–1–2 against the likes of Thiel, Bucknell, Drake, Scranton and Carnegie Tech in 1931 and '32. School officials were looking to Warner to elevate their team to the level of such eastern titans as Pitt, Penn, Army and Notre Dame, and possibly add some of those teams to Temple's schedule. They had done their part by building a state-of-the-art stadium and recruiting the most celebrated coach in the country. It was now up to the coach to do his part.

Warner traveled to Philadelphia in late January to meet with Erny, graduate manager Earl R. Yeomans and university president Charles Beury to discuss long-term plans and formally sign his contract. On January 31, Pop attended a luncheon sponsored by the Philadelphia Sportswriters Association at the Benjamin Franklin Hotel and was met by an enthusiastic crowd of nearly 1,000 reporters, dignitaries and sports enthusiasts. After declaring his happiness with returning to the East and pointing out the advantages of eastern football over western, he discussed the team's immediate future. "I don't know much about my prospects at Temple," he told the gathering. "I have met but a few of the players so far and don't know the caliber of the material. A great team can't be developed in a season or two. It may take several seasons and even then the accomplishment rests upon the material. There are no miracle coaches."[2]

Warner blew the whistle on his first practice at Temple Stadium on March 27 with 56 candidates present, 21 of whom were returning from the previous season. Assisting him was a fairly large staff—by Warner's standards—consisting of Swan, Winterburn, Miller, and De Benneville "Bert" Bell, who had been the Owls' backfield coach during Miller's tenure as head man.[3] Prior to the camp's opening, Warner had arranged to have a crew build a platform upon which the coaches could stand while monitoring practices. He also had them construct—to his own exacting specifications—tackling machines and blocking sleds that were employed to a great extent during the first three weeks. Then it was on to scrimmaging and the implementation of the single and double wing formations.

Pop found he had some fine ballplayers on the squad, including quarterback Don Watts, halfback Danny Testa and guard Edgar Smith, the team's captain. The Owls, however, were similar to Warner's Carlisle teams of the late 1890s and early 1900s—a relatively light team that was going to have trouble matching up against the bigger teams with which Temple officials wanted to compete. Pete Stevens, a 210-pound fullback on the 1932 squad, was moved to center to add bulk to a line that otherwise averaged less than 190 pounds per man. At the end of the six-week camp, Warner and Winterburn returned to California, where they stayed in constant contact, mapping out the master plan for the Temple football team.

The Owls, dressed sharply in cherry and white jerseys, officially welcomed their new coach on September 29 by presenting him with a victory over South Carolina in his first game with the team. Ed Zoukas ushered in the Warner era when he returned a punt 80 yards to paydirt in the opening quarter. From there the outcome was never in doubt as the Owls cruised to an easy 26–6 win in front of a jubilant sellout crowd at Temple Stadium. The buzz permeating campus was stilled a week later, however, when the Owls traveled to Pittsburgh and were skunked by Carnegie Tech, 25–0.

Week 3 pitted the Owls against the Haskell Indians, led by Gus Welch, the former Carlisle quarterback in his first year as Haskell's head football coach and athletic director. Since leaving Carlisle, Welch had earned his law degree at Dickinson College and served valiantly in the U.S. Army during World War I. After his discharge, Welch found success in the coaching ranks, beginning with Washington State in 1919, and later at Randolph-Macon College and the University of Virginia. In 1933, he assumed the reins at Haskell Institute, replacing his former Carlisle teammate, Lone Star Dietz, who had left the school after accepting the head coaching position with the Boston Braves of the National Football League.[4]

The press, of course, played up the contest between mentor and student, which was to become a fairly common occurrence as more and more of Warner's players found their way into the coaching ranks. "Teacher and pupil of 20 years ago meet on the gridiron tonight as enemies," wrote the *Lawrence Daily Journal-World.* "Two decades back, Welch learned his football at the old Carlisle Indian school with Warner as coach. Tonight, he is confident his Braves can take his old teacher's team."

Welch's confidence notwithstanding, the Indians were totally outclassed and fell in a rout, 31–0. The Owls then defeated West Virginia, 13–7, but lost to Bucknell, 7–0, a week later. They rebounded to beat Drake (20–14) and Washington & Jefferson (13–0), then lost the season finale against Villanova, 24–0.

It had been an up-and-down season for the Temple football team. The 5–3 final record was disappointing when compared to the 5–1–2 finish they had posted the year before under Heinie Miller. Though this mark was certainly not in keeping with the quick turnarounds Warner engineered in the first seasons at his three previous stops (10–1 at Carlisle, 8–0 at Pitt, and 7–1–1 at Stanford), he was nevertheless happy with the results. Warner felt this team was on the verge of becoming the power Temple fans and officials were expecting him to make it. He was, it turned out, just a year away.

The Owls were entering the 1934 season with the luxury of having 21 lettermen returning with a full year's training in the Warner system, and optimism was swirling throughout the campus. "The upperclassmen were now more experienced," the coach recalled, "and their confidence and superb execution was beginning to show."[5] Adding to Warner's sanguinity was the arrival of triple-threat fullback David "Dynamite Dave" Smukler, a sophomore transferring to Temple after spending his freshman year at the University of Missouri. It wasn't long before Warner was exalting the six-foot, one-inch, 212-pound Smukler as his next great back. By season's end, the coach would be comparing him favorably to Ernie Nevers and Jim Thorpe.

When the Owls opened the season against Virginia Tech on September 29, however, it was halfback Danny Testa making headlines for scoring three touchdowns in a 34–0 whitewash. The win gave Warner enough confidence to leave captain Pete Stevens to run things the following week against Texas A&M while he and Fred Swan traveled to Columbus to scout Ohio State and Chuck Winterburn was in Morgantown scouting West Virginia. The coachless Owls didn't miss a beat, easily defeating the Aggies, 40–6. Warner was back on the sidelines a week later when Temple tied Indiana, 6–6. The Owls then defeated West Virginia (28–13) before traveling to Milwaukee, Wisconsin, for their only scheduled road game against Marquette, winning 28–6. They returned home to defeat Holy Cross (14–0). A week later, the boys in cherry and white faced a plucky squad from Pittsburgh-based Carnegie Tech. With Smukler hurling three touchdown passes, two of which went to Horace Mowrey (who also had a 64-yard interception return for a score), the Owls rolled to an easy 34–6 win.

Smukler had been enjoying a fine season, though a nagging knee injury had prevented him from reaching the high bar his coach had set for him back in training camp. But his breakout performance against Carnegie Tech finally opened the eyes of napping newspapermen, who were now scurrying to get some sort of scoop on the husky fullback. Warner, who obviously knew a good football player when he saw one, raised the eyebrows of more than a few reporters when he boldly declared Smukler to potentially be the greatest player he ever coached. Said Warner: "He is a better fullback now than Nevers was in Nevers' sophomore year. Dave is the best sophomore fullback I have ever seen. He may become the greatest fullback I have ever seen, a greater player than Nevers or Jim Thorpe."[6]

Smukler continued his brilliance when Temple faced Villanova, carrying the ball 29 times for 154 yards and a touchdown, and adding a field goal and extra point in guiding his team to a 22–0 win. The Owls then finished the regular season undefeated by playing Bucknell to a scoreless tie on Thanksgiving Day.

The headlines the Owls were making had not gone unnoticed by the Mid-Winter Sports Association of New Orleans, which had for several years been planning to stage a season-ending football extravaganza along the lines of the West Coast's Rose Bowl, pitting the best northern team against the best team from the South. The very first Sugar Bowl, as it was to be called, was finally going to take place at Tulane Stadium in New Orleans on January 1, 1935. The association's executive board selected 9–1 Tulane University to represent the South in the inaugural game, and invited undefeated Temple to provide the opposition. Induced by a $15,000 guarantee, and the prospect of gaining credibility for their nascent football program, Temple officials readily agreed.

The coach, however, did not seem so keen on accepting the invitation. The publicly reticent Warner may have felt his team wasn't quite ready yet, or that they didn't belong on the same field as Tulane's formidable Green Wave. Perhaps he was using a bit of psychology to appeal to his players' collective pride. Whatever his true feelings may have been, Pop was acting as if he wished the game had never been arranged. "Yea, we had a pretty good season," he told reporters in the days leading up to the contest, "but it's just like those [expletive] alumni to get me into this thing against Tulane. We'll get massacree-ed *(sic)*, and they'll be after me worse'n ever."[7]

With more than 22,000 football fanatics on hand, the first Sugar Bowl Game kicked off in New Orleans on New Year's Day, 1935. Warner's boys dominated early on, with Smukler tossing a touchdown strike to John Stonik in the opening frame and then running 25 yards for another score in the second to give the Owls a 14–0 lead before halftime. But Tulane stormed back to tie it up at 14–14 midway through the third. The Green Wave took the lead on a touchdown pass with about three minutes remaining in regulation. The Owls blocked the extra point try, leaving them trailing by six. They made a valiant march down the field on the ensuing drive, but were unable to get to the end zone before the final whistle. Tulane University staked its claim to history with a 20–14 win.

Despite the loss, the 1934 season had been a resounding success for both the Temple football team and its famous coach. The Owls' undefeated regular schedule had brought them into the national spotlight, and would have been Pop's sixth unbeaten campaign had they not played the Sugar Bowl game. Nevertheless, being invited to the bowl game provided Warner with vindication against critics who had been declaring him over the hill when he was still at Stanford. In just two seasons, Warner had taken Temple from its place as a regional power to one of national prominence. These were indeed exciting times for followers of the Temple football team, but they proved to be short-lived. With the level of competition from rival schools increasing and recruitment efforts falling short, the team's fortunes eventually turned and the Owls would find themselves losing ground with each successive season.

Temple faithful had reason to be optimistic when the 1935 season began. The Owls were coming off a brilliant 7–1–2 season that brought national attention and earned them an invitation to the very first Sugar Bowl Game. With two full seasons of training in the Warner system and Dave Smukler returning with a clean bill of health, the team seemed poised to reach unprecedented heights in the upcoming campaign.

The Owls burst from the gate by crushing Philadelphia's St. Joseph's College (coached by former Temple head man Heinie Miller), 51–0, in the season opener. Smukler was spectacular, scoring three touchdowns and throwing for two more. The Owls then rolled over Centre (25–13), Texas A&M (14–0) and Vanderbilt (6–3) before heading out on the first extended road trip (two games) of the Warner era. The streak continued as the Owls defeated Carnegie Tech (13–0) and West Virginia (19–6). Warner's boys were riding high when they returned to Philadelphia at 6–0, but when they met up with Michigan State in Week 7, the master of chicanery had met his match.

Finding new ways to flout rules and hoodwink opponents was both a vocation and an avocation for the Old Fox. It was not for nothing that his admirers—along with some of his detractors, no doubt—had conferred that sobriquet upon him. Warner's formations, shifts and trick plays had been wreaking havoc on opposing defenses for decades. Since the Owls' jerseys did not have numbers on the fronts, the Michigan State players had trouble discerning which players were which in Pop's perplexing schemes. Sid Wagner, the Spartans' star guard, devised a solution. Early in the game, Wagner grabbed a piece of black chalk from the sidelines and tucked it under the cuff of his own jersey. At the end of each play, Wagner drew a large X on the Temple backs' jerseys as they lay prone on the turf. "After the first few scrimmages, every Temple back had a large black X on his white jersey front," the Fredericksburg *Free Lance-Star* reported. "Also, Wagner was armed with a piece of lip stick he was going to use if Pop crossed him up and numbered his boys."

Wagner's strategy worked like a charm, neutralizing the effectiveness of the Owls' shifts and allowing the Spartans to pull off a 14–7 upset win. The Owls bounced back to defeat Marquette (26–6), but then lost to Villanova (21–14) and Bucknell (7–6) to finish the season with seven wins and three losses.

While 7–3 was not good enough to earn a bowl invitation, Pop was pleased nevertheless for the fact that it had been earned against what he felt was an unusually tough schedule. Temple officials were equally pleased, and demonstrated their gratitude by offering to extend the coach's current contract for another two seasons. Warner was loath, however, to sign an extension due to a degenerative hip injury that was causing great discomfort and making it difficult for him to get around. He had sustained the injury while on a hunting trip in South Carolina some 30 years earlier. The condition had worsened over the past ten years, and by this time Pop was able to ambulate only with the aid of a cane. He wasn't sure he was going to be able to remain upright at all beyond his current contract, which ran through the 1937 season. He was no longer able to stalk the practice field like he had in his early days, and was now more likely to assume a spot on the coach's platform and remain there for the duration. If he felt the need to get closer to the action, he would gingerly mount a horse and steer it up and down the field.[8]

Warner was also growing tired of the incessant travel that went along with coaching a major college football team. He loved being back east and within driving distance of the family farm in Springville, but ultimately longed to settle down once and for all in his adopted home town of Palo Alto, California. Still, there was a nagging feeling he still had not achieved all he had set out to when he took over Temple's football program three years earlier. After mulling it over for another year, Pop finally agreed to a two-year extension at the end of the 1936 season.

As expected, the Owls breezed through the first part of their 1936 slate by knocking off St. Joseph's College (18–0), Centre (50–7), Mississippi (12–7) at home before heading to Chestnut Hill, Massachusetts, for their

first road game of the year against Boston College. This contest marked
the first meeting between two coaching legends in Warner and Gilmour
Dobie, in his debut season at BC after 16 years and two national championships at Cornell. Despite his successes, Dobie was known for a dour
countenance that earned him the regrettable nickname of "Gloomy Gil."
He had entered the coaching profession in 1906 and had known Warner
for several years, but until this year had never faced him on the field of
play. By the time this one was over, Dobie was wishing their first meeting
had been indefinitely postponed, as Temple prevailed for a 14–0 win to
remain undefeated.

Temple's great start was spoiled a week later, however, when the team
returned home and was shocked by Carnegie Tech, 7–0, providing the Tar-
tans with their only win of the season. The Owls bounced back to beat Holy
Cross (3–0) and tie Michigan State (7–7), but then dropped two straight
to Villanova (6–0) and Iowa (25–0). The 25-point loss to Iowa represented
the team's worst setback in three years. The tailspin continued with a
scoreless tie against Bucknell and a season-ending loss to St. Mary's.

Another promising start had gone to waste, as the Owls went 2–3–
2 down the stretch to finish 6–3–2, the worst record posted by the team
in Warner's four years.

Temple fans were reserved in their enthusiasm as they watched their
team open the 1937 campaign at 2–0–1. Since the team's boosters had
seen the Owls squander fast starts in each of the last two campaigns, their
reservations were certainly justified.

The Owls' first road trip of the year took them to Chestnut Hill to
face the Eagles of Boston College. Though they didn't lose, the game was
a boring affair that resulted in Temple's second scoreless tie of the campaign. Syndicated columnist Red Smith recalled the scene in the locker
room as two-fourths of football's living Mount Rushmore rehashed the
farce over which they had just presided. "Pop and Gil sat having a bit of
something to warm their bones, glowering stone-faced across a table, each
telling the other how lucky he'd been to let off with a tie. Gil said BC had
worked all season on a long gainer which no defense could stop but he
hadn't the heart to use it against his old friend. Pop said that was good,
because Temple had been prepared to retaliate with some dazzling forward
laterals that never missed. They made a picture—two old guys who probably had no wish to add to each other's troubles, positively had no taste
for losing, and wouldn't admit how ticked they both were with the tie."[9]

The up-and-down season continued as the Owls rebounded to beat Carnegie Tech (7–0), then tied Holy Cross (0–0), lost to Michigan State (13–6), played Bucknell to another scoreless tie, and then closed out the season with the team's worst loss in the Warner era, a 33–0 drubbing from Villanova.

It had been one of the strangest campaigns of Warner's career. While suffering just two losses could be viewed as an improvement over the previous season (three), the Owls played in four scoreless ties and were shut out a total of five times. This team simply lacked offensive punch, an area in which Warner had always excelled. The final straw, however, was the season-ending walloping the Owls received at the hands of Villanova. Predictably, Temple alumni—just like their Stanford counterparts before them—were becoming impatient. It seemed clear to them that the pace and scope of directing a major college football program were becoming too much for the gimpy, overweight, 66-year old coach.

In hopes of finding a resolution, Temple officials decided to exercise the disability clause that had been written into Warner's contract and forced him to undergo a physical examination by Dr. John Royal Moore, the internationally renowned orthopedic surgeon at Temple University Hospital who doubled as the football team's physician. According to a story appearing in the *Philadelphia Evening Bulletin*, Dr. Moore had come to the conclusion that Warner was "in no condition to actively assume charge of a football squad. Warner has a hip ailment, finding it necessary to lean heavily on a cane. When he gets up from a chair it requires a great deal of effort. The physicians said they were certain Warner suffered excruciating pain."[10]

Despite these findings—and the mounting concerns of school administrators and alumni—Warner insisted he could continue at least another year.

When Pop Warner called in his squad to open the Owls' training camp on September 5, 1938, there were suspicions that it was going to be his last. Despite having signed a contract extension that was supposed to carry him through the '39 season and his declarations to the contrary, it was obvious to anyone observing Temple workouts that the findings of his recent medical examination were spot on. The man clearly was no longer able to bear the physical demands of the job. Julian Ertz, a reserve fullback that season, recollected that Warner did not stand unless aided by his ubiquitous cane. The coach, said Ertz, would simply perch himself upon the raised platform and observe the entire practice from there. "On each play, he knew what all twenty-two players had done," Ertz recalled. "He'd point and say very softly, 'OK, so-and-so, you didn't do this. And so-and-so, you didn't do that.' He never gave you hell in front of the other players. He was always analyzing." And though he no longer stormed up and down the practice field the way he once did, there was at least one thing that hadn't changed: "He always had a cigarette," said Ertz. "He'd finish one and use it to light the next."[11]

The season started out, appropriately enough, like a sentimental journey for Warner, since the first two opponents were being coached by men who once played for the Old Fox. First up was Albright College, coached by Lone Star Dietz, the former Carlisle tackle, assistant coach and artist. Despite keeping the score close, the final stats tell a different story. Temple outgained the Lions 222 yards to 23, while tallying 13 first downs to Albright's two. But Dietz' plucky defenders broke only once, and that was all the Owls needed to escape with a narrow 6–0 victory.

Next on the slate was his former team, the Pittsburgh Panthers, who were still under the watchful eye of Pop's most successful protégé, Jock Sutherland. This time, the student got the better of the teacher as the Panthers rolled to an easy 28–6 win.

If the first two games were a sentimental journey for Pop, the rest of the campaign was more like a bad dream, for the loss against Pitt was just the beginning of what proved to be the worst season for a Warner-coached team in 24 years. The Owls would go 2–5–1 the rest of the way to finish with 3–6–1, the most losses of any team with which he was associated since losing eight games in 1914, his final season at Carlisle. When a reporter dared ask Warner if was considering retirement after seeing his team suffer an embarrassing 33–0 loss to Holy Cross on November 5, the coach exploded.

"No, I'm not retiring!" Warner bellowed. "What gave you that idea? I'm not retiring as long as I'm sure I can do justice to a coaching job, and as long as I have a coaching job. Right now I feel swell. I'll keep coaching until I'm past seventy—if I still have a job."[12]

Things did not get much better over the next two weeks as Temple fell 20–7 to Villanova and 10–0 to Michigan. But the Owls, as if sensing this was going to be their coach's last hurrah, saved their best performance of the year for the season finale, scoring a resounding 20–12 victory at the University of Florida. Jimmy Powers paced Temple with a 102-yard return of a kickoff in the second quarter.

Though it wasn't known publicly at the time, Warner had already discussed with Temple officials the possibility that he would retire at season's end, though both sides had agreed to wait until March 1 before making a final decision. But with some school boosters and alumni grumbling over their team's recent downturn, Yeomans and university president Charles Beury sought a more expedient resolution that could make all interested parties happy. What they came up with was an idea that they hoped would gently nudge Warner toward the door while allowing the proud coach to pass through it on a positive note with his dignity intact. Yeomans and Beury proposed that Warner retire at this time, despite having a year left on his contract and, if he agreed to do so, the school would honor the final year of his pact.

In late January, Yeomans telephoned Warner at his home in Palo Alto to discuss the proposal. Whether the idea was presented as an ultimatum is not clear, but it didn't take Warner long to respond. The next morning, January 28, Yeomans entered his Philadelphia office to find a telegram awaiting him. It was the coach's resignation. In it, Pop explained that he saw no need for further delay.

But as it turned out, Warner was playing Temple every bit as much as they were playing him. In a private letter written shortly afterward to *Pittsburgh Press* sports editor Chester L. Smith, Pop revealed that he never intended for his resignation from Temple to be a permanent retirement. Rather, he saw another season of futility on the horizon and felt the offer given by Yeomans and Beury was his chance to get while the getting was good. "My resignation did not necessarily mean that I was retiring from active coaching," he wrote. "I just did not want to go through another losing season which that suicide schedule was likely to bring about. It is no fun coaching a losing team, and my reputation could not stand many more seasons like last year. I do not want anything published that might displease Temple because they treated me fine—that's why I did not announce my reasons for resigning."[13]

When reached for comment, Warner publicly denied having any immediate plans despite rampant speculation he would be returning to Palo Alto in the role of advisory coach of the Stanford University football team. While Pop did make his way back to the West Coast, rumors of a return to Stanford were put to rest on March 1, 1939, when it was announced he had accepted a similar position at nearby San Jose State University. San Jose State was coached by Dudley DeGroot, who had been Stanford's first All-America footballer back in 1922, Warner's first year as advisory coach with the Cardinals. Since becoming head coach of the Spartans in 1932, DeGroot had delivered a solid 47–19–7 record while employing Warner's famous system.

"I accepted the invitation of San Jose State," he explained, "only after DeGroot agreed to remain on the job as head coach. I will act in an advisory capacity. DeGroot suggested I advise on offensive work, and I will be very happy to do this. I believe it will be lots of fun and I am glad I will be back in the harness." Since San Jose State played a large number of Friday night games, and its campus was less than a half-hour's drive from Warner's residence, this job would allow him ample opportunity to attend other games in the area over the weekend. "At the same time," he added, "I will be out here on the coast where I want to live."[14]

Surprisingly, Warner declined remuneration for his services, asking only that the school cover his expenses for travel and meals. He didn't need the money—he still had a year's salary from Temple coming to him.

TWELVE

San Jose State

The arrival of Pop Warner as a member of the San Jose State coaching staff provided an immediate boost for the school's football program. Not only did Warner's name attract national media attention, it acted as a magnet for a large number of area players who transferred to State with the hope of playing for the most famous coach in the nation.

"Glenn S. (Pop) Warner pulled on his cleats again today and took over his new job as advisory coach at San Jose State College," observed the *Berkeley Daily Gazette.* "Nearly 80 candidates answered Warner's whistle at the opening of the eight weeks' spring training season, many of them transfers lured from junior colleges by his name. Thirteen transfers registered Tuesday. Warner preceded the training season with a chalkboard talk, outlining his new ideas for the 1939 season."[1]

After just a single day assessing the squad, Warner was expressing his satisfaction with the talent and the prospects for the upcoming campaign. "Dud has plenty of fine material and from what I've seen today, we should have a great team. The boys are well versed in my system. This makes it easy to drill new plays and formations."[2]

If there were any doubts that Warner's system was still relevant as he entered his 45th year stalking gridiron sidelines, they were obliterated within the first half-dozen weeks of the season as the Spartans rolled to a 6–0 record and outscored their opponents by a whopping 157–6. The highlight of the year, as far as Warner was concerned, came in Week 7 when the Spartans met up with the small, Stockton, California-based school commonly known as the College of the Pacific, which was currently being coached by Pop's old rival, Amos Alonzo Stagg. The two had last met on the field 32 years earlier—November 23, 1907, to be exact—when Warner's Carlisle Indians visited the University of Chicago and spoiled the Maroons' otherwise perfect season with an 18–4 upset win that he considered one of the greatest of his career.

Lost in the media hype stirred up in anticipation of the clash of the aging titans was the fact that DeGroot, not Warner, was the Spartans' head coach. Newspapers made so much of the matchup between Warner and the 77-year-old Stagg that DeGroot was virtually forgotten. "Far from the scenes of their greatest triumphs, in a tiny stadium on the campus of a tiny college," remarked the *Sarasota Herald-Tribune*, "two old men will pace the sidelines this week during a game that will add a colorful bit of history to the spirit of football."

The underdog Tigers took the game's first lead on a field goal early in the opening frame, but that was all the offense they would muster. The Spartans responded with 13 unanswered points and cruised to an easy win. As the teams made their way toward the dressing rooms at the conclusion, Warner and Stagg met at midfield and shared an embrace.

"Well, Glenn," said Stagg, "we were simply out-played. The better team won."

"Pshaw!" Warner responded. "Just a bit of luck, Lonny. It was a fine game your boys played."[3]

The Spartans continued their winning ways, defeating their final six opponents to finish the season with a spotless 13–0 mark while outscoring them by an aggregate 324–29! Warner had proven yet again that, despite being of feeble body, he was still capable of putting together a highly effective offensive machine. At season's end, Pop let it be known just how much he was enjoying being back on the Coast. "I have enjoyed my work at San Jose even more than I figured I would when I reached an agreement with Dud DeGroot last spring. The entire setup has been highly satisfactory and I hope to start in next season where I left off this year."[4]

Ever since Knute Rockne's untimely death in March 1931, his family, friends and nearly everyone associated with Notre Dame had been clamoring for a movie that would memorialize the iconic figure for future generations. Nine years to the month after the tragic plane crash that killed Rockne and seven others in a Kansas wheatfield, Warner Brothers studios began production. Veteran actor Pat O'Brien was cast in the titular role, with a young thespian named Ronald Reagan portraying Rockne's immensely talented—but equally troubled—halfback, George Gipp.

Pop Warner and three other famous coaches were invited to play themselves in a dramatic scene in which Rockne gives an impassioned speech before a board of college educators who were discussing the possibility of banning the sport of football. In mid–May 1940, Warner gath-

OFFICIAL PROGRAM ◼ FIFTEEN CENTS

The American Way
45 YEARS OF COACHING

GLENN S. "POP" WARNER

WILLAMETTE U.
VS.
SAN JOSE STATE

MULTNOMAH STADIUM   ::   8:00 P. M.   ::   OCTOBER 4, 1940

He wasn't the head coach, but who would have known? Game Program featuring Pop Warner on the cover—San Jose State versus Willamette University, October 4, 1940. (Courtesy Alan V. Manchester, Springville, New York.)

ered with fellow grid mentors Amos Alonzo Stagg, Howard Jones and William H. Spaulding (of UCLA) on a Warner Bros. soundstage to shoot their parts. Each coach had at least one speaking line in the fictionalized sequence (Stagg had two). Despite the brevity of their parts, the four lent an air of believability to the movie simply by their appearance in it.

Knute Rockne: All-American opened the following October to rave reviews and packed theaters, and was subsequently voted the second-best-liked film of 1940 by the American Institute of Public Opinion. The film remains culturally significant, as evidenced by its selection in 1997 for preservation in the Library of Congress' National Film Registry.[5]

Unfortunately for Pop, the Spartans were not—as he had hoped—going to be starting the 1940 season where they left off in 1939. On February 3, San Jose State head coach Dudley DeGroot announced he was leaving the school to take the same post at the University of Rochester. This came as a blow to Warner, who had accepted the job with the Spartans in large part because of his history with DeGroot. To replace DeGroot, however, the school hired another student of the Warner system in Ben Winkelman. Winkelman had been, until recently, serving as an assistant at Stanford under Tiny Thornhill.

With Winkelman at the helm and Warner guiding the offense, the Spartans tore through the 1940 schedule with a 10–1 record. The highlight of the season was a 28–7 win over Stagg's College of the Pacific eleven on November 8.

As had been the custom at the end of the past several seasons, speculation regarding Warner's future began circulating throughout the football world. As the summer months passed, however, San Jose State officials had no reason to believe that Warner was not going to be returning for a third season as the team's offensive coordinator. But all guesswork ended a week before the school's football camp was set to open. In a letter sent from his summer home in Springville on August 21, 1941, the 70-year-old coach advised San Jose State that he would not be returning. He planned, said Warner, to take a year off to "travel and loaf."[6]

Whether he intended for this to signal an official retirement is uncertain, for within days of resigning his post at San Jose State, Warner was telling reporters that he was hoping for one more opportunity to coach at a big school with good material. But the phone never rang, and Pop Warner never coached another down of football.

THIRTEEN

Retirement
and Legacy

Upon Pop's resignation from San Jose State, he and wife Tibb retreated to their home on Escobita Avenue in Palo Alto. The coach became a familiar figure at college football games in and around the city. Well into his 70s, he was known to attend as many as three games in an autumn weekend. "I'm just a grandstand quarterback now," he told a reporter from the *Pittsburgh Post-Gazette* in 1948, "but I don't miss a game if I can help it. There's plenty of football around Palo Alto and I have been averaging about three games a week."

Observing so many games allowed the Old Fox to keep up with the latest trends in the sport. Every football season he would be tracked down by reporters seeking his opinion about some rule change or innovation, many which he felt were actually ruining the game, such as the resuscitated T formation and the adoption of unlimited substitution. The modern T had been gaining in acceptance in recent years, eclipsing the popularity of old offensive attacks such as the Notre Dame box shift and Warner's venerable single and double wings. "The T formation … is ancient stuff," Pop argued. "When you have superior material, any formation will work." The double wing, he insisted, "has more striking power than any system in football. There are a lot of coaches using the double wing today, but few can teach it."

As for unlimited substitution, Pop believed "the rules committee made a bad mistake when they put in that unlimited substitutions rule. It will permit the coaches to run the game and it will slow it up. I believe it will benefit the smaller colleges where the squads are small, but the disadvantages and delay are too great."

Years after coaching his last game, Pop was still answering the inevitable question: Who was your greatest player: Jim Thorpe or Ernie Nevers?

**Pop Warner pictured during one of his frequent trips to his hometown of
Springville, New York, 1943. (Courtesy Alan V. Manchester, Springville, New
York.)**

Warner's opinion apparently had mellowed over the years, or he simply no longer wished to appear that he favored one over the other. Since 1925, he had repeatedly stated that Nevers was the best player he ever coached, but at the age of 77, Pop was singing a different tune. "Thorpe was the better man in the open and was more versatile while no one could punch a line like Nevers. Thorpe was the best all-time halfback and Nevers the best fullback."[1]

Regard for Pop within the football community remained strong. In July 1944, it was reported that Warner had turned down a $10,000 offer to coach the San Francisco Packers of the new professional Pacific Coast Football League. He declined the offer upon the advice of his doctor, who felt the coach was not physically up to it.

The Warners continued to travel between the West Coast and their childhood home town of Springville for several years, until Pop's bum hip made long-distance travel too uncomfortable for him to bear. Pop made his final sojourn to Western New York in 1948, at which time he sold off all of his holdings, including the Warner family home at 292 East Main Street. In October of that year, he attended a football game at the University of Pittsburgh between his former team and the Fighting Irish of Notre Dame. He had been invited as a guest of honor and was treated to a nostalgic weekend that included spending time with several of his former players, many of whom had come to town specifically for the occasion.

The same hip ailment that forced him to decline a lucrative coaching job and prevented extended travel eventually made it impossible for Pop to attend even local football games as a spectator. By the early 1950s, he was forced to retreat to his living room and tune in to whatever games were being broadcast live on television. It also prevented him from attending the world premiere of *Jim Thorpe: All-American*, the major motion picture based on the life of Pop's most famous protégé, whose profile had enjoyed a major resurgence since being named by the Associated Press as the greatest football player of the century and greatest male athlete of the half-century. The project had been in development for several years, but Warner Bros. Studios—the same company that produced the Knute Rockne biopic a decade earlier—did not begin production until the summer of 1950. Pop was given the opportunity to review the script prior to the start of filming. He sent a note to the studio stating that he approved of "the very nice way my part in the story has been handled."[2]

Jim Thorpe: All-American starred Burt Lancaster in the title role and veteran character actor and three-time Academy Award nominee Charles Bickford as Warner. Bickford narrated the movie from Warner's point of view, telling the somewhat fictionalized story of Thorpe's athletic rise and fall. It opened in August 1951 to mixed reviews, but proved wildly popular at the box office.

Pop was able to endure one last long-distance excursion when he traveled to Cincinnati, Ohio, in early 1952 to accept the Coach of All the Years Award from the National Collegiate Athletic Association. The award was the brainchild of Columbia coach Lou Little, who conceived the idea of polling active coaches for their choice of which living coach they felt had done the most to advance the game of football. The Old Fox was said to have won easily. The ceremony was held on January 10 at the Netherlands Plaza Hotel in downtown Cincinnati. Dudley DeGroot, Pop's former player and onetime head coach at San Jose State, presented his old mentor with the bronze plaque. Warner, however, might not even have made the trip had it not been for the fact that he was accompanied by current Stanford head man Chuck Taylor, who was being honored by the NCAA as Coach of the Year.[3]

Though he ultimately would lose his ability to travel, Pop never lost his passion for the arts. He continued to paint watercolors and carve walking canes in his Palo Alto home until the very end. Several articles written about Pop in his latter years featured photographs of him tinkering in his workshop—whether applying brush strokes to a new landscape or perhaps a rasp to a new cane—watched over by his trusted canine companion, Teddy.

By 1954, decades of chain-smoking finally caught up with him. In July of that year, Pop entered Palo Alto Hospital for an operation to remove a cancerous tumor in his throat. A month later, Warner appeared to be improving, but lapsed into a coma in mid–August. On September 6, a hospital spokesman announced that Warner was at death's door. "He probably will go within the next day or two. Mr. Warner has been critically ill for some time, but he has shown extraordinary persistence."[4] But that legendary fortitude that carried him to the pinnacle of his profession finally gave out on the afternoon of September 7. With his wife Tibb, niece Jane, and friends Mr. and Mrs. Ben Winkelman at his bedside, Warner passed away quietly at the age of 83.

Condolences and memorials poured in from across the nation. From Amos Alonzo Stagg: "He was a great leader in football and one of the excellent creators. He was not just a coach but helped develop part of the game." From Ernie Nevers: He was the greatest, that's all. He could fix a brace better than a doctor; he had more psychology than the trainer; he had more energy than the student manager—and as for football, no one knew as much as Pop."[5] Wrote Claude Thornhill: "Pop was undoubtedly one of the greatest coaches that ever lived. He was like a big, warm-hearted farmer who was never severe in his coaching. We always had a lot of fun playing for Pop."[6]

A funeral was held at Palo Alto's First Methodist Church under the auspices of the local Masonic Lodge, of which Warner was a long-standing member. Pallbearers were all former Stanford football players, including Nevers, Bill Corbus, Jack Holwerda, Jim Lawson, Hal McCreery, Ted Shipkey and Robert Sims. Warner's remains were cremated and flown back to Springville, accompanied by Ben Winkelman, his friend and head coach in Pop's final year at San Jose State. After a memorial service at the Weismantel Funeral Home—located just a few doors from the Main Street house in which he spent his childhood—Pop's ashes were buried in the family plot in Maplewood Cemetery alongside his father, mother and maternal grandparents.

Tibb outlived her husband by seven years, passing away on November 10, 1961, at the age of 92. Her body was returned to Springville and laid to rest next to Pop.

Within days of the announcing his resignation from San Jose State, Warner was letting it be known that he was hoping for one more chance to be a head coach. He had been seeing his single and double wing formations supplanted by the modern T formation. The T had been enjoying a surge in popularity in recent years, culminating in 1940 when Clark Shaughnessy's Stanford Indians used it to go undefeated and claim victory in that season's Rose Bowl Game. Shaughnessy had coached the University of Chicago from 1933 to '39, and during that time had become acquainted with George Halas, owner and head coach of the NFL's Chicago Bears, and a fellow T adherent. Halas brought Shaughnessy in to help prepare the Bears' game plan for their meeting with the Washington Redskins in the 1940 title game. The Bears completely dominated the single-wing based Redskins, rolling to a 73–0 rout that still stands as the most lopsided score in NFL playoff history. Despite the implications of these monumental victories, Warner insisted that his system, if properly executed, was superior to the T. "I'd like to prove," he said, "that the double wing style of attack is the best system in football."[7]

Unfortunately, he would never get the chance. Warner, like the offensive system that bore his name, was by this time cast as a relic in the sport which he once was considered the greatest innovator. The single and double wing formations were eventually tossed aside by a younger generation of coaches who favored the T, until only a handful of college and high school teams were still using it. The last pro team employing the single wing as its primary offense was the 1951 Pittsburgh Steelers, who abandoned its use after going 4–7–1 and tying for last in the league in total points scored.

Many successful coaches of the early part of the century had direct ties to Warner, either as players or assistants, and most applied his methods or philosophies to their own coaching styles. Warner's coaching tree includes several men who enjoyed at least a fair amount of success, among them Charley Bowser (played under Warner at Pitt—later head coach at Bowdoin and Pitt), Clifford "Doc" Carlson (played for Warner at Pitt—later became a very successful basketball coach at Pitt, winning two national championships in 32 years), Dudley DeGroot (played at Stanford while Warner was advisory coach in 1922—later head coach at San Jose State, Rochester, West Virginia and New Mexico, as well as the Washington Redskins of the NFL and the Los Angeles Dons of the AAFC), Jimmy DeHart (played for Warner at Pitt—later head coach at Washington & Lee and Duke), Lone Star Dietz (played for and assisted Warner at Carlisle and Stanford—later head coach at Washington State, the Mare Island Marines, Purdue, Louisiana Tech, Haskell Indian, and Albright, as well as the Boston Redskins of the NFL), Albert Exendine (played for and assisted Warner at Carlisle—later head coach at Georgetown, Washington State, Occidental, Northeastern State, Oklahoma A&M), James Herron (played and assisted Warner at Pitt—later head coach at Indiana, Duke and Washington & Lee), Andy Kerr (assistant under Warner at Pitt and Stanford—later head coach at Stanford, Washington & Jefferson, Colgate, and Lebanon Valley), Ernie Nevers (played for and assisted Warner at Stanford—later head coach at Lafayette, as well as the Duluth Eskimos and Chicago Cardinals of the NFL), Ted Shipkey (played for Warner at Stanford—later head coach at Arizona State, New Mexico and Montana), Jock Sutherland (played for Warner and assisted at Pitt—later head coach at Lafayette and Pitt, as well as the Brooklyn Dodgers and Pittsburgh Steelers of the NFL), Fred Swan (played for Warner at Stanford and later assisted at Stanford and Temple—later head coach at Temple), Claude Thornhill (assistant under Warner at Pitt and Stanford—later head coach at Stanford), Jim Thorpe (played for Warner at Carlisle—later head coach of NFL Cleveland Indians and Oorang Indians), Bill Warner (Pop's younger brother who spent several seasons as a guest coach under him at Carlisle—later head coach at Cornell, North Carolina, Colgate, St. Louis, and Oregon), and Gus Welch (played for Warner at Carlisle—later head coach at Washington State, Randolph Macon, Virginia, Haskell Indian, and American University).

There are still a handful of high school and college teams employing the single wing today, as the attack enjoys a rabid following among coaches who adhere to it in almost cult-like fashion. Each year, several of these grid mentors gather at what is called the National Single Wing Symposium in Liberty, Missouri, to watch old black-and-white game film, study ancient playbooks, and share thoughts and tips on the formation that ruled the football world so many decades ago.[8]

Even at the NFL level, supposedly innovative coaches have in recent years injected elements of Warner's basic concepts into their playbooks with great success. "A century after Pop Warner's eternal tinkering with formations evolved into the single wing," said noted Carlisle scholar Tom Benjey, "coaches at all levels saw the advantages of snapping the ball to a back who would run with it or pass it while gaining a blocker lost with conventional formations. Some called the version they used the Wildcat formation." Indeed, nearly every pro team used some variant of the single wing at some point during the early part of the 21st century. "It will be interesting," Benjey continued, "to see how long NFL coaches run the Wildcat or other versions of the single wing before they admit that the fundamental formation was developed a century ago by Pop Warner for the Carlisle Indians. Some think that NFL coaches will continue to obfuscate this point so as not to appear to be behind the times by 100 years."[9]

Aside from his signature single and double wing formations, Warner is credited with either conceiving or significantly improving several elements of the game, including the three-point stance for backfield men, the cross-body (or "Indian") block, the bootleg play, the screen pass, improvements to shoulder and thigh pads, improvements to tackling dummies and blocking sleds, and the use of deception over brute strength to gain the advantage over the opponent. Additionally, by representing Jim Thorpe in his negotiations with professional baseball teams in 1913, Pop pioneered the field of sports agency.

The Pop Warner Museum, located at the corner of Main and Franklin streets in Springville, serves as a shrine honoring the village's most famous son. The building, originally constructed in 1840, was purchased by the Concord Historical Society in 1953 utilizing funds provided by Pop and Tibb Warner to serve as a repository for Pop's Native American artifacts and area history items. The following May, it was officially designated as the Warner Museum and Historical Building. In addition to Pop's collections, there is also a room filled with artifacts and photos from his fabled coaching career, including the ring that was awarded posthumously when he was enshrined in the Greater Buffalo Sports Hall of Fame in 2001.

One of Warner's most enduring legacies was born on April 19, 1934, an unseasonably wintry night in the City of Brotherly Love. Warner had been invited, along with several other area college coaches, to speak at a banquet honoring the Junior Football Conference, a youth football league started in 1929 by a Philadelphia stockbroker named Joseph J. Tomlin five years earlier. However, because of the unexpected turn in the weather, only Warner managed to show. Since each coach was to speak for at least a few minutes, there was plenty of time to kill, so Warner regaled the crowd of some 800 players and coaches with an extemporaneous speech that touched on various subjects including sportsmanship, the value of athletic competition, and some of his own reminiscences from his long career. He stayed long enough to answer questions from the audience and sign autographs for any of the kids—or star-struck dads—who wanted a keepsake from this truly memorable evening.

Warner's appearance was a big hit, and it wasn't long before JFC officials were discussing the possibility of changing the organization's name to reflect an alliance with the great coach. Pop was agreeable, and in the fall of 1934 the 16-team Junior Football Conference became the Pop Warner Football Conference. Enrollment exploded. By 1938, the league had expanded to 157 member teams. In 1959, the organization was officially incorporated as a national non-profit organization under the name Pop Warner Little Scholars, Inc.

Today, there are approximately 325,000 boys and girls between the ages of 5 and 16 participating in Pop Warner leagues as players or cheerleaders in 42 states and several countries around the world. The mission of Pop Warner Little Scholars is "to enable young people to benefit from participation in team sports and activities in a safe and structured environment. Through this active participation, Pop Warner programs teach fundamental values, skills and knowledge that young people will use throughout their lives. Pop Warner seeks to provide fun athletic learning opportunities for children, while emphasizing the importance of academic success. Specifically, Pop Warner seeks to familiarize players and spirit participants with the fundamentals of football, cheerleading and dance. Pop Warner strives to inspire youth, regardless of race, creed or national origin, to practice the ideals of sportsmanship, scholarship and physical fitness as reflected in the life of the late Glenn Scobey 'Pop' Warner."[10]

※ ※ ※

Pop's last game as a head coach took place on December 3, 1938, with his Temple Owls defeating the Florida Gators, 20–12. That win "officially" gave the Old Fox a grand total of 313 for his career, placing him at the top of the list for career victories among major college coaches. Eight years later, however, Amos Alonzo Stagg came along and passed his old friend. The 84-year-old Stagg had stayed in the game just long enough—57 seasons—to reach 314 wins before calling it a career. But as they say, records are meant to be broken, and in 1981, Alabama head coach Paul "Bear" Bryant relegated Warner to third place by notching his 315th win. Bryant recorded eight more wins before retiring with a grand total of 323.

Bryant held a firm grip on the top spot until 1993. That's when author Mike Bynum, while conducting research for a book he was writing on Warner (*Pop Warner: Football's Greatest Teacher*), "discovered" 28 wins for which Pop had not been credited by the NCAA. Twenty-two of these victories were earned during Warner's time as head coach at Iowa State from 1895 through 1899. During this period, he was also coaching at Georgia (1895–96), Cornell (1897–98) and Carlisle (1899). In each of these seasons, Warner would oversee training camp at Iowa State before heading off to the other schools, leaving assistant coach Bert German to take charge of the team during the regular season. He would correspond regularly with German, advising him on matters of personnel, play calling, and so on. There were also five victories earned at Carlisle and another at Pittsburgh that, if credited, would give Pop a total of 341 and restore him to the number one spot.[11]

After reviewing Bynum's exhaustive research, however, the NCAA agreed that only the previously uncredited wins at Carlisle and Pitt should count, and not those earned at Iowa State. Since Warner was officially listed as coach at other schools, and was not present for Iowa State's 22 wins during that period, he could not be credited as the head coach of record. Those victories were to remain Bert German's.[12]

Although the six extra victories were not enough to vault Pop into first place among all-time coaches, they did at least move him past Stagg. However, the top spot has since been claimed by Joe Paterno, who collected 409 wins in 45 years at Penn State. The NCAA has also recognized Eddie Robinson's 408 wins at Grambling State, placing him second among Division 1 coaches, followed by Bobby Bowden (Samford University, West Virginia, Florida State) at 377, Bryant with 323, and Warner with 319.

Chapter Notes

Chapter One

1. Erasmus Briggs, *History of the Original Town of Concord, Erie County, New York*.
2. Springville Journal and Herald, January 20, 1916.
3. Alan V. Manchester, and David C. Batterson, *Springville: Images of America*, p. 62.
4. Mike Bynum, Pop Warner: Football's Greatest Teacher, p. 37.
5. Glenn S. Warner, "My Life in Football," pt. 2.
6. Alan V. Manchester, "Western New York's Pop Warner: Father of Modern Football," *Western New York Heritage*, Fall 2008.
7. Glenn S. Warner, "What's the Matter with Football?" *Collier's*, November 14, 1931.
8. Warner, "My Life In Football," pt. 1.
9. *Buffalo Evening News*, September 11, 1954. Waite was interviewed at the time of Warner's death.
10. *Sporting Life.* November 13, 1915.
11. Bynum, p. 39.
12. Warner, "My Life In Football," pt. 1.
13. Ibid., pt. 2.
14. Ibid., pt. 1.
15. Glenn S. Warner, "Battles of Brawn," *Collier's*, November 7, 1931.
16. Warner, "My Life in Football," pt. 2.
17. Ibid.

Chapter Two

1. www.CornellBigRed.com. Johanson, as captain of the Cornell football team, was also the *de facto* coach, as the team did not have a formal head coach until Marshall Newell was hired in 1894, Warner's senior year. This was customary in the early days of organized collegiate football.
2. It was not uncommon in those days for collegiate athletes to enjoy more than four years of varsity eligibility, as rules restricting players to four seasons were not adopted until the early part of the twentieth century.
3. Warner, "My Life in Football," pt. 3.
4. Warner, "What's the Matter with Football?" and "Football's New Deal," *Saturday Evening Post*, October 7, 1933.
5. Warner, "Battles of Brawn."
6. Warner, "My Life in Football," pt. 3.
7. Warner, "Battles of Brawn."
8. www.CornellBigRed.com. Cornell athletic teams did not adopt the nickname "Big Red" until 1905. Prior to that time, the school's teams were usually referred to as the "Red Men" or "Redmen."
9. Bynum, p. 46.
10. Glenn S. Warner, *Football Forty Years Ago*, newsreel film produced by Universal Pictures, 1936.
11. Some accounts credit Johanson with being the first to call Warner "Pop," while others give credit to one of the other players on the Cornell team. Warner's ghost-written autobiography states that he received the nickname from "one of my teammates" (Bynum, p. 53).
12. Warner, "My Life in Football," pt. 4.
13. CornellBigRed.com. The dressing quarters at Percy Field, home field for the Cornell football team during the 1890s, was named Witherbee Club House in George Witherbee's honor.

14. Ed Hardy, "He Kept Us on Our Toes," *Cornell Alumni News*, September 1992.

15. "The Greatest Player Ever?" *College Football Historical Society*, XI, no. III (May 1998).

16. *New York Times*, October 18, 1894.

17. The value of a touchdown at that time was four points.

18. Lars Anderson, Carlisle vs. Army: Jim Thorpe, Dwight Eisenhower, Pop Warner, and the Forgotten Story of Football's Greatest Battle, p. 30.

Chapter Three

1. Philadelphia Record, November 30, 1894.

2. *Springville News*, February 4, 1897.

3. Bynum, p. 57.

4. Powers, p. 12.

5. Bynum, p. 60.

6. Warner, "Battles of Brawn."

7. Warner, "My Life In Football," pt. 13.

8. Ibid., pt. 9.

9. Jack Newcombe, The Best of the Athletic Boys: The White Man's Impact on Jim Thorpe, p. 86.

10. Philip L. Brooks, Forward Pass: The Play that Saved Football, p. 22.

11. Warner, "My Life in Football," pt. 9.

12. Brooks, pp. 22–23.

13. Warner, "My Life in Football," pt. 9.

14. *Atlanta Constitution*, November 27, 1896.

15. Warner, "My Life in Football," pt. 9.

Chapter Four

1. *Springville News*, February 4, 1897.

2. Warner, "My Life in Football," pt. 11.

3. Bynum, p. 77.

4. *Washington Post*, April 5, 1914. Former Auburn quarterback Reynolds Tichenor claimed in interview that he had been part of a hidden ball play against Vanderbilt on November 9, 1895, predating Warner's use of the play by two years.

5. Whiting quote from Ed Hardy, "He Kept Us on Our Toes," *Cornell Alumni News*, September 1992.

6. *The Free Lance*, December 1897.

7. The Syracuse Standard, September 18, 1898.

8. Anderson, *Carlisle vs. Army*, p. 37.

9. Philadelphia Record, October 9, 1898.

10. Carlisle Daily Herald, October 9, 1898.

11. Bynum, p. 79.

12. Ibid., p. 80.

13. The Syracuse Standard, December 6, 1898

14. Warner, "My Life in Football," pt. 15.

15. Ibid.

16. Sally Jenkins, The Real All Americans: The Team That Changed a Game, a People, a Nation, pp. 20–22.

17. Warner, "My Life in Football," pt. 15.

Chapter Five

1. Historical information regarding the establishment and early years of the Carlisle Indian Industrial School derived from several sources, chiefly from Richard Henry Pratt, *Battlefield & Classroom: Four Decades with the American Indian, 1867–1904*; also Robert Wheeler, Tom Benjey, *Jim Thorpe: World's Greatest Athlete; Keep a-Goin': The Life of Lone Star Dietz*; and Sally Jenkins, *The Real All-Americans: The Team That Changed a Game, a People, a Nation*.

2. Pratt, p. 317.

3. Ibid., p. 318.

4. Ibid.

5. Ibid.

6. Glenn S. Warner, "The Indian Massacres," *Collier's*, October 17, 1931.

7. Ibid.

8. Glenn S. Warner, A Course in Football for Players and Coaches, p. 8.

9. Bynum, p. 84

10. Glenn S. Warner, "Heap Big Run-Most-Fast." *Collier's*, October 24, 1931.

11. Ibid.

12. Warner, "The Indian Massacres."

13. Ibid.

14. Moss Hall, Go, Indians: Stories of the Great Indian Athletes of the Carlisle School, p. 31.

15. Glenn S. Warner, "The Indian Massacres."

16. *Philadelphia Record*, October 29, 1899.

17. *New York Times*, November 11, 1899.

18. Warner, "The Indian Massacres."
19. *Philadelphia Record*, December 1, 1899.
20. Warner, "My Life in Football," pt. 20.
21. Jack Newcombe, *The Best of the Athletic Boys*, p. 86.
22. Warner, "The Indian Massacres."
23. *The Indian Helper*, January 17, 1900, and Warner, "The Indian Massacres."
24. *New York Times*, December 26, 1899.
25. The definitive score of this game remains a mystery. The 83–6 final given here is from Warner's ghost-written autobiography (Bynum). However, the game account given in the Carlisle school's newsletter, *The Indian Helper*, provides a final score of 86–6. The internet website for the College Football Data Warehouse (www.cfbdatawarehouse.com) gives the final score as 104–0.
26. Jenkins, p. 177.
27. Warner, "My Life in Football," pt. 18.
28. Glenn S. Warner, "Red Menaces," *Collier's*, October 31, 1931.
29. Warner, "My Life in Football," pt. 20.
30. Warner, Glenn S. "My Forty Years in Football," pt. 27.
31. Interview with Lois Batt Lane (cousin to Tibb Warner by marriage), March 2, 2015.
32. Observations on Tibb Warner drawn from letter written by Calvin W. Dunbar to Alan V. Manchester, May 12, 2005.
33. Warner, "Football's New Deal."
34. Newcombe, p. 64.
35. Jenkins, p. 189.
36. *Philadelphia Record*, October 28, 1900.
37. John S. Steckbeck, Fabulous Redmen: The Carlisle Indians and Their Famous Football Teams, p. 33.
38. Warner, "Heap Big Run-Most-Fast."
39. Steckbeck, p. 34.
40. *New York Times*, October 18, 1901.
41. *Buffalo Express*, October 20, 1901.
42. Warner, "My Forty Years in Football," pt. 27.
43. *New York Times*, November 3, 1901.
44. *New York Times*, November 12, 1901.
45. Walter Camp, "Football Development in 1901," *Outing*, November 1901.
46. Allison Danzig, Oh, How They Played the Game: The Early Years of Football and the Heroes Who Made It Great, p. 342.
47. *Springville News*, July 30, 1903.
48. *The* (Carlisle Indian School) *Arrow*, January 25, 1907.
49. Warner, "My Forty Years in Football," pt. 27.
50. www.baseball-reference.com.
51. Newcombe, p. 79.
52. Warner, "Heap Big Run-Most-Fast."
53. *New York Times*, November 29, 1902.
54. Glenn S. Warner, "What's the Matter with Football," *Collier's*, November 14, 1931.
55. PFRA Research, "The First Football World Series: Experiment in the Garden," *The Coffin Corner*.
56. Warner, "Battles of Brawn."
57. New York World and Syracuse Post Standard, December 30, 1902.
58. Warner, "My Life in Football," pt. 21.
59. *New York Times*, September 13, 1903.
60. Warner, "The Indian Massacres." Warner listed Johnson as the greatest quarterback ever to play at Carlisle.
61. Bynum, p. 105.
62. Ibid.
63. Newcombe, p. 79.
64. Warner, "The Indian Massacres."
65. Bynum, p. 107.
66. Ibid., p. 108.
67. Warner, "My Forty Years in Football," pt. 24.
68. Bynum, pp. 111–112.
69. Letter from Colonel Richard H. Pratt to Glenn S. Warner, February 1, 1904.

Chapter Six

1. *New York Times*, March 4, 1903
2. Tom Benjey, "Where Did Bill Warner Go?" (www.tombenjey.com) July 13, 2012.
3. Warner, "My Forty Years in Football," pt. 24.
4. Cornell Daily Sun, October 31, 1904.
5. Bynum, p. 112.
6. Warner, "My Forty Years in Football," pt. 26.
7. Jenkins, pp. 216–220.
8. Brooks, *Forward Pass*, p. 22.

9. Warner, "My Forty Years in Football," pt. 26.
10. Ibid.
11. Ibid., pt. 36.
12. Danzig, p.186.
13. *Buffalo Courier*, September 30, 1906.
14. Troup quote from email to author, November 28, 2014.
15. Warner, *Football for Coaches & Players*, pp. 136–139.
16. Cornell Daily Sun, October 1, 1906.
17. Warner, "My Forty Years in Football," pt. 26.
18. Newcombe, pp. 94–95.
19. *Cornell Daily Sun*, December 14, 1906.
20. Warner, "My Forty Years in Football," pt. 26.

Chapter Seven

1. Jenkins, p. 233.
2. Ibid.
3. *Buffalo Courier*, September 11, 1906.
4. Letter written by Jim Thorpe to the *Shawnee News Star*, October 20, 1943, in Robert Wheeler, *Jim Thorpe, World's Greatest Athlete*, p. 291.
5. Robert L. Whitman, Jim Thorpe and the Oorang Indians: N.F.L.'s Most Colorful Team, pp. 2.
6. Wheeler, p. 8–12.
7. Jenkins, p. 211.
8. Ibid., p. 212
9. Ellen C. Labrecque, Jim Thorpe: An Athlete for the Ages, p. 10.
10. Wheeler, p. 19.
11. Ibid., p. 20.
12. Bynum, p. 120.
13. Wheeler, p. 52.
14. Bynum, p. 121.
15. Warner, "The Indian Massacres."
16. Ibid.
17. *New York Times*, October 6, 1907.
18. *Buffalo Courier*, October 13, 1907.
19. Wheeler, p. 62.
20. Warner, "Heap Big Run-Most-Fast."
21. Wheeler, p. 58.
22. Warner, "The Indian Massacres."
23. Jenkins, p. 238.
24. Harper's Weekly.
25. Glenn S. Warner, "Athletics at the Carlisle Indian School," *The Indian Crafts-*

man: A Magazine Not Only About Indians But Mainly by Indians, February 1909.
26. Warner, "The Indian Massacres."
27. Ibid.
28. Bynum, p. 124.
29. Letter from W. G. Thompson to Dr. C. Montezuma, in John W. Larner, Jr., editor. *The Papers of Carlos Montezuma* (Wilmington, DE, Scholarly Resources, Inc., 1984).
30. *New York Times*, December 7, 1907.
31. *The Arrow*, December 13, 1907.
32. *Hearings Before the Joint Commission of the Congress of the United States, 63rd Congress, 2nd Session, Part II.* Warner estimated the cost of construction of the athletic quarters "at ... ten, twelve or thirteen thousand dollars."
33. Newcombe, p. 113.
34. Ibid., p. 120.
35. *New York Times*, December 28, 1907.
36. Jenkins, p. 249.
37. Wheeler, p. 63.
38. Ibid., p. 64.
39. Spalding's Official Foot Ball Guide for 1908.
40. Bynum, p. 126.
41. Wheeler, p. 67.
42. Steckbeck, pp. 75–76.
43. Newcombe, p. 132.
44. Edwin Pope, Football's Greatest Coaches, p. 107.
45. Newcombe, p. 134.
46. William A. Cook, *Jim Thorpe: A Biography*, p. 43.
47. *St. Louis Star*, November 24, 1909.
48. Newcombe, p. 143, and Buford, pp. 90–91.
49. Newcombe, p. 143.
50. Welch quote from interview in *Spokane Daily Chronicle*, January 9, 1933.
51. Steckbeck, pp. 103–104.
52. Newcombe, p. 143.

Chapter Eight

1. Newcombe, p. 149.
2. Wheeler, pp. 80–82.
3. Glenn S. Warner, "Red Menaces," *Collier's*, October 31, 1931.
4. Arthur Martin, oral history project, Cumberland County Historical Society, and Pope, p. 294.
5. Pope, p. 293.

6. Newcombe, p. 156.
7. Hyland quote from Pope, p. 293.
8. Danzig, p. 344.
9. Warner, "Red Menaces."
10. Bynum, p. 129.
11. Warner, "My Forty Years in Football," pt. 29.
12. For the 1911 season, Walter Camp and Caspar Whitney published identical top five rankings, which placed Princeton at number one followed, in order, by Minnesota, Penn State, Yale, and Carlisle.
13. Bynum, p. 132.
14. Warner, "My Forty Years in Football," pt. 30.
15. Warner, "Red Menaces."
16. Bynum, pp. 132–133.
17. Letter from Pete Dygert to author, March 1, 2015.
18. Cook, pp. 54–55, and Jenkins, pp. 270–271.
19. Warner, "My Forty Years in Football," pt. 30.
20. Bynum, pp. 136–137.
21. Wheeler, pp. 118–119.
22. Newcombe, p. 196.
23. Benjey, p. 65.
24. Warner, "My Forty Years in Football," pt. 32.
25. The rouge, or "single" as it is generally called today, is a method of scoring exclusive to Canadian football by which a team is awarded one point when the ball is kicked into the opposing end zone by any legal means, other than a successful field goal, and the receiving team fails to return the ball beyond its own goal line.
26. Newcombe, p. 201.
27. Danzig, p. 338.
28. Tom Bennett, The Pro Style: The Complete Guide to Understanding National Football League Strategy, p. 210.
29. In Warner's 1927 book, *Football for Coaches & Players*, the single wing was designated "Formation A" and the double wing "Formation B."
30. Wheeler, p. 128.
31. Ibid., p. 131.
32. Warner, "My Forty Years in Football," pt. 32.
33. *The* (Sumter, South Carolina) *Daily Item*, February 15, 1973.
34. Wheeler, pp. 151–152.
35. Cook, p. 75.
36. Letter written by Thorpe to James E. Sullivan (secretary of both the Amateur Athletic Union and the American Olympic Committee), January 27, 1913, in *Olympic Review (Révue Olympique)*, March 1913, pp. 36–37.
37. Warner quote from Danzig, p. 173.
38. *Sporting Life*, February 15, 1913.
39. Mack Whelan, "Football Coaches—Drivers and Diplomats," *Outing*, November 1913.
40. Bynum, p. 147.
41. (Gettysburg, PA) *Star and Sentinel*, July 11, 1914.
42. New York Times, May 26, 1914.
43. Bynum, p. 150.
44. Warner, "My Forty Years in Football," pt. 35.
45. *Pittsburgh Gazette*, November 10 and 12, 1914, and *New York Times*, November 12, 1914.
46. Warner, "The Indian Massacres."

Chapter Nine

1. *Sporting Life*, October 16, 1915.
2. Bynum, p. 153.
3. *Sporting Life*, October 16, 1915.
4. Bynum, p. 156.
5. Pitt's selection as 1915 champion by Parke H. Davis is recognized as official by the NCAA. In the 1933 edition of *Spalding's Football Guide*, Davis, after exhaustive research, cobbled together what is now considered the definitive listing of all national champions going back to 1889.
6. Warner, "My Forty Years in Football," pt. 50.
7. Warner, "Here Come the Giants!" *Collier's*, November 21, 1931.
8. Bynum, pp. 158–159.
9. *New York Times*, October 26, 1916.
10. *Pittsburgh Press*, July 23, 1929.
11. Danzig, p. 348.
12. www.whoislog.info/profile/jock-sutherland-1.html.
13. John M. Heisman, *Heisman: The Man Behind the Trophy*, p. 160.
14. The Heisman (or "jump") shift is considered to be the precursor to the modern "T" formation. The Heisman shift began with the center standing over the ball while the other linemen stood in a tight formation about one yard back and the backfield men stood in a classic "T" grouping. The backfield men would then shift into a single wing formation, either

to the left of the right. Just as the backs' fingers touched the turf in their three-point stance, the center snapped the ball, giving the defensive players little or no chance to adjust. The tactic was highly successful until 1921, when a new rule was adopted requiring players in motion to come to a complete stop before the snap of the ball. Heisman, p. 171.

15. *Pittsburgh Gazette Times*, November 22, 1918.

16. Warner, "My Forty Years in Football," pt. 51.

17. Pope, p. 294.

18. *Pittsburgh Post-Gazette*, March 25, 1942.

19. *Pittsburgh Post-Gazette*, October 2, 1948.

20. *New York Times*, November 27, 1919.

21. Pope, p. 298.

22. *New York Times*, October 31, 1920.

23. Bynum, p. 185.

24. *New York Times*, December 4, 1921.

25. Bynum, p. 188.

26. Warner, "My Forty Years in Football," pt. 52.

27. Ibid., pt. 51.

28. Ronald A. Smith, "Football Coach Salaries and the Hiring of Pop Warner at Stanford," *North American Society for Sport History Proceedings and Newsletter.* 2007

29. *New York Times*, October 24, 1922.

30. Bynum, p. 192.

31. Warner, "My Forty Years in Football," pt. 52.

32. Herb McCracken, *Glenn "Pop" Warner: Football Innovator*, video produced by the University of Pittsburgh (www.225.pitt.edu/story/glenn-pop-warner-football).

Chapter Ten

1. Bynum, p. 194.

2. Chuck Frederick, Leatherheads of the North: The True Story of Ernie Nevers & the Duluth Eskimos, pp. 49–53.

3. Bynum, p. 200.

4. Murray Goodman and Leonard Lewin, My Greatest Day in Football: Thrilling Stories of the Gridiron.

5. Rockne's box shift was merely a variation of Warner's single wing. The box shift, however, featured a balanced line

with the wing back playing in more tightly, giving the backfield the appearance of a square. The formation provided more options, allowing offenses to run to either side of the line, where the single wing was limited to running mainly to the strong side. Because of the frequent shifting in the backfield, the formation's effectiveness was more in deception than power. Tom Bennett *The Pro Style: The Complete Guide to Understanding National Football League Strategy*, p. 210.

6. Glenn S. Warner, "Pigskin Sherlocks," *Liberty*, November 30, 1935

7. Spokane Daily Chronicle, January 2, 1925.

8. Warner, "Here Come the Giants!"

9. Letter from Stanford University president Ray Lyman Wilbur to Glenn Warner, January 2, 1925.

10. Warner, "What's the Matter with Football?"

11. *Quad 1925* (Stanford University's annual yearbook), p. 103.

12. *The Reading* (Pennsylvania) *Eagle*, December 1, 1925.

13. George H. Dacy, "Glenn Warner Put the Win in Football," *Athlete and Sportsman*, December 1925.

14. Warner, "My Forty Years in Football," pt. 53.

15. Robinson, p. 190.

16. Heisman, p. 198.

17. *Pittsburgh Press*, August 19, 1927.

18. Warner, "My Forty Years in Football," pt. 53.

19. McCreery quote from *Sports Illustrated*, September 20, 1954.

20. Warner, "My Forty Years in Football," pt. 53.

21. In the typical "Statue of Liberty" play, the quarterback receives the snap from center and drops back as if he were getting ready to throw a pass. He raises his throwing arm and makes a throwing motion while keeping the ball in his non-throwing hand, stealthily hiding it behind his back. As this is happening, a runner sweeps in behind and takes the ball from the quarterback's non-throwing hand and heads upfield. If executed properly, the defense will be confused into thinking a pass is being attempted, and that split second will give the offense ample opportunity to make a large gain against a defensive squad whose initial steps have

been away from the line of scrimmage. The play receives its name from the positioning of the quarterback as he hands the ball to the runner (one hand in the air and the other either behind his back or at his side), which, if done correctly, resembles the pose of the famous statue.

22. Bynum, p. 238.

23. *Palm Beach* (Florida) *News*, January 8, 1928.

24. Danzig, pp. 346–347.

25. Bynum, p. 251.

26. Ibid., p. 158.

27. *Sarasota Herald-Tribune*, September 24, 1930.

28. *Berkeley Daily Gazette*, April 1, 1931.

29. Robinson, pp. 264–265.

30. Glenn S. Warner, "Is the Notre Dame System Slipping?" *Saturday Evening Post*, October 6, 1934.

31. Article found on Stanford athletics' official web site, www.gostanford.com.

32. Glenn S. Warner, "Football's New Deal." *Saturday Evening Post*, October 7, 1933.

33. *The* (St. Petersburg, Florida) *Independent*, February 13, 1932.

34. *Time*, October 31, 1932.

35. Bynum, pp. 263–266.

36. *Milwaukee Sentinel*, December 6, 1932.

37. *Berkeley Daily Gazette*, December 6, 1932.

38. *Spokane Daily Chronicle*, December 6, 1932.

39. Bynum, p. 269.

40. *Berkeley Daily Gazette*, December 6, 1932.

41. Danzig, p. 344.

42. Telegram from Leland W. Cutler to Glenn S. Warner, December 6, 1932 (punctuation added by author).

43. *Pittsburgh Press*, December 29, 1932.

Chapter Eleven

1. *Buffalo Evening News*, (no date), 1955.

2. *Pittsburgh Press*, January 31, 1933.

3. Warner eventually dismissed Miller and Bell, and within a year Bell became a co-owner of the new Philadelphia Eagles franchise of the National Football League.

In 1946, he was named commissioner of the NFL.

4. According to family tradition, Boston Braves owner George Preston Marshall changed the name of the team to "Redskins" in 1933 in Dietz' honor. (In 1937, Marshall moved the team to Washington, where the Redskins have been located ever since.) Benjey, p. 160.

5. Bynum, p. 277.

6. *Los Angeles Times*, November 20, 1934.

7. Pope, p. 294.

8. *The Deseret* (Utah) *News*, February 1, 1939.

9. *Sarasota Journal*, September 13, 1954.

10. *Philadelphia Evening Bulletin*, January 28, 1938.

11. Ertz interview from *Orange County Register*, October 23, 2012.

12. *Lodi* (California) *News-Sentinel*, November 12, 1938.

13. Smith revealed the contents of Warner's letter of February 7, 1939, in a column published in *Pittsburgh Press* on the occasion of Warner's death, September 8, 1954.

14. United Press, March 1, 1939.

Chapter Twelve

1. *Berkeley Daily Gazette*, March 30, 1939.

2. *San Jose Evening News*, March 30, 1939.

3. *Pittsburgh Press*, October 21, 1939.

4. *San Jose Evening News*, November 23, 1939.

5. *Toledo Blade*, February 26, 1941.

6. *Reading Eagle*, August 21, 1941.

Chapter Thirteen

1. *Pittsburgh Post-Gazette*, October 2, 1948.

2. Letter from Glenn S. Warner to Warner Brothers Studios, October 1, 1951, in Kate Buford, *Native American Son*, p. 345.

3. *Pittsburgh Press*, January 11, 1952, and *Springville Journal*, January 24, 1952.

4. *Sarasota Herald-Tribune*, September 7, 1954.

5. *Buffalo Evening News*, September 8, 1954.

6. *Pittsburgh Press*, September 8, 1954.

7. *Buffalo Evening News*, August 26, 1940.

8. *NFL Films Presents: The Single Wing*, NFL Films, 1999.

9. Email from Benjey to author, February 26, 2015, and "The Single Wing May Be Off Life Support," www.tombenjey.com, December 5, 2008.

10. www.popwarner.com, Internet site of Pop Warner Little Scholars, Inc.

11. Bynum, pp. 23–25.

12. *The* (Lexington, North Carolina) *Dispatch*, November 17, 1993.

Bibliography

Books

Anderson, Lars. *Carlisle vs. Army: Jim Thorpe, Dwight Eisenhower, Pop Warner, and the Forgotten Story of Football's Greatest Battle.* New York: Random House, 2007.

Benjey, Tom. *Keep a-Goin': The Life of Lone Star Dietz.* Carlisle, PA: Tuxedo Press, 2006.

_____. *Wisconsin's Carlisle Indian Immortals.* Carlisle, PA: Tuxedo Press, 2011.

Bennett, Tom. *The Pro Style: The Complete Guide to Understanding National Football League Strategy.* New York: National Football League, 1976.

Briggs, Ersamus. *History of the Original Town of Concord, Erie County, New York.* Rochester: Union and Advertiser Co.'s Print, 1883.

Brooks, Philip L. *Forward Pass: The Play That Saved Football.* Yardley, PA: Westholme, 2008.

Buford, Kate. *Native American Son: The Life and Sporting Legend of Jim Thorpe.* New York: Alfred A. Knopf, 2010.

Bynum, Michael J., ed. *Pop Warner: Football's Greatest Teacher.* Birmingham: Gridiron Football Properties, 1993.

Cook, William A. *Jim Thorpe: A Biography.* Jefferson, NC: McFarland, 2011.

Crippen, Kenneth R. *Turmoil vs. Triumph: The History of the Syracuse Athletic Association Football Team (1890–1900).* Lincoln: iUniverse, Inc., 2007.

Danzig, Allison. *Oh, How They Played the Game: The Early Days of Football and the Heroes Who Made it Great.* New York: Macmillan, 1971.

Goodman, Murray, and Leonard Lewin. *My Greatest Day in Football: Thrilling Stories of the Gridiron.* New York: A. S. Barnes, 1948

Hall, Moss. *Go Indians! Stories of the Great Athletes of the Carlisle School.* Los Angeles: Ward Ritchie Press, 1971.

Heisman, John M., and Mark Schlabach. *Heisman: The Man Behind the Trophy.* New York: Howard Books, 2012.

Herget, James E. *American Football: How the Game Evolved.* Middletown, DE: Self-published, 2013.

Jenkins, Sally. *The Real All Americans: The Team That Changed a Game, a People, a Nation.* New York: Doubleday, 2007.

Labrecque, Ellen C. *Jim Thorpe: An Athlete for the Ages.* New York: Sterling, 2010.

Layden, Tom. *Blood, Sweat and Chalk: The Ultimate Football Playbook.* New York: Sports Illustrated Books, 2010.

Manchester, Alan V., and David C. Batterson. *Images of America: Springville.* Charleston, SC: Arcadia, 2012.

Maxymuk, John. *NFL Head Coaches: A Biographical Dictionary, 1920–2011.* Jefferson, NC: McFarland, 2012.

Newcombe, Jack. *The Best of the Athletic Boys: The White Man's Impact on Jim Thorpe.* Garden City, NY: Doubleday, 1975.

Pope, Edwin. *Football's Greatest Coaches.* Atlanta: Tupper & Love, 1956.

Pratt, Richard Henry. *Battlefield & Classroom: Four Decades with the American Indian, 1876–1904.* Norman: University of Oklahoma Press, 2003.

Reising, Robert. *Jim Thorpe: The Story of an American Indian.* Minneapolis: Dillon Press, 1974.

Robinson, Ray. *Rockne of Notre Dame: The Making of a Football Legend.* New York: Oxford University Press, 1999.

Shaughnessy, Clark, Ralph Jones, and George Halas. *The Modern "T" Formation with Man-in-Motion.* Chicago: Self-published, 1941.

Stanford University. *Quad 1925,* (Stanford University's annual yearbook).

Warner, Glenn S. *A Course in Football for Players and Coaches—Offense.* (Reprint of 1908–11 pamphlets originally bound and published in book form by Warner in 1912, edited by Tom Benjey). Carlisle, PA: Tuxedo Press, 2007.

Warner, Glenn S. *Football for Coaches & Players.* (Reprint of Warner's book published in 1927, edited by Tom Benjey). Carlisle, PA: Tuxedo Press, 2007.

Wheeler, Robert W. *Jim Thorpe: World's Greatest Athlete.* Norman: University of Oklahoma Press, 1979.

Whitman, Robert L. *Jim Thorpe and the Oorang Indians: N.F.L.'s Most Colorful Franchise.* Mt. Vernon, IN: Windmill Publications, 1984.

Magazine Articles

Dacy, George H. "Glenn Warner Put the Win in Football." *Athlete and Statesman,* December 1925.

Camp, Walter. "Football Development in 1901." *Outing,* November 1901.

"The Greatest Player Ever?" *College Football Historical Society* XI, no. III (May 1998).

Hardy, Ed. "He Kept Us On Our Toes." *Cornell Alumni News,* September 1992.

Manchester, Alan V. "Western New York's Pop Warner: Father of Modern Football." *Western New York Heritage,* Fall 2008.

PFRA Research. "The First Football World Series: Experiment in the Garden." *The Coffin Corner.*

Smith, Ronald A. "Football Coach Salaries and the Hiring of Pop Warner at Stanford." *North American Society for Sport History, Proceedings and Newsletter,* 2007.

Spalding's Official Foot Ball Guide for 1908.

Sporting Life. February 15, 1913; October 16, 1915; November 13, 1915.

Warner, Glenn S. "Battles of Brawn" *Collier's,* November 7, 1931.

_____. "Football's New Deal." *The Saturday Evening Post,* October 7, 1933.

_____. "The Football 'Tramp' in Our Colleges." *Liberty,* October 17, 1936.

_____. "Heap Big Run-Most-Fast." *Collier's,* October 24, 1931.

_____. "Here Come the Giants." *Collier's,* November 21, 1931.

_____. "The Indian Massacres." *Collier's,* October 17, 1931.

_____. "Is the Notre Dame System Slipping?" *The Saturday Evening Post,* October 6, 1934.

_____. "Pigskin Sherlocks." *Liberty,* November 30, 1935.

_____. "Red Menaces." *Collier's,* October 31, 1931.

_____. "What's the Matter with Football?" *Collier's,* November 14, 1931.

Newspapers

The (Carlisle Indian School) *Arrow*
Atlanta Constitution
Berkeley Daily Gazette
Buffalo Courier
Buffalo Evening News
Carlisle Daily Herald
Cornell Daily Sun
The (Sumter, South Carolina) *Daily Item*
The (Lexington, North Carolina) *Dispatch*
The (Fredericksburg, Virginia) *Free Lance-Star*
Gettysburg (Pennsylvania) *Star and Sentinel*
The (St. Petersburg, Florida) *Independent*
The (Carlisle) *Indian Helper*
Lodi (California) *News-Sentinel*
Los Angeles Times
Milwaukee Sentinel
New York Times
New York World
Orange County Register
Palm Beach (Florida) *News*
Philadelphia Evening Bulletin
Philadelphia Record
Pittsburgh Press
Pittsburgh Post-Gazette
Reading (Pennsylvania) *Eagle*
St. Louis Star
San Jose Evening News
Sarasota (Florida) *Journal*
Springville Journal

Springville News
(Gettysburg, Pennsylvania) *Star and Sentinel*
Spokane Daily Chronicle
Syracuse Standard
Toledo Blade
Washington Post

Internet Sites

baseball-reference.com. Internet site for Baseball Reference.com.

cfbdatawarehouse.com. College Football Data Warehouse.
cornellbigred.com. The official internet site for Cornell University athletics.
owlsports.com. Official internet site of Temple University athletics.
popwarner.com. Official internet site of Pop Warner Little Scholars, Inc.
profootballresearchers.com. Professional Football Researchers Association.
tombenjey.com. Internet site of author and historian Tom Benjey.

Index